AIRCRAFT of WORLD WAR II

Published by Collins
An imprint of HarperCollins Publishers
Westerhill Road
Bishopbriggs
Glasgow G64 2QT
www.harpercollins.co.uk

HarperCollins Publishers
Macken House,
39/40 Mayor Street Upper,
Dublin 1, D01 C9W8, Ireland

1st edition 2025

© HarperCollins Publishers 2025
Published in association with Imperial War Museums

Collins® is a registered trademark of HarperCollins Publishers Ltd

All rights reserved. No part of this publication may be reproduced, stored in a retrieval system, or transmitted, in any form or by any means, electronic, mechanical, photocopying, recording or otherwise without the prior permission in writing of the publisher and copyright owners.

The contents of this publication are believed correct at the time of printing. Nevertheless the publisher can accept no responsibility for errors or omissions, changes in the detail given or for any expense or loss thereby caused.

HarperCollins does not warrant that any website mentioned in this title will be provided uninterrupted, that any website will be error free, that defects will be corrected, or that the website or the server that makes it available are free of viruses or bugs. For full terms and conditions please refer to the site terms provided on the website.

A catalogue record for this book is available from the British Library.

ISBN 9780008704179

10 9 8 7 6 5 4 3 2 1

Printed in India

If you would like to comment on any aspect of this book, please contact us at the above address or online.
e-mail:collins.reference@harpercollins.co.uk

This book contains FSC™ certified paper and other controlled sources to ensure responsible forest management.
For more information visit: www.harpercollins.co.uk/green

AIRCRAFT of WORLD WAR II

A History of Second World War Aircraft from 1939 to 1945

KIERAN WHITWORTH

CONTENTS

Introduction	6

ALLIED POWERS

Allied Aircraft	10
#01 Avro Lancaster	12
#02 Avro Manchester	32
#03 Bell P-39 Airacobra	36
#04 Bell P-63 Kingcobra	38
#05 Boeing B-17 Flying Fortress	40
#06 Boeing B-29 Superfortress	54
#07 Bristol Beaufighter	60
#08 Bristol Blenheim	64
#09 Consolidated B-24 Liberator	68
#10 Consolidated PBY Catalina	74
#11 Curtiss P-40 Warhawk	78
#12 de Havilland Mosquito	82
#13 Douglas A-20 Havoc (Boston)	90
#14 Douglas C-47 Skytrain	94
#15 Douglas SBD Dauntless	98
#16 Fairey Firefly	102
#17 Fairey Swordfish	104
#18 Gloster Gladiator	110
#19 Gloster Meteor	112
#20 Grumman F4F Wildcat	116
#21 Grumman F6F Hellcat	118
#22 Grumman TBF Avenger	120
#23 Handley Page Halifax	124
#24 Hawker Hurricane	128
#25 Hawker Tempest	138
#26 Hawker Typhoon	142
#27 Lockheed Hudson	146
#28 Lockheed P-38 Lightning	148
#29 Martin B-26 Marauder	152
#30 North American B-25 Mitchell	156
#31 North American P-51 Mustang	160
#32 Northrop P-61 Black Widow	168
#33 Republic P-47 Thunderbolt	170
#34 Short Stirling	174
#35 Short Sunderland	178
#36 Supermarine Spitfire	182
#37 Vickers Wellington	196
#38 Vought F4U Corsair	200
#39 Yakovlev Yak-9	206

AXIS POWERS

Axis Aircraft	212
#40 Dornier Do 17	214
#41 Focke-Wulf Fw 190	216
#42 Focke-Wulf Fw 200 Condor	222
#43 Heinkel He 111	224
#44 Junkers Ju 88	226
#45 Junkers Ju 87 Stuka	228
#46 Messerschmitt Bf 109	232
#47 Messerschmitt Bf 110	238
#48 Messerschmitt Me 163 Komet	240
#49 Messerschmitt Me 262	242
#50 Mitsubishi A6M Zero	244
Index	250
Acknowledgements	256

Introduction

The aircraft of World War II were both exceptional and terrifying.

From biplanes to jet-powered aircraft, the rapid development of these fighting machines would change the face of aerial warfare forever and produce iconic aircraft that would eternally belong to the era. This book features 50 key aircraft from both the Allied air forces, primarily Britain and its empire and the United States, and the Axis powers, Germany and Japan.

A common theme throughout this book is that many aircraft were often hindered by the limitations of technological development during the war. This ranged from insufficient engines to materials that could not produce a desired performance, in a constant drive to produce aircraft that could fly faster, higher, further and for longer, whilst delivering a knockout blow to the enemy.

Delve into the origins, development and operations of these iconic aircraft, and stories of the brave crew members that would fly in them. These were the people who would make some of these aircraft the legends they have become today, often paying the ultimate sacrifice in the fiercest air battles seen during World War II.

An Avro Lancaster I on the runway at RAF Waddington in early 1942.

ALLIED POWERS

Allied Aircraft

The aircraft used throughout World War II by the Allies were war winning.

But it did not start that way. At the beginning of the war in 1939, Britain and her Allies were plunged into a conflict in response to the German invasion of Poland, that had been on the horizon since the rise of the German Nazi party in the 1930s, with generally obsolete aircraft like the Gloster Gladiator and Fairey Swordfish. However, the development of two modern fighters, the Hawker Hurricane and the Supermarine Spitfire, in the 1930s would prove pivotal when a decisive battle over the skies of Britain in the summer of 1940 would take place, allowing the RAF to thwart the Luftwaffe and a possible German invasion of Britain.

The development of long-range aircraft, both for maritime patrol to protect vital shipping routes for Britain's global empire and 'heavy' bombers for strategic bombing of enemy cities, would see the development of powerful aircraft, such as the Avro Lancaster, Short Sunderland and de Havilland Mosquito. Throughout, the British would supplement its forces with American-built aircraft, including the Lockheed Hudson, Consolidated B-24 Liberator and Douglas C-47 Skytrain. Towards the end of the war, the rapid development of British aviation would lead to the jet, with the Gloster Meteor being the first Allied jet-powered fighter to enter service during World War II.

The United States would join the conflict with under-performing aircraft when facing the Japanese 'Zero' fighter, with the Grumman F4F Wildcat and Curtiss P-40 'holding the line' before more superior aircraft were rapidly developed. The industrial might of the United States and its vast factory production lines would mass produce iconic aircraft. These ranged from bombers, including the Boeing B-17 Flying Fortress, North American B-25 Mitchell and the most advanced long-range bomber to serve in the war, the Boeing B-29 Superfortress, to fighters, including the Lockheed P-38 Lightning, Republic P-47 Thunderbolt and the exceptional North American P-51 Mustang.

The Soviet Union would also be jolted into war when its former ally, Nazi Germany, invaded the Soviet Union in June 1941, with the Luftwaffe decimating obsolete Soviet aircraft. Initially reliant on support from Britain and America, the Soviets would successfully reverse the German invasion over vast land battles using aircraft like the Bell P-63 Kingcobra and Hawker Hurricane, before rapid development in Soviet wartime industry would finally produce modern aircraft, including the Yakovlev Yak-9 fighter bomber.

The technological development of aircraft for the Allies was rapid, as the need to fly faster, further and higher, whilst carrying increasingly more weapons, would push the wartime industries of the Allies to maximum capacity. But the sheer quantity of aircraft delivered, along with the vast numbers of Allied pilots trained to fly them, would ensure that the Allied air forces would gain air superiority across the globe and lead to the eventual dropping by Allied aircraft of the ultimate weapon, an atomic bomb, to end the war in 1945.

#01
Avro Lancaster

GREAT BRITAIN

Introduction

The Avro Lancaster 'heavy' bomber is widely recognised as one of the most iconic aircraft of World War II.

This British heavy bomber played a pivotal role in the defeat of Nazi Germany. Not only was it to become a decisive weapon of war, but it would also become a unifying symbol for the many nationalities that served in these huge planes and supported them on the ground, forging an unbreakable bond that for many veterans would last a lifetime.

It was as much a symbol of defiance against Nazi Germany, allowing the Allies to strike back after earlier losses in the war, as the equally famous Supermarine Spitfire. The remaining surviving airworthy examples of the Lancaster bomber are frequent favourites at modern-day air shows and are often seen flying during grand occasions of the British state. For all the modern celebratory pomp that surrounds the plane, it also represented for many the increasingly barbaric nature of aerial bombing during World War II, and its significant and appalling impact on civilian populations across Europe. The Lancaster was to be one of the decisive aircraft, along with the American B-17 Flying Fortress in the Allied bombing campaign, that would become a totemic icon for the destructive nature of war.

Lancaster B Mk Is of No.50 Squadron RAF, flying in spread formation.

Origins

The Avro Lancaster evolved from an earlier British bomber, the Avro Manchester. The Manchester was designed specifically to meet a British Air Ministry specification for a twin-engine heavy bomber, due to the emerging threat from a rapidly rearming Nazi Germany in the 1930s. The main criteria, and one that would later prove to be a pivotal key to the success of the Lancaster, was for any new aircraft to be able carry a bomb load up to 8,000 lb. This requirement came at a time when many of the aircraft flying in the skies were still antiquated biplanes.

The specification also preferred the selected manufacturers to use the Rolls-Royce Vulture engine, to save the more powerful Rolls-Royce Merlin engine for the development of British fighters, the Hurricane and Spitfire. Whilst this engine was to ultimately lead to the demise of the Avro Manchester, it would also become the principal reason for the successful development of the Lancaster. This was because a good aircraft design can often be improved significantly by an increase in its engine power and this concept would be a crucial factor to the Lancaster's success.

The initial design of the Avro Manchester had been a good one for its designer, Roy Chadwick, principal designer at the Avro manufacturing company, for he had developed a strong and reliable all-metal-skinned airframe, which could meet the Air Ministry requirements. Despite this, the Manchester suffered from a lack of power from its twin Vulture engines. The resulting Manchester bomber was plagued by this issue, with the aircraft having a reputation with its crews for being dangerously underpowered.

Another concern was that on a long bombing mission over Germany, if an aircraft only had two engines, the likelihood of returning would diminish if anything happened to one or both engines. However, Chadwick was convinced that the Manchester aircraft was a good design overall. Luckily, there had been prototypes built during the development of the Avro Manchester Mk III that had changed the Manchester to a four-engine aircraft, and so this larger four-engine bomber adopted a new name and became the first Avro Lancaster Mk I.

A Lancaster B Mk III in flight.

Development and Manufacturing

The newly named Avro Lancaster Mk I had four Rolls-Royce Merlin engines which would give it significantly more power than its predecessor, and the wingspan expanded to just over 100 ft to accommodate this increase in the number of engines.

The increase in power produced a maximum speed of 275 mph at an altitude of 15,000 ft and, most crucially, allowed the Lancaster to carry a bomb load of nearly 7,000 lb to a maximum distance of 2,350 miles, meeting pre-war requirements. The new bomber was also going to be manufactured by a consortium of British aircraft companies, including Avro, Vickers-Armstrong and Armstong Whitworth.

The manufacture of the Lancaster was coordinated by the Ministry for Aircraft Production in Britain and early in the war this was led by a friend of Prime Minister Winston Churchill, Lord Beaverbrook. Beaverbrook was a media baron and industrialist who had been tasked by Churchill to significantly improve the rate and number of aircraft provided to the war effort by British industry. He had the ability to simplify processes, was cut-throat in rooting out inefficiency and removing 'red tape' to get the most out of Britain's factories and place them on a more productive war footing, and the Rolls-Royce Merlin engine once again became a problem for Avro and Roy Chadwick. The Rolls-Royce Merlin engine was used heavily in the development of British fighters and so the Vulture engine was prioritised for the Lancaster project. Luckily, Rolls Royce managed to 'quietly' supply a small number of Merlin engines to Avro for the new prototype Lancaster and the new heavy bomber could finally take to the skies.

An advantage that became apparent during the Lancaster's production was that even though it was made up of over 55,000 separate parts, 70 per cent of these parts were the same as the Avro Manchester. This meant any significant cost of building machines and tools had already been paid for, which significantly brought down the cost of each Lancaster. The existing tools also meant production could be carried out by a relatively unskilled workforce and produced in high quantities, ideal when factories were being filled with largely, and at least initially, unskilled women plugging the gap in the workforce.

A fast rate of production would be crucial for RAF Bomber Command needing to build up large numbers of new heavy bombers to be able to hit back at the Germans in Europe.

Such a large bomber also required larger factories to produce it. Avro had built one such factory in 1939 at Yeadon in Yorkshire. At the time of its construction the

GREAT BRITAIN

Avro Lancaster bombers nearing completion at the A. V. Roe & Co. Limited factory.

factory was thought to be one of the largest in Europe. A factory of such immense size was a huge target for the German Luftwaffe, but the Yeadon factory was never bombed, in large part due to it being hidden in plain sight. Using large earthworks to disguise shadows from its buildings and having a unique camouflage resembling the English countryside above it, the factory would go on to produce over 700 Lancasters during the war.

The maiden flight of the Lancaster prototype, BT308, took place in January 1941, and initial feedback showed that it was easy to fly and was 'comfortable' to be inside. Part of this 'comfort' derived from a system that used some of the excess heat from the four engines to warm the inside of the aircraft, useful when flying for long distances at high altitude, where cold would hamper the effectiveness of the crew. It was robust and reliable,

Rear fuselage sections of the Avro Lancaster aircraft under construction at the A. V. Roe & Co. Limited factory.

offering its crew a chance of returning to base. Like other contemporary bombers being developed in the United States, the cabin was not pressurised so the crew required oxygen masks at high altitude. The Lancaster would consist of a crew of seven: pilot, flight engineer, navigator, wireless operator, bomb-aimer, mid-upper gunner and a rear gunner. However, losses of crews, when the Lancaster began to enter the war, would often mean available crew to fly the Lancaster would frequently be in short supply.

The initial design for the Lancaster included a gun turret under the belly of the plane, a 'ventral' ball turret, but this was later removed to allow for a large, unobstructed bomb bay that was 33 ft long. This meant the Lancaster had the largest bomb bay of any World War II bomber until the American B-29 Superfortress came into service later in the conflict. Indeed, when American crews first saw the Lancaster, they called it a 'flying bomb bay'. The sight of the Lancaster bomb bay is still awe-inspiring today and can be seen first-hand on surviving Lancasters, including one at Imperial War Museum Duxford in Cambridgeshire. The size of the bomb bay meant that the design of the Lancaster would progress through the war with relatively few changes. As the bay was unobstructed it allowed for adaptions for different types of bombs of varying size and design that would enable the Lancaster to inflict its bomb loads to devastating effect.

Three Avro Lancaster B Mk Is flying above the clouds.

GREAT BRITAIN

Operations

By April 1942, two squadrons of the RAF had been equipped with the Lancaster, and one of its first operational raids was a low-level daylight attack on the M.A.N factory in Augsburg, Germany, which was making U-boat engines. Bomber Command was under pressure to release aircraft to hinder the U-boat threat in the Battle of the Atlantic, but their Commander-in-Chief, Arthur Harris, wanted to attack associated U-boat factories instead, so he could argue that he was helping the Allies in the fight against the U-boats.

The daylight raid on 17 April 1942 was an audacious gamble, and it was hoped that the Lancasters could achieve surprise and provide accurate bombing, despite the threat from enemy fighters, in bombing a target that was over 500 miles beyond the French coastline and roughly the size of a football pitch.

The raid itself was claimed to be a success by British propaganda, but it was at a cost. Seven of the 12 Lancasters that took part in the raid were shot down, but despite heavy damage the factory was not put out of action. It would prove to be the longest low-level bombing raid of the war and demonstrated the potential of the Lancaster bomber. But daylight raids were proving to be difficult for Bomber Command without fighter cover. It would hasten plans for the development of a Pathfinder Force that could mark targets for the following bomber groups and also saw the Lancasters switched to mainly bombing targets by night from higher altitudes.

Harris needed to demonstrate that Bomber Command, with its new Lancaster bomber, could become a war-winning part of the Allies, and the new Lancasters were tasked with joining an 'eye-catching' 1,000-bomber raid, in May 1942, on the German city of Cologne. The raid was successful in proving that big bomber forces could inflict large areas of damage on enemy cities, and it proved a propaganda hit. However, Bomber Command was still slowly moving over to new heavy bombers like the Lancaster, and so the impact of the raid was not yet at a desired 'war-winning' level for Harris.

GREAT BRITAIN

A further audacious raid was planned for the Lancaster bomber in May 1943. Code-named Operation Chastise, it is now more commonly known as the 'Dambusters Raid', which took place on the night of 16/17 May. It has gone down in the collective memory of the British, helped by a classic 1950s film, which saw a new RAF 617 Squadron, led by Wing Commander Guy Gibson, knock out crucial dams in Germany. These dams helped power the Ruhr industrial heartland. The Lancasters were equipped with just one bomb, a secret weapon that had a unique ability: a 'bouncing bomb'. For the raid to be a success the new Lancaster squadron crews had to perfect flying at a height of 60 ft and at a speed of 232 mph to deliver the spinning bomb, which would bounce over nets guarding the dams before sinking at the dam wall and exploding at the dam's base. All of this was to take place at night and under anti-aircraft fire.

The three dams were the Möhne, Eder and Sorpe, and they were surrounded by difficult terrain. On the night of the attack, 19 Lancasters took off with 133 aircrew and, following waves of bombing runs, two of the dams were finally breached. But it came at a cost, with 53 crewmen killed and three captured, whilst around 1,300 people were killed on the ground in the subsequent flooding. The impact on industrial production in the Ruhr was not as large as first hoped, but it was a further propaganda success for Bomber Command and a boost to British morale. It also showed the German High Command that the RAF bomber force was becoming a significant threat to Nazi Germany in tandem with American bombers now entering the European air war, and more resources of pilots, aircraft and anti-aircraft defences would be needed to protect the German Reich homeland.

The port city of Hamburg was targeted in July 1943. Operation Gomorrah was a series of raids in which Lancasters played a central role from mid-July 1943. The night of 27/28 July was the most destructive. It is estimated around 40,000 people died that night as RAF bombing produced a firestorm that lasted for over three hours, partly due to unseasonably warm and dry weather, which led to many people suffocating in bomb shelters as streets melted above them, as flames reached nearly 1,600 ft high. This also resulted in over a million people fleeing the city after the firestorm and further prompted Nazi officials to prioritise home defences at the expense of the fighting forces at the front. For Harris and Bomber Command, the destruction was also a vindication that the war could be won using 'area bombing' tactics and the Lancaster bomber.

With ever-increasing numbers of Lancasters arriving in Bomber Command, and in tandem with increasing American raids by day as part of the Allied Combined Bomber Offensive, the emphasis of strategic bombing shifted from industrial targets to the symbolic capital of Nazi Germany, Berlin. Hoping to deliver a war-winning blow to Hitler's regime, the air Battle

The crew of Dambuster Lancaster ED285/'AJ-T' sitting on the grass, under stormy clouds, July 1943.

21

for Berlin began in November 1943, but German air defences were improving with more efficient German night fighters that had new weapons such as upward firing guns, leading to more Lancasters and their crew being lost over the German capital. It is estimated that due to the narrow-bodied design of the Lancaster and the relatively small crew hatches, there was as little as a 15 per cent chance of escaping from a damaged and diving Lancaster. For those fortunate enough to escape, they also had to run the gauntlet of a local population traumatised by bombing. Treatment of some downed aircrews was often harsh and Allied 'terrorflieger' (terror fliers) began to fill up German Prisoner of War (POW) camps.

By spring 1944, Lancaster bombers and their crew had about a one in ten chance in the skies over Berlin. A further throw of the dice came with a large raid on another symbolic city for the Nazis: Nuremburg. The raid by 795 RAF bombers, including 572 Lancasters, on 31 March 1944, was to be one of the worst nights of the war for the RAF with 95 bombers shot down by German night fighters, including 64 Lancasters, the biggest Bomber Command loss of the war on one night.

The 'area bombing' strategy of Bomber Command, whilst causing massive damage in Germany by 1944, had not delivered a knockout blow. Allied attention

TOP: Buildings on fire in Hamburg following the RAF Bomber Command raids in July 1943.
RIGHT: A flight engineer on board an Avro Lancaster B Mk I.

moved to prepare and support the landings in northern France, which were planned for June. An Allied Supreme Headquarters directive in April 1944 was intended to put to an end any debate on using heavy bombers such as the Lancaster in supporting the landings. It stated that heavy bombers were to be used to disrupt rail routes to Normandy, making it difficult for German forces to be sent to the invasion area, and to destroy German air strength, with bombers proving to be the bait to draw out German fighter aircraft. Over 72 separate railway facilities in France and Belgium were bombed in the run-up to D-Day, as the Allies landed successfully in Normandy, but at the expense of French rail workers and civilians, with the Lancaster seen at the forefront of the British bomber force over northern France in the summer of 1944.

By early 1945, and with the victorious land battles of Allied and Soviet armies in Europe, the borders of Nazi Germany were rapidly shrinking. The Lancaster was a prominent aircraft in the Allied air superiority, with over 1,000 of them in service, and now facing more depleted German air defences, despite the appearance of faster German fighter jets like the Me 262. However, one of the most controversial attacks of the war that included Lancasters was to occur on the night of 13/14 February 1945, with the bombing of the German city of Dresden. The city had been one of the largest urban areas left in Germany that had been unscathed from the main bombing raids and was packed full of refugees from the front line. The railway station was also thought by the Allies to be a hub for transporting German forces from the Western to the Eastern Fronts and it was situated in the heart of the historic city centre.

The Lancasters that flew over Dresden carried over 200,000 incendiary bombs and the subsequent firestorm, like at Hamburg earlier in the war, killed thousands.

Post-war analysis has estimated the number killed in Dresden at around 25,000. Almost as soon as the raid had ended – and the end of the war was near – the controversy began, with Churchill distancing himself in written communications from 'terror bombing'. The historical debate around the bombing continues to this day, but it was also a demonstration of the power of the Lancaster bomber and of its bombing capability that would continue until the end of the war in Europe in May 1945.

With the war against Japan continuing after victory in Europe, many Lancasters were prepared for transfer to the Pacific, but with the end of the war against Japan finally in August 1945, they were never sent. The destructive power of the Lancaster was also used for more humane missions towards the end of the war in Europe. Operation Manna was a relief effort with Lancasters alongside American bombers dropping food supplies in the Netherlands in the last days of the war, due to the starvation of the Dutch population during German occupation. The Lancaster also provided a flight home for many POWs on their liberation in 1945, as Operation Exodus saw Lancasters deliver home many of its former crews from German captivity. From 1942, the Lancaster had been the principal bomber of British RAF Bomber Command and was regarded as the best night bomber in service, delivering a significant contribution to the Allied war effort before it finally retired from service in 1953.

LEFT: A gathering of men of No.467 Squadron Royal Australian Air Force to celebrate the completion of 100 operations by the Avro Lancaster 'S for Sugar' after its mission on 11/12 May 1944.

RIGHT: Canadian wireless operator of an Avro Lancaster bomber, carrying two pigeon boxes. Homing pigeons served as a means of communication in the event of a crash, ditching or radio failure.

Avro Lancaster B Mk I drops a 22,000-lb 'Grand Slam' bomb over the viaduct at Arnsberg, Germany.

Specialist Bombs

The size of the Lancaster's bomb bay led to it being modified for several special bombs during the war, most from the mind of British inventor Barnes Wallis. Wallis' first and most famous bomb, the 'bouncing bomb', was code-named 'Upkeep' and was successfully used by Lancasters during the Dambusters Raid in 1943.

To accommodate the bouncing bomb, which was actually a mine, Lancaster Mk IIIs were modified by removing the bomb bay doors. The bomb was suspended in the bay using a V-shaped strut and it was rotated to provide the spin needed to make it 'bounce' using a hydraulic motor. This bomb was used to successfully breach two of the dams and demonstrated that specialist bombs used for certain targets could achieve success.

Wing Commander Guy Gibson (front left) with members of his crew. Gibson was not interested in the 'fame' he received following the Dambusters Raid and wanted to return to operational duty.

No.617 Squadron went on to become a high-altitude precision bombing squadron after the Dambusters Raid and was tasked with preparing to use more of Wallis' inventions. The Lancaster was adapted significantly to carry his next large bomb, 'Tallboy', weighing over 5,000 lb and intended to rotate while descending, which helped it to burrow deep into a target before exploding. To assist the Lancaster to carry the bomb, the planes were lightened by removing armour plating in the cockpit and used even more powerful engines. Successful uses of 'Tallboy' included attacking a V-2 assembly bunker and, on a hill in Normandy, preventing German tank reinforcements from reaching the Normandy battlefield. It was most famously used against the German battleship *Tirpitz*, which was sunk by two 'Tallboys' whilst in a Norwegian fjord in November 1944.

GREAT BRITAIN

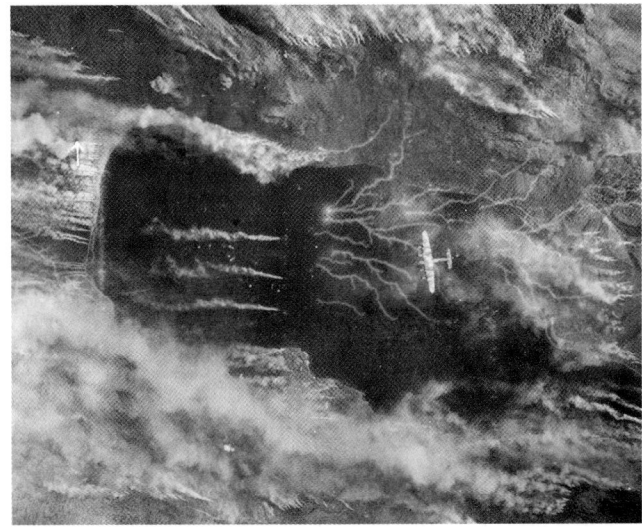

TOP LEFT: Portrait of Dr Barnes Wallis.

TOP RIGHT: A Lancaster flies towards the German battleship *Tirpitz*.

MIDDLE LEFT: A practice run with the 'bouncing bomb'.

MIDDLE RIGHT: Aerial photo showing the breach in the Möhne Dam on 16 May 1943.

BOTTOM RIGHT: Debriefing Wing Commander Guy Gibson's crew, whilst Air Chief Marshal Sir Arthur Harris (back left) looks on.

A further bomb, originally called 'Tallboy Large', was later given the code name 'Grand Slam'.

It was another Wallis invention, an 'earthquake' bomb, weighing in at a vast 22,000 lb. Thirty-two Lancasters were specially adapted to carry it and reduced in weight further. Even then crews found the adapted Lancasters were difficult to manoeuvre when carrying such a large bomb, devised to penetrate deeply into the ground and on explosion produce an 'earthquake' causing buildings or structures to collapse.

Lancasters were to drop 42 'Grand Slams' on Germany in 1945. It proved particularly effective against bridges and viaducts, but it was only used in the final months of the war when the total defeat of Nazi Germany was already imminent.

Crews

The total number of Lancasters produced during World War II was over 7,000 and with a crew number of seven, many saw service with it. As a result, families today across Britain and the Commonwealth have a direct connection to the Lancaster. Although many of the veterans are no longer with us, this connection to a shared aviation history with the aircraft remains as strong as ever. One such crew member was Sergeant Navigator Ken Brown. His story highlights that of many crews from around the world and what they were to experience flying in Lancasters whilst serving in RAF Bomber Command.

Ken joined the RAF in November 1941, just after his 19th birthday. Following basic and then advanced training he qualified as a Sergeant Navigator, and was to move on to the OTU (Operational Training Unit). Ken described how the OTU assembled all the pilots, navigators, wireless operators, bomb-aimers and gunners together, and asked them to sort themselves out into their 'own' crews. Many airmen described this process and whilst many, including Ken, had no idea how it worked out, he became settled in a crew, and 'from that

The seven-man crew of an Avro Lancaster bomber wait near the crew room at Waddington, Lincolnshire for transport out to their aircraft.

time a bond existed between us that was immutable'. Bomber Command was to have one of the most diverse pool of men to call upon, with many from across the British Empire. A colour bar on officers had been relaxed by the RAF as the need for more crews grew, which saw over 500 men from the Caribbean and West Africa also serving with Bomber Command.

Ken and his crew joined 207 Squadron based at RAF Spilsby in Lincolnshire and he went on to fly in nine operational flights in a Lancaster over Berlin, Brunswick and Leipzig. However, on the night of 30 January 1944, Ken was part of a raid to Berlin. On the way there his Lancaster Mk III, EE173, 'K for King', suffered a minor engine problem, which meant that rather than aborting, the crew arrived about one minute later over Berlin, and as Ken said, 'Even that small error seemed to suggest that we were on our own over Berlin'. At 8:25 p.m., after releasing their bombs and moving away from the target area at 19,000 ft, a German night fighter with upward firing cannon attacked and 'the aircraft went into a vertical dive'. Although the pilot managed to recover to a straight level, 'K for King' had two engines that had stopped, a third was failing and the port wing was on fire. Ken recalled: 'I actually saw the shells coming up through the floor and hitting the armour on the back of the pilot's seat. How we escaped injury was unbelievable.' The crew prepared to jump out.

Ken managed to bail out and was relieved when his parachute opened. For him, the descent was 'as light as day, with a full moon and fighter flares drifting about'. His luck in escaping the burning plane was not to last, as he landed on the roof of a house, hitting the guttering and sliding down the side of it to land on his backside, directly opposite a public bomb shelter. Ken recalled: 'I was immediately surrounded by air raid wardens. Someone pulled my hair; another brandished a revolver and someone else pulled out a damn great knife.' The knife was used to cut his parachute cords and he was led down to the air raid shelter where he was abused by the local population. His pilot and other crew members were rounded up and joined him in the shelter: 'We weren't allowed to talk, I threw a rueful grin in Dick's

The personnel required to keep one Avro Lancaster flying on operations.

GREAT BRITAIN

direction and the Germans didn't like that one bit. They childishly made me stand in the corner facing inwards for about half an hour, in spite of my obvious back pain.'

Ken's flying days were now over. As he was marched off to captivity, he learnt later that 'K for King' had crashed into Lake Krumme, on the edge of the Grunewald Forest. He had landed in the village of Teltow, around 12 miles southwest of Berlin. Sadly, Sergeant Arthur Pulman, the rear gunner for this raid, went down with the plane. Passing through transit camps and witnessing first-hand the destruction the Lancasters that he had been part of had wreaked on the Germans, he eventually became prisoner no.1091 at Stalag Luft VI in the village of Heydekrug. This was not before his parents, back home in Ipswich in Suffolk, were made aware of his capture as his name was read out by German propaganda broadcaster William Joyce, also known as 'Lord Haw-Haw'.

As the Soviet armies progressed in their advance from the east in 1944, Ken could begin to hear the distant gunfire at his camp, and so was moved to Stalag 357 at Fallingbostel, close to the city of Hamburg. By April 1945, just about surviving amongst the disintegration of Nazi Germany, Ken, like many other Allied POWs, was forced to march away from the advancing Allies. With little food, he suffered hardships, including his column being mistaken for Germans and being attacked by rocket-firing Typhoons, which killed 31 of his fellow POWs. He was eventually liberated on 2 May by soldiers of the British Royal Dragoon Armoured Division, having been marched from farm to farm. He was repatriated as part of Operation Exodus from the Reiner Aerodrome on the Dutch/German border, on what he described as a 'battle-scarred Lancaster, with strict instructions not to touch anything'.

Ken's connection to the Avro Lancaster was to have one final twist. Some 25 years after jumping from the burning 'K for King', he received a phone call at work. It was the British Ministry of Defence and he was asked to go straight home, due to the Official Secrets Act, to find out that his Lancaster had been discovered at the bottom of Lake Krumme. Due to the aircraft leaking oil, his Lancaster would be raised from the bottom of the lake, a difficult task as the German authorities were unsure whether bombs were still on board. It proved to be safe and no bombs were found when the work to raise the plane began in October 1970, with one of his former crew able to witness its raising.

Ken Brown would go on to return many times to Germany in later life and was responsible, along with the local mayor, for developing a memorial to his fellow POWs at Stalag 357 at Fallingbostel. He stayed in touch with his crew members and visited many of them across the Commonwealth throughout the rest of his life. They had forged an immense 'unbreakable bond' that those crews who served on the Lancaster with RAF Bomber Command were to forever feel, and that would forever secure the Lancaster its place in World War II aviation history.

Avro Lancaster B Mk I (Special), May 1945.

#02
Avro Manchester

The Avro Manchester was a twin-engine British heavy bomber that has gone down in World War II history as a failure.

But despite its flaws it would go on and be developed further, evolving into the successful Avro Lancaster, one of the most significant heavy bombers of the war.

Origins

The Manchester was developed and built by the Avro company in response to British Air Ministry Specification P.13/36, issued in May 1936, detailing the requirement for a twin-engine medium bomber for the RAF.

A number of aircraft designs from different aircraft manufacturers were developed in response, including the more successful Handley Page Halifax, but Avro's design, whilst robust and sturdy, had one central weak point: its two Rolls-Royce Vulture engines. These engines did not provide sufficient power for the Manchester and suffered from reliability issues. Despite this, the Manchester made its maiden flight in July 1939, just before the German invasion of Poland in September that year, and entered service with No.207 Squadron RAF in November 1940.

The original design for the Manchester included a twin tail with a central fin. However, after an initial number

The crew of Avro Manchester Mk I, of No.207 Squadron RAF, standing by the nose of their aircraft at Waddington, Lincolnshire.

An Avro Manchester Mk IA with enlarged twin fins and without a central fin, flying above Saxilby, Lincolnshire, November 1941.

of Mk I aircraft were made, the central tail fin was removed following handling trials at Boscombe Down in Wiltshire, leaving the twin-fin configuration of the Mk IA with larger twin fins at the tail. Other features included a strong two-spar wing, a smooth external surface of aluminium alloy with flush rivets, self-sealing fuel tanks housed in the wing, which in turn gave it a large bomb bay covering the length of the aircraft. The Manchester had three hydraulic gun turrets, in the nose, rear and midway along the upper part of the aircraft, but plans to add a turret on the underside were not concluded, leaving more space for the bomb bay, a crucial feature that would contribute to the eventual success of the Avro Lancaster. Avro had also considered the need for manufacturing and maintenance, which would later aid the development of the four-engine Avro Manchester Mk III, which was to be renamed 'Lancaster'.

Operations

RAF Bomber Command used the Avro Manchester operationally from December 1940 to June 1942, with some continuing to operate as instructional aircraft until being retired in 1943.

The operational Manchesters that flew in this period conducted over 1,200 missions, but the big Allied bomber raids on Berlin that began in November 1941 contained only a small number of Manchesters. As an instructional aircraft it was used to train crews for the Avro Lancaster, as the layout was closely aligned to the new Lancaster with crew positions in the aircraft the same. In this role, in the evolution of the four-engine Lancaster, the Avro Manchester would play its most significant role of the war.

RIGHT: Interior view of the cockpit of an Avro Manchester Mk I, showing the captain seated at the controls and the bomb-aimer leaving his seat in the nose section. The similarity with the Avro Lancaster meant the Manchester was used to help train crews for flying the Lancaster.

GREAT BRITAIN

#03
Bell P-39 Airacobra

The Bell P-39 Airacobra was an innovative American-built single-seat fighter when compared to many other fighters manufactured in the war.

It can be considered as one of the few aircraft to be built around its principal weapon, a Browning T-9 cannon, which was mounted in the nose of the P-39, giving it a unique nose shape and placing the engine further back in the aircraft over the main wing.

It was limited in performance at higher altitudes which meant it was unsuited for combat in the skies of Western Europe, but it was used successfully by Soviet Air Forces on the Eastern Front in Europe, operating with the Soviets up until the end of the war in 1945.

Airacobra Mk I, of No.601 Squadron RAF, on the ground at RAF Duxford. No.601 Squadron was the only RAF unit to use the P-39 in operations, but its limited performance at higher altitudes meant it was deemed ineffective for the air war in Western Europe.

Origins and Operations

The P-39 evolved from a United States Army Air Corps pre-war requirement for an interceptor fighter to attack enemy aircraft at high altitudes.

The Bell Aircraft Corporation developed an unusual prototype that placed its Allison V-1710 engine to the rear of the aircraft, sited just over the wing, to be able to centre the aircraft's principal weapon, the Browning T-9 cannon, in the nose. This meant the cannon would protrude from the front of the nose and a long shaft would power the propeller, which ran from the engine and under the pilot's cockpit. As a result of this layout, the P-39 Airacobra also used a tricycle landing gear configuration for stability, with three wheels including one under the nose, which made landing and taking off simpler for the pilot. Unfortunately, the performance of this radical design was lacking, as the Allison engine gave the P-39 poor speed when at higher altitudes.

The fate of the P-39 as a front-line fighter was sealed at a meeting in August 1939, when a decision was made to continue development without fitting a turbocharger to the engine, which would have helped with the aircraft's poor speed at altitude. A cooling duct would have hindered the drag on the aircraft, but when the P-39 went into production the lack of the turbocharger gave a crucial altitude of 12,000 ft before the performance of the aircraft declined, at a time when the air war was being fought in Europe above this altitude.

In 1940 the British Direct Purchase Commission ordered over 600 of the P-39, believing the aircraft to be faster and more efficient than it actually was. After very limited operations with the RAF, the British order was cancelled due to the aircraft's issues. However, the P-39 went on to perform well with the Soviet Air Forces over the Eastern Front, where its sturdy airframe and cannon made it a success.

TOP RIGHT: The cannon projecting through the hollow hub of the airscrew of the Bell P-39 Airacobra. The unique design of the aircraft stemmed from this central weapon system and ensured the design would be radically different to other contemporary fighters.

BOTTOM RIGHT: The Bell Airacobra in flight.

#04
Bell P-63 Kingcobra

The Bell P-63 Kingcobra was an American-built single-seat fighter based on the earlier Bell P-39 Airacobra, but greatly improved based on feedback from P-39 pilots.

It would go on to serve most notably with Soviet Air Forces, shipped to the Soviet Union under the Lend-Lease Act, designed to aid the defence of the United States by supplying material to its wartime Allies.

Origins and Operations

The P-63 Kingcobra was an 'improved' P-39 which had some key changes to the radical design of the earlier Bell aircraft, built around its centrally mounted cannon in the nose and with its engine placed behind the cockpit.

It had a new semi-laminar flow wing and was overall larger than the P-39. Initially the engine was changed to a different one in early prototypes, but when the Kingcobra went into service it had reverted to using a newer version of the Allison V-1710 engine. The modifications persuaded the United States Army Air Forces (USAAF) – in 1941 US Army Air Corps became USAAF – to put the P-63 into production, as Allies such as the Soviet Union were still in need of modern aircraft, even though by 1943 it had been deemed to be inferior to the P-51 Mustang and as a result it never saw combat with the Americans.

The first variant, the P-63A entered production in October 1943, but due to the Soviet Union being the principal operator of the P-39, the Soviets sent an experienced test pilot to help with the development of the Kingcobra. This resulted in changes that included better armour to protect the pilot and extra fuel tanks. Over 2,000 P-63 Kingcobras were shipped to the Soviet Union under Lend-Lease. These planes would take a long route to the Soviet Union, transported by female pilots of Air Transport Command to Canada, and through to Alaska, where female Soviet ferry pilots would fly the planes to Siberia. There is some debate as to whether the P-63 was operated by the Soviet Air Forces in Germany; official Soviet records indicate they were only used on the Eastern Front, but according to some German pilots they encountered several P-63s in the skies over Germany towards the end of the war.

For the Western Allies, the lack of performance at higher altitudes meant the USAAF would use the P-63 mainly as a training and target aircraft, painted in a bright orange, earning it an unofficial nickname of 'Pinball'. In Britain, the P-63 was evaluated by the Royal Aircraft Establishment, with a particular focus on the performance of the aircraft's laminar flow wings. Although the P-63 would have limited service in the war, the Kingcobra was an improvement on its predecessor and served the Soviets well in their march onto Berlin.

Three P-63 Kingcobras made by Bell to replace and improve upon the P-39 Airacobra, flying in formation as part of a training unit. Although not used in combat by the Americans, they would serve the Soviet Air Forces well on the Eastern Front in Europe.

UNITED STATES

#05
Boeing B-17 Flying Fortress

The Boeing B-17 Flying Fortress was an American four-engine heavy bomber, which was to spearhead the American daylight bombing campaign against the German Luftwaffe in the skies over Europe.

It was a formidable aircraft, carrying a vast array of defensive weapons. Early belief by commanders (nicknamed the 'Bomber Mafia') in its defensive capabilities and accurate precision bombing in daylight was to be severely tested in early operations over Europe. The reality of fast interceptor German fighters, and cloudy skies and harsh weather, led to many aircraft and crew losses for the USAAF, and limited precision bombing.

It wasn't until the P-51 Mustang single-seat American fighter arrived in Europe, capable of providing continuous fighter support to B-17 bombers with its very long range, that the Flying Fortress would realise its potential for the Allies in helping to gain control of the skies of Europe. It became a potent symbol for all who flew and operated the B-17 as a very real definition of American air power.

B-17 Flying Fortresses of the 91st Bomb Group fly in formation during a mission. Early missions suffered from heavy losses in Europe, which only significantly improved with the introduction of the P-51 Mustang long-range fighter.

Origins

UNITED STATES

In 1934, the US Army Air Corps put forward a proposal for a new multi-engine daylight bomber that would have a speed over 200 mph and could carry a bomb load at an altitude of 10,000 ft.

It ideally also wanted the aircraft to have a flying distance range of up to 2,000 miles, to support far-flung areas of the United States such as Alaska and Hawaii.

The decision would be made between the Boeing company prototype B-17 against the designs by other US aircraft manufacturers, including Martin and Douglas.

The initial B-17 prototype, known simply as Model 299 at Boeing, was based on two other Boeing development aircraft: the Model 294 (also called the XB-15 by the Army Air Corps), a large bomber with four engines; and the Boeing Model 247 airliner, notable for its all-metal semi-monocoque skin and cantilevered wing, which included retractable landing gear. The Boeing team working on Model 299 incorporated four Pratt & Whitney Hornet radial engines into the design, which gave it superior performance when placed alongside the competitors in the race to win the best bomber design. Model 299 was also given defensive armament of five .30 calibre machine guns, and this initial large array of guns prompted a US journalist to describe the prototype when seeing it for the first time as a 'flying fortress'. The name appealed to Boeing, who had funded the initial development, and the company was quick to trademark the nickname, and the B-17 Flying Fortress had been born.

The Model 299 B-17 was to fly for the first time in the summer of 1935, and proved superior when placed against the twin-engine aircraft from both Martin and Douglas. However, a test flight in autumn 1935 ended suddenly when Model 299 crashed, with the loss of both test pilots, which disqualified Boeing at this point from fulfilling the Air Corps 1934 requirements. Later investigation into the crash would determine pilot error and some aviation historians attribute the crash to the development of preflight checklists in aviation.

Although the crash of Model 299 was to be a setback for Boeing, the US Army Air Corps had been impressed with the performance of the four-engine bomber. In 1936 they funded and ordered a small number of B-17s (designated YB-17) for testing, which had seen improvements since the prototype, including more powerful engines. One B-17 was also adapted with turbo-superchargers attached to the engine exhausts (which became YB-17A), increasing its maximum speed. Following successful testing, these test aircraft were designated B-17 and B-17A, with the letter 'B' simply defining 'bomber'.

By late 1937, further small orders were placed by the US Army Air Corps to equip a bomber group on both the east and west coasts of the United States. Despite the ongoing development of the B-17 and its production line through various types and modifications, the numbers of manufactured and equipping bomb groups were relatively small up until the entry of the United States into the war in 1941. After that, production would significantly accelerate to place the B-17 at the heart of the air war across all theatres of World War II, and especially in the dangerous skies over occupied Europe.

Crewman of the 303rd Bomb Group, in position inside the ball turret of a B-17 Flying Fortress. This was altered to the powered 'Sperry' ball turret in the B-17E variants.

Variants and Developments

The initial variants of the B-17 designated with a letter at the end were 'B' through 'D' and were developed from 1939 to 1941.

These saw alterations to the aircraft, including larger rudders and flaps to improve speed, changes to the side gun windows to make them open positions, and a gun turret that was placed in the lower part of the fuselage. The B-17E in 1941 became the first B-17 to be produced in larger numbers, with over 500 built. This version was developed to include a longer fuselage by 10 ft and a larger tail fin. It also saw the addition of a rear gun position and the lower fuselage gun position was changed to a 'Sperry' manned ball turret, whilst another electrically powered gun position, also built by the Sperry company, was added to the upper fuselage just behind the cockpit. The increases in armaments also added to the overall aircraft weight and the engines were upgraded to Wright Cyclone engines to compensate for this weight gain.

The B-17F became the main initial version used by the USAAF in Europe, with over 3,000 being built from 1942. Its main modifications were to standardise the 'Sperry' ball turret and improve the glazing in the nose to be an almost frameless 'Plexiglass' design. At this point there were some further experiments, including a modified B-17 designated the YB-40. This aircraft was an even more heavily armed and modified B-17, with the thought that it would support the bomb groups on missions by providing enhanced firepower against enemy fighters, and it could carry up to 11,000 rounds of ammunition. But the additional firepower came at a cost and increased the weight of the aircraft, which meant it struggled to keep up with the bombers it was supposed to be accompanying. This led to the modified YB-40 being scrapped, and B-17 aircraft and their bomber crews being left alone on missions deep into Germany until the introduction of the P-51 Mustang.

The abandoned YB-40 did have one innovation that would emerge in the next variant and the main production model, the B-17G, – an automated 'chin' gun turret. Previous versions had been equipped with manually operated forward-firing gun positions, although these were ineffective and often not accurate as they required the skill of the crew. But the addition of the Bendix Corporation manufactured and remotely operated 'chin' turret directly under the bombardier's position at the front of the nose, comprising of two .50 calibre Browning machine guns, greatly enhanced the forward firepower of the B-17. This became a standard gun position in the B-17G, which from 1943 would lead to over 8,000 aircraft of this type being built. This version of the B-17 would go on to see considerable combat over Europe. This mixture of continuous design and manufacturing improvements and combat experience had seen the defensive armaments of the B-17 Flying Fortress evolve from seven guns to 13.

Rear gunner of a Flying Fortress; the tail gun position was added to B-17E variants from 1941.

Cockpit view of the B-17 Flying Fortress. IWM undertook years of extensive conservation work to return this B-17 to its current condition and it is found in the American Air Museum at IWM Duxford.

Cockpit view of the B-17 Flying Fortress steering column.

The radio operator's position in the B-17 Flying Fortress located at IWM Duxford.

View of the B-17 Flying Fortress waist gun positions. These were originally oval 'blisters' in earlier versions of the B-17 but were altered to open windows. The waist gunners at these positions would wear oxygen masks and were subject to extreme cold at altitude, as the B-17 was not a pressurised aircraft. The fuselage was made of thin metal sheets, providing little protection to the crews on missions, but despite this the B-17 gained a reputation for sturdy reliability in getting damaged aircraft back to base. This example is found in the American Air Museum at IWM Duxford.

Such a large plane would inevitably be expensive. By 1945, a single B-17 would cost $250,000 to build, the equivalent to approximately $2.6 million today. But it could be manufactured quickly, with over 12,000 being built, spread between Boeing, Lockheed and Douglas factories. The ability to mass produce the B-17 allowed the USAAF to be re-equipped following early losses over Europe, which was necessary as around 5,000 B-17s would be lost before eventual Allied victory in 1945.

Many B-17G Flying Fortresses were to form the core of the USAAF Eighth Air Force Bomb Groups that would fly from airfields in East Anglia until the end of the war. Some were converted for other uses, including for cargo or for search and rescue, but all the B-17s operating on bombing missions over Europe would be equipped with a 'secret weapon' that would allow its crews to attack with precision accuracy: the 'Norden Bombsight'.

Norden Bombsight

The Norden Bombsight was a bomb-aiming system that was developed by the Norden company and invented by a Dutch immigrant to the United Sates, Carl Norden, in the 1920s.

Bombsights had gradually evolved since World War I, but the Norden sight combined three primary areas to produce a piece of equipment that could, in theory, deliver bombs on a target precisely. To do this it combined an optical sight with a small analogue computer and an autopilot. In its simplest terms, this combination allowed a bombardier to sight an enemy target through the optical lens, whilst the computer was able to continuously recalculate the bomb's release and impact point based on changing flying conditions, such as wind or altitude, whilst the autopilot could alter the aircraft in flight for optimum bomb release.

UNITED STATES

The Norden Bombsight was developed at a time when the Americans were primarily concerned with their own defence, with the aim to destroy any seaborne invasion on the United States by using the B-17 bomber and Norden Bombsight to drop bombs with precision on any enemy invasion fleets. Other nations in the pre-war period developed torpedo bombers to counter sea-invasion threats, and although other bombsights were also being developed, these did not have the same combination of parts as the Norden and were deemed less effective. Although the sight was not as precise at low altitudes, it was still of interest to both the Army Air Corps and US Navy. It helped with a strategy and doctrine that formed in the thinking of senior US commanders (the 'Bomber Mafia') that high altitude precision bombing in daylight against industrial and military targets inside enemy territory could win any war.

The development of the sight and its adoption in aircraft such as the B-17 led to a high level of security before and during the war. The Americans were resistant to sharing their technology, even with their British Allies who were aware of the bombsight and enquired about buying it, which was rebuffed. Despite the secrecy, the British had developed a similar system and details had been passed to Germany even before war had begun. Its existence was not declared publicly until 1944, and crew bombardiers were required to disable any bombsight by shooting it if it were possible that it could fall into enemy hands if an aircraft were shot down or landed in enemy territory.

It was also removed from B-17s after every mission by the crew and locked in a secure area of the base.

Despite the initial enthusiasm and belief in the Norden Bombsight in tandem with the B-17, which led to claims that the B-17 'was the best bombardment aircraft in existence', real combat experience, and a later change in strategy, meant the Norden Bombsight did not deliver the precision it had initially promised. However, it remains probably the most famous bombsight ever developed.

View of the B-17 Flying Fortress bomb bay. Whilst the bomb 'load' of the B-17 bomber was not as large as the Allies contemporary heavy bomber (the RAF's Avro Lancaster) when the B-17 was combined with the Norden Bombsight, the Americans initially came into the air war over Europe in the belief that this combination of the Norden Bombsight within the B-17 could deliver precise and targeted daylight bombing raids.

At an airfield in the United States, ground personnel work on the engines of a B-17 Flying Fortress nicknamed 'Hannah'.

Operations

UNITED STATES

As the US entered the war in 1941, the USAAF started to build up its forces in Europe, with the first B-17s arriving in England in May 1942.

Initial B-17 daylight raids took place over France in the summer of 1942, accompanied by Spitfires. These were generally successful and helped ease British fears over the effectiveness of daylight raids, as the few B-17s that had been delivered to the RAF that had already seen combat had been withdrawn from bombing missions by the RAF due to aircraft losses, before being transferred to RAF coastal patrol missions.

Part of the USAAF in Europe was the Eighth Air Force, which was activated in the state of Georgia in 1942. Its aims on activation were two-fold: to gain air superiority over the German Luftwaffe and to take the war to Nazi Germany by bombing key strategic targets. If achieved, this would pave the way for an invasion of occupied Europe, but with the RAF also bombing Germany as their own heavy bombers began to be delivered in numbers to RAF squadrons, a unified approach was needed. This was to arrive after the Casablanca Allied Conference in January 1943, which would see the Eighth Air Force bombers, with the B-17 as its main aircraft, attack with precision daylight raids, whilst the RAF would attack the same targets using more broad 'area bombing' by night, resulting in an Allied Combined Bomber Offensive that would target Nazi Germany 'round the clock'.

Crew of the 91st Bomb Group sit on the bonnet of a jeep in front of a B-17 Flying Fortress in 1943. Early missions to attack German aircraft manufacturing facilities would lead to heavy losses for the USAAF.

To support the arrival of so many American aircraft needed to mount this combined offensive, the 'flat' lands of the east of England were an ideal location to base the USAAF, with their close flying proximity to Europe, and they would become a massive land-based 'aircraft carrier' for the Eighth Air Force. Around 100 air bases were constructed for bombers and fighters by US engineering units in the initial phase of the American deployment. The large influx of American service personnel would have a profound impact on rural English villages and towns, especially across the East Anglian region, during what was termed the 'friendly invasion'.

General Carl Spaatz was in command of the Eighth Air Force, whilst Brigadier General Ira Eaker would command the bomber group of the force. In the summer of 1943, Eaker directed the growing number of B-17s stationed in England on missions to important German aircraft manufacturing plants, after raids on German air bases had not reduced the Luftwaffe's ability to fly up and meet the Allied bombers.

The bombing raids in 1943 on factories at Schweinfurt and Regensburg proved costly for the Eighth Air Force, despite disrupting German aircraft manufacturing, with many B-17s and their crews lost. In October 1943, raids on several locations including Munster and Schweinfurt would decimate the B-17 bomber groups, so much so that it would become known as 'Black Week'. In that week alone, 148 bombers were lost, and nearly 1,500 crew were shot down and killed or captured. The 100th Bomb Group, featured in the TV series *Masters of the Air*, lost all but one of 14 B-17s on the Munster raid in October 1943. During 'Black Week' the USAAF would lose 13 per cent of its attacking aircraft and, despite the ability of US industry to quickly make more aircraft to replace these losses, it was not sustainable. The air war over Europe would have to change.

TOP RIGHT: B-17 Flying Fortresses of the 381st Bomb Group are escorted during a practice mission by a P-51 Mustang of the 355th Fighter Group. The use of long-range escort fighters, especially the P-51 Mustang, to support American bombers from England into Germany and back to base would prove a turning point in the air war for the Allies. As the war progressed and the enemy fighter threat diminished, B-17s could roam through the skies with fewer losses than the initial American raids in 1943.

Big Week

In the autumn of 1943, the USAAF Eighth Air Force was faced with a dilemma.

It could not call off its campaign to attack the Luftwaffe, yet it could not sustain the ongoing high losses that raids deep into Germany were amassing, when escort fighters could only travel part of the way due to the fighters' limited fuel capacity. Also, the USAAF could not switch to night bombing, already covered by the RAF and who themselves were struggling with more deadly Luftwaffe night fighters, as the US crews were not trained for night bombing raids. As a result, missions were suspended until

fighter development could provide cover fully to the bomber 'streams' of aircraft on daylight bombing raids.

The first units of a new aircraft, the North American P-51 Mustang, began to arrive in England in November 1943. These sleek and streamlined fighters, powered by Merlin engines, could use extra fuel drop tanks mounted under their wings to fly to Berlin and back, and provide fighter support for the full length of a B-17 bombing mission. After training with bombing formations, the Eighth Air Force was ready to resume bombing missions in 1944 and this was also to coincide with a change at the top.

Major General James Doolittle, of the famous raid on Tokyo from earlier in the war when he flew bombers from an aircraft carrier, replaced Ira Eaker, but Doolittle decided to change tactics. Rather than have fighters escort the B-17 formations closely, the newly arrived Mustangs were tasked with flying ahead of the bombers and attacking the Luftwaffe both on the ground and in the air, hoping the approaching bombers would tempt the German fighters to fly up to meet the bomber streams. Then the P-51s would attack enemy positions on their way back to base. The USAAF would also move away from precision targeted raids and move to target area bombing, with a lead aircraft bombing the mark, and the rest of the bomb group following the leader and releasing their bombs at the same time.

Bombs falling away from a formation of Boeing B-17 Flying Fortresses of the US Eighth Air Force on a daylight raid over Europe. As in this photograph, heavy cloud cover and the need to maintain defensive formation meant that the B-17s often simply released their bombs on a signal from the formation leader, who used radar to identify the target. This method produced a pattern of bombs around an aiming point, which was vastly different from the precision bombing on which American pre-war planning had been based. During 'Big Week', large formations of B-17s attacked whilst the new P-51 Mustangs supporting the bombers would decimate the Luftwaffe.

The tactics proved successful, as between 20 and 25 February 1944, Operation Argument saw the USAAF by day and the RAF by night attack the Luftwaffe and its manufacturing industries. However, this was not wholly a bombing campaign but also a ploy to destroy the Luftwaffe and gain control of the skies of Europe before an Allied invasion. The operation was a success and became known as the 'Big Week'. Combining the US Eighth Air Force from England with the Fifteenth Air Force based in Italy, 1,000 bombers and 700 fighters would attack 12 targets. Although the USAAF would lose 200 bombers during this week, the impact on the Luftwaffe was far graver, with over 1,000 experienced pilots lost by the end of April 1944. The Allies were gaining the upper hand and really becoming masters of the air in Europe.

As the Luftwaffe continued to become worn down by the Allied Combined Bomber Offensive in the early part of 1944, thoughts were turning to the Allied invasion of Europe. B-17s of the Eighth Air Force would take part in missions to support the landings, scheduled to take place in Normandy. The heavy bomber groups of the Allies, including the B-17 Flying Fortress, coupled with a receding threat from German fighters, allowed the Allies to effectively 'seal' the battlefield for the landings, attacking vital infrastructure such as railways, which was to hinder any German attempts to move troops against the Allied landing forces. D-Day successfully delivered the Allies into Europe on 6 June 1944 and B-17s of the Eighth could resume their bombing missions over Germany.

By the end of the war, B-17 aircraft losses had become so low that replacement aircraft were no longer being delivered and this allowed for other, more humanitarian missions. The 100th Bomb Group used its B-17s to drop food to the starving Dutch population between 1 and 7 May 1945 as part of Operation Manna, just days prior to the final victory in Europe. Many of the crew who flew these missions to drop much-needed supplies would describe them as the most satisfying of the war for those involved.

Pacific

In the Pacific, the B-17 was to arrive with a baptism of fire. Twelve B-17s flying to the Philippines made a stop where they landed to refuel at Pearl Harbor.

It was 7 December 1941 and the crew were attempting to land during the Japanese attack on the American naval and air bases in Hawaii. Luckily for the crews there were only limited injuries and, diverting to a different base, the B-17s managed to land, with 10 of the 12 B-17s surviving the ordeal. In the Philippines, on hearing of the attack, commanders of the Far East Air Force were attempting to send the limited numbers of B-17s and fighters on air patrol to avoid a similar fate to the forces at Pearl Harbor that had been attacked on the ground. Unfortunately, internal disputes during the battle for the Philippines allowed the Japanese to attack and a force of B-17s was destroyed.

Early in the Pacific campaign, commanders thought the B-17 would be ineffective in the theatre. This was re-enforced by a lack of success attacking the Japanese from high altitudes, although B-17s played a key role in the destruction of several Japanese troopships during the Battle of the Bismark Sea. But by 1943, the B-17 was phased out of Pacific operations to be replaced by the B-24 and B-29, although some that remained were adapted for other roles, such as search and rescue.

B-17G of the 100th Bomb Group bombing beach defences near Boulogne as part of the 'Overlord' deception plan, 5 June 1944.

Crew

The B-17 had a crew of ten. There was a pilot and co-pilot in the cockpit; below in the glass nose were positioned the bombardier and navigator; behind them were the flight engineer and the radio operator. Four gunners were positioned: two at the waist gun openings and one each in the tail and underside ball turret.

Conditions were cramped and, when in combat, frightening. The B-17's fuselage was thin sheet metal that was no protection against cannon fire from enemy fighters or red-hot shards of metal from shrapnel thrown up into the air around the B-17s. German anti-aircraft guns could fire an 88-mm projectile into the sky at the B-17s that exploded at altitude, which could tear through the aircraft and kill all the crew on board. The fuselage was also not pressurised, which subjected the crews to cold temperatures at high altitudes of up to minus 50 degrees. Exposed skin could freeze instantly at altitude and frostbite was a frequent problem that the crews faced; they wore thick, sheepskin-lined clothing to keep warm, especially during winter.

B-17 Flying Fortress gunner of the Eighth US Air Force is shown wearing combat headgear with oxygen mask and knitted wool cap, neck and chest covering, used while attacking German targets from high altitudes. This style of flying helmet offered little protection from flak and as a result a metal helmet was modified to fit over the flying helmet, allowing for the googles and oxygen to be worn, becoming the M3 helmet.

The crew of a B-17 also had to use oxygen at altitude and missions deep into enemy territory could last for up to ten hours. To combat anti-aircraft fire, known as flak, crews were issued with a metal helmet, originally a flying helmet which contained earphones as the crew communicated using microphones attached to their throats. But these 'soft' flying helmets were no protection from the flak. In 1943, aircrew of 306th Bombardment Group adapted metal helmets to be worn over the top of the softer flying helmets that had headphones. This modified steel helmet was adopted and became the M3 helmet, which gave the crew room for both the oxygen mask and goggles to be worn. Some positions were also extremely lonely posts in the B-17, especially the personnel in the confined ball turret.

The best defence for crews facing enemy fighters was the ability to fly in formation, which allowed all the guns to provide a 'cone of fire' and removed the risk of firing on other friendly aircraft in the formation. Despite this successful tactic, life for aircrew was frightening and exhausting, concentrating in difficult conditions for hours on end. The crew, when they returned to base, would partake in the local pubs; many described the surreal atmosphere of at one moment being safely back at base and enjoying life before returning the next day to the stress and danger of bombing missions. It seems unsurprising that superstition was commonplace, with crews adopting mascots, some as bizarre as a donkey, as was the case for 96th Bomb Group B-17 Flying Fortress, whilst B-17s were given nicknames and adorned with elaborate 'nose art'.

The pre-war aim of using B-17s in strategic bombing to provide precision attacks and avoid unnecessary casualties was to become seriously challenged towards the end of the war. B-17s took part in bombing missions and were at the forefront of raids deep into Nazi Germany that exacted a terrible price on the civilian populations towards the end of the war in 1945. These included the infamous raids on the eastern German city of Dresden, killing an estimated 20,000 people. The B-17s of the Eighth Air Force in Europe would, after difficult real combat experience that evolved the tactics for the war in the air, deliver air superiority for the Allies.

Although the Combined Bomber Offensive did not deliver a knockout blow to Hitler and his regime alone, it did pave the way for a fightback that began a year before the Allies landed in Europe. The B-17 was at the spearhead of this fightback. This remarkable aircraft, which would be produced in vast numbers, would secure its place in aviation history by dropping over 640,000 tons of bombs and flying over 290,000 sorties in Europe. The losses of crew were also huge though, and before the P-51 Mustang joined the fight providing continuous air support to the B-17s, the air war over Europe would see 26,000 American crew members killed. The legacy of those lost continues with the B-17s that still fly today, including at IWM Duxford where a B-17 can still be seen soaring over East Anglian skies, just as thousands of B-17s had done during World War II.

B-17 Flying Fortresses of the 381st Bomb Group fly in formation during a practice mission. The contribution of the B-17 to the eventual Allied victory in 1945 would come at a high price for the aircrews who flew them.

#06
Boeing B-29 Superfortress

The Boeing B-29 Superfortress was the world's first 'super' bomber.

It was the result of the most expensive development and manufacturing project of the war in the United States, totalling $3 billion, over $1 billion more than the wartime development of the atomic bomb. It was operated by the Americans from 1944 onwards, solely in the Pacific theatre of war. Its unique design and cutting-edge technology resulted in it being selected to controversially drop the first and only atomic weapons ever used in combat, on the Japanese cities of Hiroshima and Nagasaki in August 1945, securing a polarising legacy as arguably the most important bomber in history.

B-29 Superfortresses of 20th Air Force fly in formation during a mission. The cost of the development of the B-29 was the most expensive of the war and would even eclipse the development of nuclear weapons.

Origins

Even before the start of war, the US Army Air Corps had decided that the principal strategic heavy bomber the Americans would operate in the war, the Boeing B-17 Flying Fortress, would be insufficient for operations in the Pacific against an increasingly confident and expansionist Imperial Japan.

It would require a bomber to fly over 3,000 miles and deliver 20,000 lb of bombs, which was way above the limits of the Flying Fortress, to dominate the Pacific and become the ultimate 'hemisphere weapon'. But to achieve this range the new super bomber would have to fly at higher altitudes and this would require a pressurised aircraft.

The US aircraft manufacturer Boeing already had considerable experience of building pressurised cabins on their airliners and in 1940 the company was offered a contract to build a prototype, the XB-29. This prototype flew for the first time on 21 September 1942. Even before this first flight, the aircraft had been ordered by the US military, with an order for 1,500 in place by January 1942, despite the cost of each aircraft being $500,000. But the project had been given enhanced priority following the Japanese attack on Pearl Harbor in December 1941.

The level of technology on the new design would push the manufacturers, scientists and engineers to the maximum, with the B-29 built across a range of factories in the United States, including facilities of the Bell Aircraft Corporation and Martin. The first evaluation bomber, YB-29, was delivered in July 1943 to the 58th Bomb Wing. The main variants used during the war arrived a few months later. These were the B-29A-BN, which had a four-gun upper turret, and the B-29B-BA, which had reduced armament to allow for a larger bomb load to be carried. Despite the technological developments and large expense, the B-29 also suffered problems, specifically with regard to its engines, a similar problem that was to plague many aircraft developed during the war. To permit such a large and heavy aircraft to take to the air, the B-29 was fitted with four Wright R3350 Duplex Cyclone supercharged engines. However, these were prone to overheating and reliability issues, including the crash of one on its first test flights into a factory in Seattle, which killed all 11 crew and 20 factory workers. This engine problem would not be solved until after the war when they were replaced with Pratt & Whitney engines.

Technology

UNITED STATES

The development of the B-29 made use of much innovative technology and, combined with its airframe, it would produce an aircraft design that looked more like today's airliners.

The sleek circular body was vastly different to the B-17 Flying Fortress, partly because it would reduce drag, and a circular cockpit would be easier to pressurise. The B-29 had a crew of ten, with six crew housed in the first pressurised cabin at the front of the aircraft. There had been discussion on whether the bomb bay should also be pressurised. Instead, a second crew compartment to the rear of the aircraft was connected by a small pressurised tunnel, which housed the gunner crew, and the fire control system for the guns was located here.

As the B-29 was intended to fly at high altitudes, traditional crewed turrets found on the B-17 were not suitable for the new super bomber. As a result, the defensive armaments on the B-29 were all controlled by a computer fire control system. This allowed all the gunner 'seats' to operate all the guns, so concentrated fire could be directed if an attack was coming from a certain direction. The unmanned turrets would also be automated, and smaller in profile, which would help with the bomber's aerodynamics. The central fire control gunner sat in an elevated seat with a viewing dome, which gained it the nickname 'Barber's Chair'. From this position the gunner could control all the guns and direct them as required.

The B-29 was also designed to use on-board radar to aid with bombing during the night or when targets were obscured by cloud. This radar had its antenna fitted into a small dome on the underside of the aircraft's fuselage, but this innovation was often removed from photos of the bomber by wartime censors as it was deemed too sensitive to reveal. The bomber needed to carry a large bomb load, and this was housed in the B-29's two bomb bays, which released the bombs alternately between the bays and were designed to keep the aircraft stable in flight when the bombs were released.

A tail gunner of 20th Air Force cleans the windows on his B-29 Superfortress. The fire control systems of the B-29 were computer controlled, so the gunners did not sit directly in the turrets. The technology on the aircraft also included radar to assist with bombing accuracy.

Operations

At the start of the war the USAAF planned to use the B-29 against Germany and Japan, with B-29s to be based in North Africa.

But as the war developed and production of the B-29 took longer to be delivered as a front-line aircraft, the decision was made that the B-29 would be used solely in the Pacific. The first B-29s entered service with the 58th and 73rd Bomb Wings, and flew from bases in India and China, with the first B-29 raid on 5 June 1944 on the Japanese-held Thai city of Bangkok. However, operating from these bases, especially in China, was difficult and dangerous as all the supplies had to be flown over the Himalayas over what became known as the 'Hump' (a section of the Eastern Himalayas between India and China), which also proved costly. A further frustration operating B-29s from China was that not all the Japanese islands could be reached.

A solution to this problem was to set up bases amongst the Marianas Island chain in the Pacific, from which the B-29 could operate, and by late 1943 American chiefs approved plans to seize these key islands. US forces invaded Saipan in June 1944, followed by Guam and Tinian in August. With the islands secured, Naval Construction Battalion, the 'Seabees', quickly constructed bases for the B-29, with the first B-29s arriving in Saipan in October 1944. The first raid on Tokyo from the Marianas Islands since the famous 'Doolittle Raid' of 1942 was on 24 November 1944 by 88 unescorted B-29s. The final endgame of the war in the Pacific was about to begin.

The initial bombing missions over Japan at high altitude, now only 1,500 miles away from the new American bases in the Marianas, were disappointing. Mechanical issues and failures saw many B-29s turn back to base. Strong jet streams at higher altitudes over Japan also hindered accurate bombing, despite the new on-board radar. As this expensive project and aircraft was failing to deliver a knockout blow to the Japanese, the US switched to a new tactic under General Curtis LeMay: dropping incendiary firebombs on the wood and bamboo houses found in the cities of Japan.

A B-29 Superfortress of the 497th Bomb Group, 20th Air Force. The development of bases in the Pacific Marianas Islands allowed the B-29s to reach all of mainland Japan.

These missions began in February 1945. The B-29 crews altered tactics to bombing at lower altitudes and at night, with their guns removed to allow for more bombs. The success of these raids was devastating. They reached a climax with a raid on Tokyo on the night of 9/10 March 1945. The fires that were created by the Tokyo firebombing combined to devastate an area of 16 square miles, with accounts referring to people burning alive or jumping into water to escape the flames. It is estimated that 100,000 people died because of the attack. Fourteen B-29s were shot down over Tokyo during the raid and, unsurprisingly with such a huge loss of life on the ground, B-29 pilots who jumped out over Japan were to be on the end of equally brutal treatment.

The results of the raids in 1945 seriously damaged the Japanese cities and wartime economy. The B-29 also took part in the mining of Japanese waters from April 1945: Operation Starvation seriously hampered the Japanese and their ability to feed the population and move troops to support its army operations. The war was not yet won and with Allied planners suggesting the invasion of Japan would lead to huge losses of Allied troops, the B-29 was to deliver the ultimate weapon. For the Japanese, the worse was still to come.

The Atomic Bomb

The B-29 had been identified early on as the only aircraft that could deliver an atomic weapon, which had been developed under great secrecy in the United States.

The 'Manhattan Project' would come to fruition in the desert of New Mexico in July 1945 with the successful test detonation of a nuclear device. The 'Silverplate' fleet was a code name for the B-29 atomic bombing fleet, initially referring to the modification B-29s would require to carry the bombs, but which later also covered the training and operational requirements to deliver the bombs.

A B-29 named *Enola Gay* took off from a US base in the Marianas from the island of Tinian, and at 8.15am on 6th August 1945, dropped its bomb, nicknamed 'Little Boy', over the Japanese city of Hiroshima. The device exploded at 2,000 ft above the city; the blast, with the equivalent force of 12,000 tons of TNT, destroyed around 5 square miles of the city, killing 100,000 people. A second device was dropped from a B-29, *Bock's Car*, on 9 August 1945 over the city of Nagasaki, killing a further 70,000. In the face of such a potent weapon delivered from the B-29 Superfortress, the Japanese agreed to an unconditional surrender on 15 August 1945. The B-29 had played a leading role in ushering in the atomic age, but at a controversial and staggering cost.

The B-29 would continue to serve in the post-war period, including in Korea. But by 1950 this technologically advanced bomber had already become obsolete, with considerable losses suffered at the hands of jet-powered MiG aircraft, so was retired from active front-line duty. This most expensive technological aircraft of the war undeniably brought the conflict to an end, but its role in the dropping of the only atomic bombs in combat would forever place it as a controversial and expensive gamble.

ABOVE: The B-29 *Enola Gay*, which dropped the atomic bomb on Hiroshima, and her pilot, Colonel Paul Tibbets.

RIGHT: The mushroom cloud over Nagasaki, photographed from an escorting American B-29 aircraft, *The Big Stink*, after the atomic bomb had been dropped by USAAF B-29 *Bock's Car* on 9 August 1945. The Japanese Supreme War Council agreed later the same day to accept the Potsdam Declaration of 26 July 1945, which demanded the unconditional surrender of Japan.

Beaufighter TF Mk Xs breaking formation during a flight along the coast of Scotland.

#07

Bristol Beaufighter

The Bristol Beaufighter was a British multi-role twin-engine fighter, an often overlooked aircraft in the history of the air war in World War II.

With a rugged and robust structure, the Beaufighter proved to be an exceptional night fighter equipped with on-board radar, before later designs excelled in the ground and maritime attack role, arguably making the Beaufighter the most important Allied anti-shipping fighter later in the war. The 'unsung hero' status saw it serve in many areas of the conflict with several different air forces, inflicting severe damage to the Axis powers.

RIGHT: Beaufighter Mk VI being rearmed. The armourers are feeding belts of ball and high-explosive incendiary ammunition into the magazines of the aircraft's four 20-mm Hispano cannon, demonstrating the large firepower of the Beaufighter.

GREAT BRITAIN

Origins

With war looming following the Munich Crisis in 1938, the Bristol Aeroplane Company recognised a need for Britain to have a long-range fighter that could deliver a large weapons payload.

Led by designer Leslie Frise, the Bristol team assessed that the Beaufort torpedo bomber could be modified to fulfil this need and, by using the same machine tools and jigs as the Beaufort, production could easily switch between the two aircraft as required. Originally equipped with two Bristol Hercules engines, the new fighter, now named the Beaufighter, made its first flight in September 1939. It went into production shortly after, with an order for 300 aircraft from the Air Ministry.

The Beaufighter's engines were situated in the wings and slightly forward of the pilot cockpit. This gave the aircraft a better centre of gravity and ruggedness. But compared to single-seat fighters such as the Spitfire, it was slow, with a top speed of just over 320 mph. What it lacked in speed, the Beaufighter made up for with its versatility and heavy armament. Although the bomb bay from the Beaufort had been removed, it could fit bombs under its wings and later models would also use rockets. Its main armament was an array of machine guns and cannons situated under the fuselage and in its wings, which evolved over the many types or 'marks', leading to the Beaufighter having one of the strongest firepower of any fighter during the war.

In total, just over 5,500 Beaufighters of different variants were produced during the war, serving with the RAF, Royal Australian Air Force, USAAF and other air forces.

Operations

The Beaufighter entered service with the RAF in September 1940. As the Battle of Britain subsided into the Luftwaffe's nightly bombing Blitz in Britain in the autumn of 1940, the Beaufighter, fitted with internal on-board radar, carried the fight to the enemy in the night skies of Britain.

Often guided by ground radar stations to within a few miles of enemy bombers, the Beaufighter could then switch to on-board radar to close in on the enemy, and with its sufficient engine power could catch and bring its ferocious armament to attack the enemy bombers. By early 1941, most German bomber losses in the Blitz were attributed to the Beaufighter.

In the Mediterranean, the Beaufighter proved a decisive weapon, from disrupting enemy shipping to ground attack in the Western Desert, supporting the 8th Army fighting in North Africa. It also continued its night-fighter role with the USAAF taking the Beaufighter into service in Africa, Italy and Sicily, before the introduction of the Mosquito and American-built P-61 Black Widow saw it moved over to other missions.

In the spring of 1941, RAF Coastal Command received its first Beaufighters, the Mk IC, the 'C' determining that these were a maritime variant of the design. Modified from the Mk XIC, the TF Mk X fitted with torpedoes became the main maritime variant, commonly known as the '*Torbeau*'. Early models were to feature Air to Surface Vessel (ASV) radar, with antenna mounted on wings or the nose. Later models saw this radar developed to sit within an enclosed nose 'radome', or dome structure, to improve all weather and night operations.

As an anti-shipping aircraft, the Beaufighter proved exceptional, accounting for enormous losses of enemy shipping from 1942. The Coastal Command wing, based at North Coates on the Lincolnshire coast, attacked shipping using large groups of the aircraft. Other assaults by Beaufighter aircraft on shipping ranged from the coast of Norway to the Bay of Biscay, accounting for half of all enemy shipping losses in Europe between 1942 and 1945.

The Beaufighter arrived in the Pacific theatre in the summer of 1942 where it was operated extensively by the Royal Australian Air Force. The Beaufighter's Hercules engines were quieter than many other engines due to being fitted with sleeve valves; consequently the aircraft was sometimes referred to as the 'Whispering Death'. Beaufighters successfully supported the US Fifth Air Force in the Battle of the Bismark Sea, which saw a Japanese task force on the way to New Guinea being destroyed. It also served as a night fighter once again, flying from India, whilst low-level raids over Burma, now Myanmar, proved to be a continued menace to the occupying Japanese forces, and its robust construction was invaluable when flying from short jungle airstrips.

With Valletta in the background, Bristol Beaufighter Mk VIF of No.272 Squadron on the taxiway at Luqa, Malta.

ABOVE: A '*Torbeau*'. Experiments in 1942 proved that the Beaufighter would make a capable torpedo bomber. Aircrew were initially wary of carrying torpedoes as they hindered escaping through the pilot's exit hatch until the torpedo had been released.

BELOW: A low-level attack by Bristol Beaufighters on two German trawler-type auxiliaries south of Heligoland. Two Beaufighters are seen clearing one of the vessels after raking it with rocket projectiles and cannon fire. This trawler was left burning fiercely whilst the other was torpedoed and blew up.

#08
Bristol Blenheim

The Bristol Blenheim was a British light twin-engine medium bomber designed by the Bristol Aeroplane Company.

The Blenheim was operated by the RAF throughout World War II, not just as a bomber but also as a fighter and crew trainer. When it entered service in 1938 it was faster than RAF biplane fighters such as the Gloster Gladiator.

A formation of five Blenheim Mk IVs in flight over the Western Desert. The extended nose area can be seen in this version.

GREAT BRITAIN

A Bristol Blenheim Mk I in Greece, showing the earlier Mk I shorter nose and 'stepless cockpit'.

Origins

The Blenheim was based on a civil aircraft that was developed from a challenge issued in 1934 by the owner of the British newspaper the *Daily Mail*, Lord Rothermere, for a small airliner to fulfil his aim of the 'fastest airline in Europe'.

The Type 142 aircraft took to the skies in 1935, but due to its performance in outpacing the fighter biplanes then currently in service with the RAF, it was put forward for trials as a medium bomber. The successful Type 142M (for military use) went into production in 1935, with a bomb bay and a machine gun modified into the design.

The Blenheim had an all-metal stressed skin, one of the first British aircraft to do so. The Mk I featured a 'stepless cockpit', where the cockpit was incorporated into the aircraft nose. This gave the earlier types a 'stub' nosed appearance before the development of the Mk IV arrived in 1939 with a lengthened nose section to aid with the navigation and bomb aiming.

Operations

The Blenheim equipped squadrons stationed from Britain to Egypt, Iraq, India and Singapore. Initial combat in September 1939 included a raid on the German naval fleet at Wilhelmshaven, but only minor damage was inflicted.

The aircraft was on the front line during the onslaught of the German 'blitzkrieg' (lightning war) in the spring of 1940. There were considerable losses of Blenheims as the faster Luftwaffe fighter aircraft decimated the bombers in the air and on the ground, whilst a small number tried to help in the Allied evacuation at Dunkirk.

The Blenheim flew during the Battle of Britain but again suffered large losses. It proved more successful as a night fighter during the Blitz, when the Mk I F (fighter) was fitted with Airborne Interceptor (AI) radar. In August 1941, the Blenheim was used for a mass low-level attack on power stations near Cologne, but suffered considerable losses during the raid. The Blenheim also saw service in the Mediterranean and in the Pacific, where it was the first Allied aircraft to attack a Japanese aircraft carrier task group. However, rapid technological progress and extra weight gained from military equipment meant its speed advantage was no longer, and in 1941 it was deemed inadequate for operations.

Despite forming the backbone of the RAF's medium bomber force at the start of the war, the Blenheim became effectively obsolete as the war progressed and it was replaced with more advanced aircraft. The Blenheim and the Canadian-built version of the Blenheim IV, the Bolingbroke, remained in service with the RAF and Royal Canadian Air Force as a trainer until the end of the war.

Goldenberg power station at Knapsack in Germany, under attack by Bristol Blenheim Mk IVs.

RIGHT: A Blenheim Mk IV undergoes servicing while crew refuel the aircraft.

GREAT BRITAIN

#09
Consolidated B-24 Liberator

B-24 Liberators of the 93rd Bomb Group fly in formation during a mission. They would carry one of the largest bomb loads for a bomber faster and further than any other aircraft in the war.

UNITED STATES

The Consolidated B-24 Liberator was an American four-engine heavy bomber with a long range and large bomb load.

The most-produced American military aircraft in history, with over 18,000 built, the B-24 was not without its flaws and critics. Loved by some crews and hated by others, the B-24 served extensively with the USAAF during the war and made an important contribution that helped turn the tide of the war for the Allies, especially during the Battle of the Atlantic. It was eclipsed by the B-17 Flying Fortress in the USAAF daylight bombing campaign in Europe, despite having been assigned some of the most difficult missions. But regardless of its often-overlooked role, the bravery of the crews that flew in the B-24 Liberator is uncontested.

Origins

Sometimes referred to as the 'Flying Boxcar' due to its shape, the B-24 Liberator emerged from the development of large heavy bombers in the United States during the 1930s.

With it came an emerging tactical doctrine of high-level precision bombing, which it was commonly believed could win any future war and certainly destroy any invasion fleets approaching the coasts of the United States. It was designed by Consolidated Aircraft of San Diego, California and built by Consolidated as well as several other manufacturers in factories across America, including the Ford factory at Willow Run in Michigan, home to the largest production line in the world at the time.

Consolidated received a request from the US Army Air Corps in 1938 to build Boeing's B-17 bomber under licence. Instead they favoured producing their own more modern design, known at Consolidated as Model 32, which had been designed around the bomb bay capacity of a B-17. It was based on previous seaplanes designed by Consolidated such as the Model 31 seaplane with its twin-tail configuration. The design of the prototype Model 32 also used a 'Davis Wing', designed by American aeronautical engineer David R. Davis in the 1930s. His wing design had a streamlined laminar airfoil (aerofoil) skin, which helped to reduce drag. This in turn led to more speed and better lift for the aircraft. Adding the wings to a large fuselage that could carry a huge bomb load gave the US Army Air Corps, who were still looking for an 'inter-continental' bomber, an opportunity that was too good to refuse. A contract for a prototype, XB-24, was signed in March 1939, with its maiden flight a brief time after, in late December 1939.

Design

The B-24 Liberator's design, whilst not the most aesthetically pleasing on the eye compared to other aircraft from the period, with its big and 'boxy' appearance, did have some unique features.

These would become both its strengths and weaknesses when it went into combat. Indeed, some RAF personnel were believed to have referred to the B-24, when seeing it for the first time, as the 'box which the B-17 came in' as it was so big.

The laminar airfoil 'Davis Wing' was long and narrow, being some 6 ft longer than the B-17, and had a smaller surface area, but it generated less drag, producing more speed and lift. This allowed for it to be a 'thick' wing, with more room for fuel and its four supercharged Pratt & Whitney R-1830 engines, which led to its long range and fast speed. The wing was mounted high on the fuselage, due to its seaplane origins. This meant the large fuselage body and bomb bay sat close to the ground, requiring a tricycle landing gear with a nose wheel and two large wheels that opened outwards into the wings after take-off. This landing gear did, however, mean that the wing of the B-24 was slightly weakened structurally to accommodate the landing wheels ascending into them, and this would impact the aircraft's performance when it entered combat.

The lack of clearance of the B-24 when on the ground also led to a unique bomb bay door. Most bomb bays on aircraft of the time had doors that opened out and down, but this configuration on a B-24 was impossible with it being so close to the ground. A retractable roller-type bomb door was added to enable ground crew to arm the bomber. This bomb door design also gave the B-24 reduced drag when opening it over targets, allowing the B-24 to maintain its speed and not slow down, like a B-17 Flying Fortress crew found happened when opening its bomb bay.

The defensive armament of the B-24 was extensive like its contemporaries and evolved over the different variants. This was especially needed for the USAAF daylight bombing raids in Europe, although long-range Liberators would have less armament to help reduce weight and to increase the flying range of the aircraft. The B-24 had gun positions in the nose, rear, waist and on top of the fuselage, and it was also fitted with a retractable underside or 'ventral' ball turret, which was remotely operated in later models. This was retracted into the huge belly of the aircraft due to its low ground clearance.

Despite this large array of weapons, the B-24 was still vulnerable to fighter attack if sent on missions unescorted by friendly fighters. Ironically for an aircraft that originated from seaplanes, the B-24 when it landed or ditched on water was liable to sink quickly. Both the British and Americans tried to remedy this vulnerability, but it was concluded that only a complete redesign of the bomb bay doors by reinforcing them would help to reduce this issue. This was not possible with factory assembly lines producing the aircraft now in full swing.

The B-24 evolved through many variants during the war. The B-24D was the first mass-produced type with just under 3,000 built. This was followed by the B-24H and J types, with improved autopilot and forward-firing armament, and over 9,000 of these variants were manufactured.

B-24 Liberators under construction at the Ford factory at Willow Run, which had the largest production line in the world.

OPPOSITE: B-24 Liberators of the 15th USAAF in flight during a mission over Ploesti in Romania, 31 May 1944. An earlier raid of B-24s unescorted by fighters in 1943 against the oil fields disastrously led to 53 Liberators being shot down and 660 crew killed or captured and imprisoned.

Operations

The B-24 first entered service with the RAF in June 1941. It had initially been ordered with the French as part of the Anglo-French Purchasing Board, but when France fell in 1940 to the German invasion, the French allocation was sent to Britain.

The RAF used the B-24 to transport aircrews across the Atlantic from Canada to Scotland, before Liberators were transferred to RAF Coastal Command in 1941. The aim was to help in the ever-increasing battle in the Atlantic between German U-boat submarines and ship convoys that were vital to the Allied war effort.

With the vast space of the Atlantic Ocean, air cover for convoys suffered in what became known as the 'Mid Atlantic Gap', an area at the farthest point between Canada and the British Isles, where U-boats could hunt convoys without fear of being attacked from the air. Modified 'Very Long Range' (VLR) Liberators were adapted to help plug this air gap, flying from both sides of the Atlantic. They were equipped with Air to Surface Vessel (ASV) radar and a powerful beam searchlight or 'Leigh Light', and were able to fly against the submarines by day or night, having some gun turrets removed and extra fuel added to increase their flying range. The VLR Liberator became a significant menace to U-boats in the 'gap' and over the U-boat bases along the Bay of Biscay, shifting the Battle of the Atlantic in favour of the Allies and allowing the vital shipping to get through, building up forces and material in Britain for the liberation of Europe.

The B-24 entered service with the USAAF in mid-1941 and was deployed to all theatres of war, in Africa, Europe, China-Burma-India and the Pacific. Due to its longer range and to simplify logistic operations, the B-24 became the leading bomber for the American and Allied forces in the Pacific, taking over from the B-17 Flying Fortress. In the Pacific and South West Pacific, the B-24 saw service from Pearl Harbor (where the first B-24 in American service was destroyed on the ground during the Japanese attack in December 1941) through to action at Midway, Wake Island, the Philippines, Guadalcanal and flying from Australia. However, by the time US forces were to come into range of the main Japanese islands, the B-29 Superfortress had entered service and was used as the primary bomber against Japan.

The B-24 Liberator first arrived in Britain with the USAAF in September 1942 with the 44th Bomb Group. It would form the backbone of the strategic bombing campaign for the Allies alongside the B-17 Flying Fortress, flying from bases in Britain, North Africa and later Italy against targets in occupied Europe. The B-24 was thrust straight into combat and by August 1943 would conduct a raid on the Romanian oil fields that supplied Nazi Germany, at low level, in Operation Tidal Wave. Flying from Benghazi in North Africa, the mission was disastrous. It was unescorted and navigational errors saw 53 out of 177 Liberators of three USAAF bomb groups fail to return, shot down by flak and enemy fighters. As with the lessons learnt by B-17 aircrew over Europe, missions in 1943 without long-range Allied fighter cover would be extremely costly for both aircraft and crew.

As the air war over Europe continued, it became apparent that the B-24 was not a 'perfect' bomber. It was harder to fly than the B-17, especially in large 'box' formations of aircraft. In 1944 several B-24s were tasked with becoming 'assembly ships', painted in bright colours with armament removed and a smaller crew quota, to help assemble the large bomber streams for missions to Europe. The B-24 could not fly quite so high on missions as the B-17, so was more susceptible to enemy anti-aircraft fire.

It also gained a reputation as being dangerous compared to the B-17 Flying Fortress. It was perceived to be vulnerable, unlike the B-17 which was known for often managing to safely return to base despite suffering heavy damage. The B-24's reputation was arguably somewhat unfair, as early crashes could be put down to inexperienced pilots in training and were at a similar level to the B-17. However, in combat there are multiple photographs showing B-24s being shot down with one of the wings breaking free. This is possibly due to the slightly weaker area around the wheel, when hit by fire, sending the B-24s into a sharp, fast dive, which was impossible to bail out from. Combined with crew bottlenecks leading to limited hatches, the B-24 was harder to escape from when hit by flak or fire from enemy fighters. The survivability of a B-24 crew would only improve with the introduction of long-range fighters such as the P-51 Mustang.

The Consolidated B-24 Liberator was a large and versatile aircraft. Despite being used as transport, including a specially fitted-out B-24 used by British Prime Minister Winston Churchill, it is often overlooked in favour of the B-17 and other American bombers. With most being scrapped after the war, the sacrifices of the many B-24 aircrew who helped win the Battle of the Atlantic, turn the tide in favour of the Allies in the Pacific and secure eventual Allied air supremacy in Europe still lives on.

A B-24 Liberator of the 93rd Bomb Group used as a flight assembly ship.

UNITED STATES

#10
Consolidated PBY Catalina

The Consolidated PBY Catalina was an American flying boat capable of operating from sea or land, which saw extensive service throughout the war.

It was used in many roles, including anti-submarine warfare, reconnaissance patrol, convoy escort, cargo transport and maritime rescue of aircrews shot down. It featured in all major theatres, helping the Allies, especially in the vast Pacific Ocean. This aircraft was one of the most versatile flying boat types of all time, serving throughout the war and in the decades after, before it finally finished military service in the 1980s. This long service history gives an insight into the exceptional performance of the Catalina for the many roles with which it was tasked.

UNITED STATES

Origins

The Catalina evolved from a US Navy requirement for a 'Patrol Bomber' in the 1930s that would have a long range for operations in the Pacific Ocean, as tensions over Japan's military conquest in China increased in the United States.

The US Navy determined any future conflict across the Pacific would require forces to be supplied over long distances that could land on water, giving the aircraft the whole of the ocean as a potential landing site. A contract was placed with Consolidated Aircraft Company in San Diego for a prototype design in October 1933. The prototype XP3Y-1, known as Model 28 internally at Consolidated, had its first flight in March 1935, after which it was sent to the US Navy for assessment. The prototype proved successful, with initial orders going into production and being delivered to the US Navy by October 1936, after it had demonstrated its long-range ability by flying from San Diego to the Panama Canal, over 3,000 miles. The design would go on to be developed further after this introduction to service.

By 1938, an updated version emerged, the PBY-4, which carried its most distinctive feature, two midship 'blister' windows for observation and gun positions. These bulging 'lizard-like' eyes on the aircraft enhanced its already unique design, becoming a defining characteristic of the aircraft. The US Navy went on to order an amphibious version, PBY-5A, which had the addition of landing wheels, allowing the aircraft to operate from land bases. It would go on to be widely used throughout the war. The PBY was also sent to the British for evaluation in July 1939 and an order for 50 swiftly followed, helping to invigorate its production in the United States. War was on the horizon in Europe and, as an island nation and global empire, British planners needed aircraft to protect vital maritime trade routes should war break out. Britain was responsible for the name of the PBY, 'Catalina' being named after Santa Catalina Island off the coast of Southern California, with the designation PBY for 'Patrol Boat' and 'Y' being the letter assigned to identify the manufacturer, the Consolidated company. The PBY Catalina would soon see service with the Allies with the outbreak of war in Europe in 1939.

A Mk I Catalina on an RAF training flight over the Irish Sea. The distinctive 'blister' windows can be seen just behind the wing.

Design

The PBY Catalina would become the most manufactured aircraft of its type and its design went a long way to ensure its long service life.

With a large cantilever wing extending up from the fuselage with its 'boat-like' bow, the powerful Pratt & Whitney Twin Wasp radial engines were mounted as high as possible, to avoid sea spray that could affect the engines and corrode them.

It carried a crew of between seven and nine, with one crew in the bow section at the front performing observation, bomb aiming or defensive gun roles. Behind the bow was the cockpit where the pilot and co-pilot sat side by side. Behind the flight deck was a central cabin housing the navigator and radio operator, and a rear cabin for the flight engineer. Here crew bunks and a wardroom were found, for rest and food on long patrols. A walkway led to the rear where the observer/gunners were situated, using its good visibility from the large bubble 'blister' windows at the rear part of the aircraft.

Consolidated Catalina, with a view from the tail looking past its distinctive 'blister' observation and gun positions to the front of the aircraft. The Catalina would be the most-produced seaplane during the war with over 3,000 built.

UNITED STATES

An RAF Catalina Mk I in flight, returning from an anti-submarine patrol over the Mediterranean.

Operations

The Catalina served with British and then with American forces throughout the war, being used extensively in anti-submarine warfare in both the Atlantic and Pacific.

It helped to reduce the German U-boat threat in the Atlantic, enabling the Allies to win the Battle of the Atlantic. RAF pilots of Catalinas would win the Victoria Cross, the highest British military award, including Flying Officer John Cruickshank. He would pilot a Catalina that sank a U-boat off the Lofoten Islands in Norway in 1944, and despite being very badly injured in the attack and having crew casualties on board, he ensured his Catalina landed hours later at its base. Cruikshank had to be given a blood transfusion on board the Catalina before he could be moved.

Notable in maritime observation roles, the Catalina contributed to important actions, as in May 1941 when a Catalina of RAF Coastal Command spotted the German battleship *Bismarck* trying to reach the French port of Brest. The *Bismarck* was the most powerful type of battleship built by Nazi Germany that evaded the Royal Navy, but after being spotted by a PBY Catalina, it was eventually sunk in the Atlantic. In the Pacific, Catalinas observed Japanese ships approaching Midway Island, leading to a decisive turning point in the Pacific campaign with the Battle of Midway.

The Catalina also played a vital role in search and rescue of downed aircrew in all areas of the war. One of the most extreme rescues came in 1945, when the USS *Indianapolis* was torpedoed in the Pacific having delivered parts for the first atomic bomb to Tinian Naval Base on a top-secret mission. Over 800 crew would enter shark-infested waters; a PBY Catalina would eventually land days later and took as many men on board as possible. Though unable to fly it would offer respite as a 'life raft' from the sharks until rescue ships arrived, a role the PBY Catalina would continue for decades after the war.

This distinctive flying boat from the 1930s would have a long and distinguished career, but its finest moments were exemplified by its crews who rescued so many of their fellow service personnel during the dark days of World War II.

#11
Curtiss P-40 Warhawk

A Curtiss 'Kittyhawk' Mk III taxiing through the scrub in the desert. The man sitting on the wing is directing the pilot, whose view is hindered by the aircraft's nose. Versions of the Warhawk were known as 'Kittyhawk' and 'Tomahawk' in service with the RAF.

The Curtiss P-40 Warhawk, also known as 'Tomahawk'/'Kittyhawk' in RAF service, was an American single-seat all-metal fighter that suffered losses against Luftwaffe fighters at high altitude, but it was sturdy, robust and quick to build, using innovative production lines.

Crucially, it arrived in the war at a time when the Allies urgently needed to stem the advances of German and Japanese forces, especially in the war in the desert of North Africa and the South West Pacific. It was to evolve into a fighter bomber and was effective in this role early in the war. It was a largely overlooked aircraft, often thought of as a 'stopgap' filler for the Allies before more advanced aircraft in development entered the war. Yet it would still go on to be the third most-produced American fighter of the war, after the P-51 Mustang and P-47 Thunderbolt.

Origins

The P-40 was designed and built by the Curtiss Wright Corporation and evolved from an earlier design, the P-36 Hawk.

In 1937 the US Army Air Corps ordered a variant of the P-36, which became the XP-40. By 1939, an order for over 500 production P-40s, which at the time was the largest-ever order for a fighter in the US since World War I, would see the first produced Warhawk fly in 1940.

The rapid development of the P-40 stemmed from the design, which added a liquid-cooled, supercharged Allison V12 engine into a P-36 airframe. This helped speed up its manufacture using existing production lines. The design was that of an all-metal monoplane, which was to be a 'pursuit' aircraft, and was a modular design, which accelerated manufacturing and simplified maintenance when in service. The production line that built the P-40 was the main Curtiss factory at Buffalo, New York. The P-40 was moved along two lines by a rig, one for the wing and the other for the fuselage, which were finally brought together at the end of the production. This would see over 13,500 built before manufacturing ended in 1944.

Operations

UNITED STATES

At the start of the war, the P-40 was also of interest to other Allied air forces, with the French placing orders before these were picked up by the British following the fall of France after the German invasion in 1940.

The early P-40 versions were not 'perfect' as they lacked armoured protection and self-sealing fuel tanks, and the Allison engine was delivering a slow top speed when compared to contemporary enemy fighters, especially at higher altitude. Later versions would use improved Allison engines that were more dependable, and Packard Merlin engines, which improved its performance. Armament was also initially lacking before the improved P-40 D Warhawk entered service, performing well in the North African desert when used in a ground attack role.

Crew work on the Allison engine of a Curtiss P-40 in a makeshift hangar. The robust modular build of the P-40 meant it was easy to maintain on the front line.

The P-40 served with the RAF and Canadian, South African and Australian Air Forces at a crucial stage of the war. The Japanese threatened Australia in the South West Pacific and in North Africa, where German forces under General Erwin Rommel threatened to break through to the Suez Canal, a vital logistics artery for the British Empire. Due to its limited performance at high altitude, it was well suited to war in the desert as battle in the skies was usually at lower altitudes where the P-40 could compete with the Luftwaffe fighters. It began to equip the Desert Air Force from 1941, taking over from earlier Hurricanes, and holding back the Luftwaffe in support of ground forces, where its fighter-bomber capabilities were realised.

In the South West Pacific, the P-40 was to become the main fighter used by the Australians and its sturdy characteristics meant it could operate in the tropical climate. Crucially, it was available in large numbers as the Japanese threatened Australia, with the P-40 holding back the Japanese in air battles over Port Moresby in Papua New Guinea from 1942, which again held up the Japanese from further advances.

The P-40 was delivered to China in 1941, where the American Volunteer Group (AVG), also known as the 'Flying Tigers', were to fly it. It was to perform well against Japanese aircraft, helping to protect the Japanese attacks on the vital Burma Road supply link to China,

Three RAF Curtiss 'Kittyhawk' Mk IIIs preparing to depart on a sortie. The robust P-40 was well suited to the desert and successfully supported the ground forces as part of the Desert Air Force.

shooting down attacking Japanese bombers. The Soviet Union also received the P-40. It became the first fighter to be supplied to the Soviet Union under the Lend-Lease deal, playing a key role against the advancing German forces on the Eastern Front in 1942–3.

The P-40 was the main fighter for the Americans when war erupted in the Pacific in 1941. Although they were destroyed during the raid on Pearl Harbor in Hawaii, limited numbers of P-40s were famously able to take to the air during the raid and shoot down attacking Japanese aircraft. It would form the backbone of fighter operations throughout the Pacific in 1942–3, putting up rugged resistance to the Japanese, and could match the famous Japanese Zero fighter when using the best altitude and tactics for the P-40.

The P-40 Warhawk would be modified continually with many variants but was obsolete by 1944. It was overshadowed by later Allied fighters that were more advanced and had better performance. However, it played a crucial role across the globe for the Allies when it was needed most from 1941 to 1943, and did just enough when it entered service in large enough quantities to halt the advance of the Japanese and Germans. Few aircraft of World War II can live up to the P-40's wartime achievements.

A de Havilland Mosquito IIF in flight. The wartime censor has scratched out the wing-tip antennae of the Airborne Interceptor (AI) radar.

#12

de Havilland Mosquito

The de Havilland Mosquito was a British twin-engine aircraft that could be called the first MRCA (Multi-Role Combat Aircraft), excelling in the various roles it was expected to perform and a vital weapon for the Allies.

Constructed mainly out of wood, the 'Wooden Wonder' (as it was often affectionately known) was one of the fastest operational aircraft at the time, and the fastest fighter bomber of the war. It also served as both a day and night fighter, as a night bomber, intruder bomber, photo reconnaissance aircraft, pathfinder and maritime strike aircraft. It was a significant combat mixture for this fast and versatile aircraft, one of the most successful Allied aircraft of World War II.

Origins

The Mosquito was based on a 1936 Air Ministry requirement for a twin-engine medium bomber capable of carrying a bomb load of 3,000 lb for 3,000 miles at a speed of 275 mph.

However, English aviation pioneer Geoffrey de Havilland had other ideas and believed he could build an aircraft that could far exceed these requirements. The main concept was to build a bomber; not a typically large bomber with defensive turret armaments, but one so sleek that its speed and performance would allow it to evade enemy fighters, the ultimate 'unarmed' fast bomber.

The de Havilland company had experience building innovative high-speed aircraft, including the DH91 Albatross passenger aircraft in the 1930s, and began to explore the concept for a fast twin-engine bomber powered by Rolls-Royce Merlin engines in 1938. But the concept of a fast unarmed bomber was not, initially, supported by air chiefs, and de Havilland continued to privately fund the project until it was finally ordered into production in 1940 for an initial 50 bomber/reconnaissance aircraft. The tumultuous race to build the wooden DH98 Mosquito had only just begun.

The prototype Mosquito design positioned a crew of two in a Perspex cockpit, which was to be part of the fuselage. But this was changed to a more solid nose with a conventional cockpit above it, which helped with armaments on later versions. It was constructed of wood; more precisely, de Havilland was testing thin veneers of wood, such as balsa. These were glued together to give a lightweight yet strong structure that could be built in

GREAT BRITAIN

OPPOSITE: Aviation pioneer Geoffrey de Havilland sitting in the cockpit of an aircraft.

TOP RIGHT: A worker prepares strips of wood to tack over gauze inside the hull of a Mosquito aircraft.

MIDDLE RIGHT: Mosquito aircraft in various stages of production at the de Havilland factory at Hatfield, Hertfordshire. Using a skilled workforce used to working with wood allowed for fast production, with one Mosquito being completed every day.

BOTTOM RIGHT: Armourers wheel a 4,000-lb HC ('cookie') bomb for loading into a de Havilland Mosquito B Mk IV (modified). The specially modified Mosquitos were fitted with bulged bomb bays to accommodate 'cookies', bombs that were powerful enough to destroy an entire street.

sections and fused together to form a long fuselage, giving enough room for the crew and a large load of bombs. Wood was an unusual choice as most aircraft at this time were being produced with alloy metal skin. But it was chosen for several reasons: it would aid quick production; it used material that would be less susceptible to wartime metal shortages; and it brought a whole workforce of wood workers into the aircraft industry. The smooth, light but sturdy wooden fuselage would also make the aircraft fast, especially with twin Rolls-Royce Merlin engines with exceptionally large propellers that were so large they barely passed clear of the nose, providing the Mosquito with 3,000 horsepower and a maximum speed in excess of 400 miles per hour.

Aircraft interception radar AI Mk VIIIB indicator and receiver in the operating position, as seen from the observer's seat of a de Havilland Mosquito NF Mk XIII night fighter.

The first prototypes flew between 1940 and 1941 when initial flight and handling issues were gradually ironed out. This was despite the production being cancelled following the British evacuation at Dunkirk with the fall of France in June 1940. Lord Beaverbrook, Minister of Aircraft Production, had prioritised the production of fighters and aircraft able to defend Britain at the time, and he asked Air Chief Marshal Wilfrid Freeman to cancel the Mosquito project. Freeman conveniently ignored the request and as a result the development of 'Freeman's Folly' continued.

Beaverbrook was impressed with the performance of a Mosquito prototype finally demonstrated to him in 1941, and it began to be assessed, including in tests against the current Spitfire version. The Mosquito easily evaded the Spitfire and it went into mass production with large orders of all variants from the Air Ministry in 1941. With the addition of machine guns and cannons, the Mosquito would evolve further to be an outstanding fighter bomber that pilots agreed was a joy to fly. It had good flying range with additional fuel tanks and could carry the bomb load equivalent to some of the heavy British bombers of the war.

Operations

By 1941, the first production Mosquito was given to the British PRU (Photo Reconnaissance Unit) and by 1942 the bomber version began to reach squadrons.

Early daylight raids were on industrial and infrastructure targets, but the advent of the Fw 190 from 1941 meant that the Germans now had a fighter with performance that would make life much harder for the Mosquito. However, Allied pilots were still able to outmanoeuvre the German fighter and escape with its speed, so Mosquito losses were not high. Another advantage the Mosquito had was due to its wooden construction, which gave it a low radar profile and meant it was difficult for German radar to detect it. This 'stealth' radar invisibility is difficult to substantiate from wartime sources; the reality was more likely a reduced radar profile due to the wooden construction and fast speed.

de Havilland Mosquito II, Malta, 27 June 1943. The four .303 machine guns in the nose section are corked to prevent dirt damaging them.

A de Havilland Mosquito FB Mk VI, firing on two moored merchant vessels with rocket and cannon fire during an attack by the Banff Strike Wing on concentrations of enemy shipping in Sandefjord, Norway. Two merchant vessels were sunk, and a tanker and three merchantmen damaged, for the loss of two Mosquitos out of 39 aircraft employed on the strike. The addition of rockets and cannon made the Mosquito a substantial maritime attack aircraft.

A Mosquito Mk VI about to take off on a night-intruder operation over enemy territory, 1944. Mosquitos were able to hunt German night fighters by tracking their radio emissions, which helped them attack the enemy fighters that were attempting to disrupt the heavy bombers of RAF Bomber Command during Allied bombing raids.

The night fighter Mosquito designated 'NF' was equipped with Airborne Interceptor (AI) on-board radar from 1942 and successfully defended the skies of Britain against the Luftwaffe, especially during the early part of 1944, taking over from the Bristol Beaufighter as the key night-fighting interception aircraft. Offensively as a night fighter, the Mosquito flew intruder roles supporting formations of heavy bombers of Bomber Command. This helped to reduce bomber losses as the Mosquito could track German radio waves emitting from the German night fighters, attacking them and protecting the heavy bombers in the formations. Its other roles were as a pathfinder as part of the 'Light Night Striking Force', marking the targets for the heavy bombers with flares. It also served as a 'nuisance' bomber, with some Mosquito bombers modified to carry and drop large 'cookie' bombs in high-speed raids that the Luftwaffe was unable to stop.

GREAT BRITAIN

During the Allied preparation for the invasion of Nazi-occupied Europe in 1943, which was scheduled to start in the following year, Mosquitos joined the Second Tactical Air Force (TAF) to support in the preparation for D-Day. The Fighter Bomber Mosquitos designated 'FB' were trialled with rocket projectiles (RPs) and FB Mk VI Mosquitos were subsequently equipped with eight rockets under each wing. In 1944, Mosquito squadrons supported the Allied landings in France, in addition to attacking the sites being used to fire V-1 Flying Bombs. Later in the war there were raids conducted using all-Mosquito bomber formations, which provided the Allies with a significant additional weapon to the larger heavy bomber formations.

The Mosquito was also used for several precise and daring low-level raids over Europe in the latter stages of the war, targeting headquarters used by the Gestapo, the German secret police, to help various resistance movements in Europe. One such raid targeted the Gestapo headquarters in Aarhus in Denmark. The Aarhus Raid took place on 31 October 1944, when four waves of Mosquitos, totalling 25, attacked the dormitories at the University of Aarhus, which were being used by the Gestapo at the time and included their archives. A reconnaissance Mosquito was sent on the raid to film it, and it was regarded by the RAF as one of the most successful low-level types of attack during the war, with the mix of bombs and incendiaries both killing many key Gestapo agents and destroying their vital documents.

After 1943, Mosquitos were also in use with Coastal Command where they intercepted and attacked U-boats and other German surface vessels. As the threat moved from the Atlantic to the North Sea following the Allied invasion of France, a Mosquito group was set up in Banff in Scotland to patrol Danish and Norwegian waters. The introduction of a large Molins anti-tank cannon under the nose of the FB Mk XVIII gave it a devastating firepower that was used successfully to attack convoys and U-boats. This version of the Mosquito was also known as the 'Tsetse'.

Mosquitos also made a significant contribution to Allied photo reconnaissance in the latter half of the war, with distinct types evolving from Mk I to Mk 34. Flying at

The daylight precision bombing raid by de Havilland Mosquito FB Mk VI on the Gestapo headquarters, Jutland, Denmark, at the University of Aarhus. A further wave of Mosquitos can be seen in the background coming in to bomb at low level the already shattered targets.

high altitude and at 400 mph, the photo reconnaissance Mosquitos could reach most places in relative safety, bringing back confirmation of V-2 rocket sites or that the Germans controlled the bridge at Arnhem during the failed Allied airborne operation there in 1944.

Mosquito crews are well documented for discussing the outstanding performance and flying ability of the Mosquito, often feeling invincible with its immense power and speed. However, the difficult and daring missions the Mosquito flew led to a number of aircrew, including the leader of the Dambusters Raid, Guy Gibson, losing their lives whilst flying Mosquitos. It undoubtedly was one of the most unconventional yet versatile aircraft in the Allies armoury, and it was the decisive 'Wooden Wonder' weapon that helped turned the tide of the war for the Allies, excelling in everything it was asked to do when it was sent up against the Germans over the skies of Europe.

A de Havilland Mosquito PR Mk XVI of No.140 Squadron RAF warms up its engines in a dispersal in Belgium, before taking off on a night photographic reconnaissance sortie. The Perspex nose housing the camera is visible at the front.

A Mosquito FB Mk XVIII banking away from the camera while in flight, showing the 57-mm Molins gun mounted underneath the nose. This version is sometimes referred to as the 'Tsetse' Mosquito.

#13
Douglas A-20 Havoc (Boston)

UNITED STATES

The Douglas A-20 Havoc (known as the 'Boston' in RAF service) was a medium twin-engine attack bomber with a crew of three, and saw service in the early stages of the war in Europe with the French and British.

It remained in service with several air forces until the end of the war. A rugged and sturdy aircraft, popular with pilots and crew who flew in it, its versatility saw it perform several roles, including night fighter/intruder, ground attack bombing and reconnaissance missions. Over 7,000 would eventually be produced, making it an often-unsung aircraft from World War II.

A Havoc Mk I, following its transfer to the USAAF, originally a Boston Mk I.

91

A Douglas Boston aircraft of No.24 Squadron South African Air Force (SAAF) at an airfield in the North African desert.

Origins and Operations

The Havoc originated from a US Army Air Corps 1937 specification for an attack bomber aircraft. The team at Douglas developed the Model 7B prototype, which initially attracted the attention of the French, and after consultation went into production as the DB-7, with an order in 1939 for the A-20 Havoc.

By this time, the US Army Air Corps also felt the bomber would meet its needs for an attack bomber and placed an order, with the first aircraft leaving the Douglas production line in California in October 1939.

The fall of France in May 1940 saw the British Purchasing Commission (BPC) purchase the remaining aircraft originally planned for the French. The British saw the aircraft's potential as a night fighter, mainly as it was large enough to house the rapidly developing AI aircraft mounted radar, renaming the Havoc in service with the RAF as the 'Boston'. The Boston would go on to replace Bristol Blenheims with the British, and A-20s would serve with the Americans from North Africa to Europe and further on to the Philippines, and with the Soviet Air Forces on the Eastern Front in Europe.

The Havoc did not always gain the same recognition as many other fighters and bombers of the war, as the aircraft did not have the necessary flight range to enable it to bomb Germany. However, in the many theatres and multiple roles in which it saw service, this rugged medium-attack bomber would be an overlooked yet successful workhorse, which played a crucial part in the Allied victory in the war.

TOP: A daylight attack on the Matford automotive works at Poissy, France in 1942. Eight aircraft successfully bombed the target. Smoke from bombs exploding inside the factory can be seen drifting across the roof.

LEFT: A Douglas Boston of No.24 Squadron SAAF flies over the target as bombs explode on the Italian gun battery on Monte San Elmo, prior to the Allied landings there. It shows the streamlined engine housing to the rear of the engines in the wing, an identifying feature of the Havoc/Boston.

#14
Douglas C-47 Skytrain

The Douglas C-47 Skytrain was an American military transport aircraft operated extensively during the war by Allied forces and would become synonymous with key airborne parachute drops that took place in the latter half of the war in Europe.

In service with the British it was named 'Dakota', with some sources suggesting this stood for 'Douglas Aircraft Company Transport Aircraft', and it would become the mainstay of Allied airborne and transport operations during World War II.

Origins

The C-47 was developed from a popular civil airliner, the DC-3 (DC stood for 'Douglas Commercial'), which revolutionised air travel in the 1930s.

The DC-3 entered service in 1936 and was a twin-engine monoplane with its wing placed in a low position on the fuselage, which was itself an improved version of a predecessor, the DC-2. As a civil airliner the DC-3 could carry between 21 and 32 passengers, and with a maximum speed of 207 mph, was fast compared to other airliners at the time, had a range of 1,500 miles and could take off from short runways. In the United States it could transport passengers in great comfort from New York to Los Angeles in 18 hours, down from 25 hours earlier in the 1930s, and all without having to change aircraft.

Some of these traits of the DC-3, including its range and take-off abilities from short runways, would lend themselves to military adaption when war broke out. However, to fulfil its wartime role the C-47 was modified from the civilian aircraft in some key areas. First, a cargo door was fitted to the C-47 and the floor was strengthened for cargo and other transport, whilst the tail was shortened to enable glider towing. The C-47 was also fitted with an 'astrodome', a transparent dome fitted above the cockpit area allowing a navigator to use the stars to navigate the aircraft at night. The 'new' C-47 would take its first flight in December 1941.

The C-47 was used by many Allied air forces during and after the war, including the transport home of wounded service personnel and in the Berlin airlift crisis of the Cold War from 1948. During the war, over 10,000 were built by Douglas at Santa Monica and Oklahoma City in the United States. It went through many modifications in its service lifespan, improving the engine power but also specific modifications for other roles such as reconnaissance.

UNITED STATES

A C-47 Skytrain with red engine covers takes off.

Operations

The C-47 gave the Allies a reliable transport aircraft, but it was in its deployment of airborne forces that it would earn its main wartime accolades.

It was used extensively in Southeast Asia, China, India and the Pacific, with it being used at Guadalcanal, whilst in Burma (Myanmar) it could supply troops fighting more mobile Japanese forces. In this theatre, the C-47 was also used to transport vital supplies to China over what was known as the 'Hump'. The Allies were desperate to supply vital material to Chinese forces from India, who were fighting the Japanese in mainland China. This was primarily to keep a large, million-strong Japanese army tied down and unable to re-inforce their other forces fighting the Allies across Asia and the Pacific theatres of war. But the only land route from Burma was threatened by Japanese military success from 1942, so an air-based route was proposed across the difficult terrain of the Himalayas. The C-47 was also the principal transport aircraft for moving American troops from different Pacific islands and back to the United States.

In Europe, the C-47 was to become famous for its role in dropping airborne parachute forces, with the first large drop taking place in July 1943 for the Allied invasion of Sicily. This was a dress-rehearsal for the D-Day operation, where British and American airborne forces were dropped prior to the landings on 6 June 1944 to secure key bridges and objectives that were to be vital to the Allies' success in landing the main forces on the beaches in Normandy. The sight of paratroopers boarding and dropping in Normandy has since been immortalised in many television shows and films, with the C-47 always depicted as a steady and dependable workhorse during the operation.

The success of the airborne troops during the D-Day operation led to the C-47 being used again in one of the most audacious, and eventually unsuccessful, airborne operations in 1944: Operation Market Garden. This British initiative of General Montgomery was to lay a 'carpet' of airborne troops across key bridges that crossed the major rivers in the Netherlands, including the Rhine. By using the captured bridges, the Allies could move its ground forces quickly to cross the Rhine and drive straight into the heart of Germany, potentially ending the European war in 1944.

Douglas Dakota Mk IIIs at Bazenville, Normandy, loading casualties for evacuation to the United Kingdom. The C-47 was responsible for dropping the Allied airborne troops during D-Day.

UNITED STATES

The C-47 delivered the troops of the US 101st Airborne to bridges in the Eindhoven area, whilst the US 82nd were to capture bridges near to Nijmegen. The furthest drop was the British 1st Airborne Division at Arnhem. The initial campaign went well and the C-47 delivered most of the troops to the designated drop zones. However, planning of the drop zones for the British landing placed it far from the target bridge and stronger German troop concentrations led to a battle the British paratroopers couldn't win. The paratroopers eventually retreated to Allied lines which had extended as a result of the American airborne landings, but which hadn't delivered a knockout blow by placing the Allies over the Rhine at Arnhem and on to the north German Plain, potentially leading to an early victory in Europe.

The C-47 Skytrain, sometimes affectionately known as the 'Gooney Bird', became the principal transport aircraft for the Allies. It played a significant part in delivering the material and, importantly, airborne troops to the European theatre, ensuring success in key operations of the Allies' war effort from Europe to the Pacific.

ABOVE: British paratroopers, inside a C-47 transport plane, that would drop with the First Allied Airborne Army on enemy-held Netherlands.

BELOW: C-47 Skytrain nicknamed 'Mary Co-Ed II' of the 434th Troop Carrier Group.

#15
Douglas SBD Dauntless

The Douglas SBD Dauntless was an American dive bomber that was also used as a scout aircraft (the letters standing for 'Scout Bomber Douglas').

It formed the backbone of American naval dive bomber aircraft in the early years of the war in the Pacific and would play a crucial role in one of the most famous American battles of World War II. With its sturdy and robust design, long range, impressive bomb load and good armaments, it would claim the most Japanese shipping sunk of any aircraft in the Pacific. Just under 6,000 SBDs were built in total before production stopped in 1944.

American Douglas SBD-3 Dauntless preparing to take off from the aircraft carrier USS Enterprise (CV-6) for a raid on Wake Island in 1941.

UNITED STATES

A Douglas Dauntless scout or dive bomber on the ground. Its sturdy design gave it a chance to withstand heavy anti-aircraft enemy fire.

Origins and Variants

The SBD Dauntless began as a proposal for a new naval dive bomber and a prototype, XBT-1, was built by Northrop based on a light bomber, the A-17, with the first flight taking place in 1935.

Modifications were made and when Northrop became part of Douglas Aircraft Company in 1937, an updated version became the XSBD-1. A first batch of SBD-1s was delivered to the US Marine Corps in 1940.

These featured a perforated flap on the rear of the wings, to aid the aircraft when diving by reducing drag on the tail, which became a distinctive feature of the aircraft.

The SBD was the main US Navy dive bomber from 1940 to 1944, and despite not having folding wings to facilitate operation from carrier ships, the SBD-2 entered service with the Navy in 1941. This variant had extra fuel-tank space, protective armour and an autopilot. The strength of the wing, rather than having a split wing, helped the aircraft remain strong when diving at high speeds. This robust characteristic of the SBD would ensure it became a favourite of its pilots, earning it the nickname 'Slow but Deadly'.

The SBD-3 followed in 1941, with increased armour and four machine guns, followed by the SBD-4 in 1942, which included radar. Then the SBD-5 was delivered, which had a more powerful version of the Wright Cyclone engine, and became the main type built with just under 3,000 being delivered to the US Navy. When production ended in 1944, the SBD Dauntless had played a pivotal role in changing the war against the Japanese.

Operations

At the outbreak of war following the Japanese attack on Pearl Harbor in 1941, the SBD Dauntless was the main strike dive bomber.

In early 1942 it fought alongside the TBD Devastator torpedo bomber (TB meaning 'Torpedo Bomber') during the Battle of the Coral Sea, which repulsed a Japanese fleet, including the light carrier *Shokaku,* which was attempting to invade Port Moresby, New Guinea.

Its main aerial success came during the pivotal Battle of Midway when SBDs flying from USS carriers *Enterprise*, *Hornet* and *Yorktown* successfully destroyed the main Japanese carrier fleet, stemming the advance of the Japanese Navy in the central Pacific. Although the SBD would eventually be eclipsed later in the war by faster aircraft, the actions of the SBD Dauntless pilots of the US Navy would secure its legacy as an unsung hero of the air war in the Pacific.

Dauntless dive bombers flying in formation during the Battle of Midway.

UNITED STATES

A Fairey Firefly Mk I fighter/maritime reconnaissance aircraft in flight.

#16
Fairey Firefly

The Fairey Firefly was a British carrier-borne fighter and anti-submarine aircraft with folding wings, which entered service with the Fleet Air Arm (FAA) in 1943.

Despite its late arrival during the war, the Firefly had a good long range, but proved to be less effective after the war when compared to newly emerging jet aircraft.

A Fairey Firefly about to land on HMS *Pretoria Castle*.

Origins

The Firefly was developed in response to a specification issued by the British Air Ministry in 1938 for a naval fighter.

The design evolved from the Fairey Fulmar, a fighter/reconnaissance aircraft built by Fairey. It was a low-wing monoplane powered by a Rolls-Royce Griffon engine and fitted with four cannons mounted in the all-metal wings. The Firefly had a crew of two, a pilot and a navigator, due to the need to navigate over open water. Pilots found the Firefly to be good to fly at low speeds and well balanced, but its overall weight meant it took some physical strength to manoeuvre the aircraft in more complex aerobatics.

Operations

The Fairey Firefly began its operational life with 1770 Naval Air Squadron in Europe in 1944, flying from HMS *Indefatigable* on reconnaissance and attacking shipping along the Norwegian coast, and supporting attacks on the German battleship *Tirpitz*, stationed in a Norwegian fjord.

The Firefly also served with the British Pacific Fleet and flew anti-submarine missions alongside attacks on oil refineries in Japanese-occupied Sumatra. The addition of radar also allowed it to fly night-fighter missions towards the end of the war. In July 1945, the Firefly became the first British-built aircraft to fly over Japan but, with the end of the war in August 1945, it was not used in an anticipated attack on the Japanese mainland islands.

After the war the Firefly went on to serve with the Royal Navy in Korea and Malaya, and remained in service with the Royal Netherlands Navy until the 1960s.

GREAT BRITAIN

Men folding the wings of a Fairey Firefly on board HMS *Indefatigable* on the aircraft's return from a carrier-borne air strike on the Japanese oil refinery at Pangkalan Brandan, Sumatra.

#17
Fairey Swordfish

The Fairey Swordfish was a British biplane reconnaissance and torpedo bomber with an open cockpit for its crew of three, which looked more in keeping with aircraft from World War I.

Despite its dated looks, the Swordfish excelled as a carrier-borne torpedo bomber. It was also a feared submarine hunter, helping many naval convoys to reach their destination ports. Even though it was already arguably obsolete as a design when the war began in 1939, it nevertheless went on to serve with the Royal Navy until 1945, outlasting its intended successor, the Fairey Albacore. The Swordfish saw action in some of the most significant Allied naval engagements in the war, especially in the Mediterranean, ensuring the 'Stringbag', as it was often affectionately known, became a most unlikely aircraft icon of World War II.

ABOVE: A Fairey Swordfish Mk I naval torpedo aircraft during a training flight. With its biplane wings, fixed undercarriage and open cockpit, the Swordfish looked more akin to aircraft from World War I.

OPPOSITE TOP: The open cockpit of the Fairey Swordfish was especially hard on the crew when flying in the cold North Atlantic or Arctic convoy operations.

OPPOSITE BOTTOM: A Fairey Swordfish aircraft, which is six years old and has flown the equivalent of five times round the world, in the process of an overhaul. Robust and straightforward to maintain, production finally ended in 1944.

Origins

The Fairey Swordfish was derived from a private venture at Fairey that became the TSR I (Torpedo-Spotter-Reconnaissance) prototype in 1933 before a modified version, TSR II, first flew in 1934.

After further successful trials and now named Swordfish in keeping with the Fleet Air Arm's naming convention, the Swordfish entered service in July 1936. It was traditional in design: built with a metal frame and covered in fabric, powered by a Bristol Pegasus radial engine, and its armaments included a fixed forward machine gun and one in the rear cockpit.

Its main weapon was the torpedo, but the low speed of the aircraft made it difficult to deliver this weapon if the target was heavily defended. The Swordfish could also carry a mine or bomb load under its fuselage or wings. With the advent of more sophisticated torpedo bombers, the Swordfish progressed to a role of anti-submarine warfare and operated from merchant ships in convoys, sometimes assisted by RATO (Rockets Assisted Take Off). The low stall speed of the Swordfish made it ideal for taking off and landing on carriers and other ships, especially in the tough conditions of the Atlantic Ocean. With its foldable wings it was ideal for storage in small spaces, prolonging its usefulness as an operational aircraft throughout the war. Later versions of the Swordfish were equipped with Air to Surface Vessel (ASV) radar, and the aircraft was credited with one of the first night-time sinkings of a German U-boat.

Operations

At the outbreak of the war in 1939, the British Fleet Air Arm had 13 squadrons of Swordfish Mk Is, including a number with floats for use from the catapults of warships.

Initial missions for the Swordfish included fleet patrols and escorting convoys, including the Norway campaign in 1940, where a Swordfish was responsible for the first sinking of a U-boat by aircraft of the Fleet Air Arm. Nicknamed 'Stringbag' by its crews, the name was not related to its strung biplane wings but after 'string' shopping bags popular at the time, which could carry a variety of different groceries. The Swordfish could similarly carry a variety of different weapons.

Fairey Swordfish Mk IIIs of No.119 Squadron RAF, with bombs being loaded, demonstrating the variety of weapons the Swordfish could carry.

In the Mediterranean, the Swordfish was to score some significant successes, with its most famous victory against the Italian Navy (*Regia Marina*) at Taranto in southern Italy in November 1940. Prior to this, in July 1940, the Swordfish was used principally against the French Navy at Mers-el-Kébir in a now infamous attack following the fall of France, to prevent the French naval vessels falling into German hands. Swordfish flying from the carrier HMS *Ark Royal* successfully used torpedoes to disable the French ships, proving that ships at anchor in harbour could be successfully attacked from the air.

This lesson was not lost on the British Admiralty, who were concerned with delivering a knockout blow to the powerful Italian battleships that were moored at Taranto. On the night of 11/12 November 1940, 21 Fairey Swordfish launched from HMS *Illustrious*, delivered a famous blow to the Italians and demonstrated the ascendancy of aircraft over battleships. The first wave of Swordfish dropped incendiaries and bombs on the oil tanks in the docks, as further waves used torpedoes to knock out and disable some of the Italian warships. This successful raid shifted the balance of naval power in the Mediterranean into British hands.

The aftermath of the raid was the profound impact it would have on naval aviation, especially at the start of the war in the Pacific in 1941. A Japanese naval attaché to Berlin, Takeshi Naito, visited Taranto to view the raid's impact, followed by further visits from other Imperial Japanese Navy delegations. The raid is believed to have influenced and accelerated an already conceived Japanese plan for attacks on ships moored in shallow ports in Southeast Asia and the Pacific, with the US naval base at Pearl Harbor one of the selected targets and subsequently attacked in December 1941.

In the Battle of the Atlantic in 1941, Fairey Swordfish flying from HMS *Victorious* proved instrumental in using torpedoes to damage and hinder the powerful German

Wheeling an 18-inch torpedo along the flight deck of HMS *Illustrious* before loading into a Fairey Swordfish. The success of the Taranto raid highlighted the importance of naval aviation over battleships in the war.

GREAT BRITAIN

battleship *Bismarck,* before Royal Navy ships could bombard and sink the enemy ship.

The Swordfish continued to operate successfully in the Mediterranean, including disabling an Italian cruiser, *Pola*, during the Battle of Cape Matapan in March 1941. However, its limitations in a torpedo attack role were starkly illustrated in 1942 when several German ships, including the battleships *Scharnhorst* and *Gneisenau*, made their way to German ports through the English Channel. The 'Channel Dash' was a success for the Germans, but it came at great cost to the six Swordfish aircraft that were sent up to attack the ships. Messerschmitt Bf 109s of the Luftwaffe intercepted the slow and lightly armed Swordfish, resulting in the flight of Swordfish being shot down before any damage could be inflicted on the German ships. The leader of the Swordfish flight, Lieutenant Commander Esmonde, was posthumously awarded the highest British honour, the Victoria Cross, for the attack, which was acknowledged

Close-up of a Fairey Swordfish Mk II. The slow speeds and light defensive armament proved inadequate during the attack on German warships in the 'Channel Dash' of 1942, hastening a change of role for the Swordfish to anti-submarine warfare.

by commanders on both sides as 'heroic' even though it had proved futile.

The Swordfish Mk II came into operation in 1943, with a lower wing that was now covered fully in alloy metal, allowing it to carry rockets. These were used to great effect by Swordfish crew on U-boats in the Atlantic and smaller vessels. Towards the end of the war the Mk III Swordfish, carrying more advanced radar, was able to hunt German midget submarines in the North Sea and on the Dutch coast, operating from bases in Belgium. Despite production finishing in 1944, the aircraft remained in service until the end of the war in 1945, but was retired very soon after, having outlasted the aircraft that had been intended to replace it.

Over 2,000 Fairey Swordfish were built. It was slow, outdated looking and aesthetically light years behind contemporary monoplane fighters and bombers. Clearly it was from an earlier era of aviation history. But the Fairey Swordifsh was undoubtedly a stubborn survivor that scored numerous successes throughout World War II, and was an unlikely pioneer in the ascent of naval aviation firepower over that of battleships. Crewed by the bravest, often flying in difficult conditions, the 'Stringbag' really did deliver its many weapons during the war, effectively and often with devastating efficiency, securing one of the most notable aerial successes of the war.

Three rocket projectile Fairey Swordfish during a training flight. The squadron has invasion stripes carried for the Normandy landings on the wings and fuselage of the aircraft.

Maintenance crew bringing a torpedo-loaded Fairey Swordfish onto the flight deck of HMS *Battler* by hydraulic lift. The folding wing of the Swordfish made it ideal for storage on carriers or merchant ships.

GREAT BRITAIN

#18
Gloster Gladiator

The Gloster Gladiator was designed by Henry Phillip Holland for the Gloster Aircraft Company in Britain in the early 1930s, with the first flight taking place in 1934.

It was the last fighter biplane to serve in the RAF, entering service in 1937; a naval variant, the Sea Gladiator, entered service with the Fleet Air Arm in 1938. The Gladiator was arguably redundant by the time the war began, due to the arrival of the new generation of monoplane fighters such as the Hurricane and Spitfire. Despite this, the Gladiator served as an important stopgap aircraft in the early years of the war for RAF squadrons in some areas of fighting, allowing the RAF to tackle emerging threats, especially in North Africa and the Mediterranean from the Italian Air Force (*Regia Aeronautica*). The Gladiator also served with the Belgian, Chinese, Finnish and South African Air Forces amongst others.

A Sea Gladiator on the ground. Although obsolete at the start of the war, it still served in the RAF as a stopgap until more modern aircraft arrived.

Origins and Operations

GREAT BRITAIN

The Gladiator was based on the Gloster Gauntlet, an open cockpit biplane.

It was made with traditional methods using wood covered in fabric with 'dope', a lacquer used to strengthen and stiffen the fabric, but this made it vulnerable to burning quickly. It was armed with two, then later four, .303 machine guns, had an enclosed cockpit and could reach a maximum speed of just over 250 mph.

The Gloster Gladiator went on to perform admirably in the early years of the war, despite coming up against faster enemy fighters and bombers. Its robust manoeuvrability saw it score some success against the Italians in the Mediterranean, including during the siege of Malta, until it was replaced by Hurricanes. The leading Gladiator ace of World War II was South African born 'Pat' Pattle, who shot down 15 planes in the aircraft.

Eventually the Gladiator was phased out of combat and served in non-combative roles, including meteorology, but by 1944 few remained in service. Most Gladiators were scrapped at the end of the war, but as an aircraft that was arguably obsolete in 1939, it is a good example of how the war in the air escalated rapidly in terms of aircraft design, production and flight capabilities. It required bravery to fly in such a slow and outdated biplane from the 1930s and the pilots that did so often paid the ultimate sacrifice.

Squadron Leader Marmaduke Thomas St John ('Pat') Pattle (left), the leading Gladiator ace of the war.

Arab guards in Iraq watch over as Glosters refuel during their journey from Egypt to reinforce the besieged garrison at Habbaniyah, Iraq.

#19
Gloster Meteor

GREAT BRITAIN

A flight of Meteors based at RAF, now IWM, Duxford.

The Gloster Meteor was the first Allied jet-powered fighter to enter service during World War II.

Its design and manufacture were comparable to other propeller fighter aircraft in the war, but alongside the German Me 262, the use of the highly secret turbojet engine to power the aircraft was to usher in a new jet age that was to change the history of aviation forever.

Origins

By 1936, British engineer Frank Whittle had developed the concept of a turbojet engine that could be applied to a new type of powered aircraft.

Independently, the German engineer Hans von Ohain had also developed a turbojet engine and, with the onset of war, the race to bring this highly secretive type of engine into practical use in an aircraft was on. In 1939, Whittle's company, Jet Power Limited, came to an agreement with the Gloster Aircraft Company to produce a twin-engine jet fighter. At the height of the Battle of Britain in August 1940, a national interest in fighters had developed; at the same time Gloster proposed their concept for a twin-engine jet fighter with a tricycle-style undercarriage.

Portrait of Air Commodore Sir Frank Whittle at his desk. Known as the 'father of the jet engine', the models on his desk include the Meteor, the first jet to enter service with the RAF.

Meteor F Mk I, EE223/G, at Boscombe Down, Wiltshire.
The tricycle undercarriage is clearly visible.

Technological Developments

The turbojet was a jet engine which, in simplest terms, sucked in air and compressed it, heating the compressed air by burning fuel, which then powered a turbine producing thrust out of the rear of the engine to propel the aircraft.

These early engines used a lot of fuel and were not vastly powerful, so both British and German engineers initially proposed designs using two engines for jet fighter development. The setting of engines either in or under wings also gave the first jets the ability to adopt a tricycle undercarriage. Without a large propeller in the nose needing to have a minimum height to clear the ground, the rear wheel in conventional propeller aircraft could move to the front, which provided an easier and safer way to take off and land. This became the standard wheel configuration for jet aircraft.

In May 1941, Gloster E28/39 'W4041' took to the skies as the first jet-powered aircraft, proving that jet-powered flight was possible and resulting in an order from the Air Ministry for the development of further prototypes. The Meteor was initially to be called 'Thunderbolt', but this was changed to avoid any confusion with the American Republic P-47 Thunderbolt. The development of the Meteor and the Messerschmitt Me 262 saw similar aircraft begin to emerge, although the Me 262 had swept-back wings with engines under the wings, giving it a slight advantage in terms of performance and speed. The fifth Meteor prototype was the first to take to the air, making its first flight at RAF Cranwell in Lincolnshire on 5 March 1943, a few months behind the Me 262's maiden flight, and exactly seven years since the iconic Spitfire flew for the first time. Despite some initial issues, which required the tail fin to be enlarged, it showed there were no problems with this new type of engine propulsion.

In January 1944, the Meteor F.1 began production, with the first operational sortie in RAF service taking place in July 1944. Only a limited number of the F.1 were produced, though, before the F.3 went into production later that summer. Further engine development with Rolls Royce saw the F.3 being fitted with Derwent engines, leading to greater power. The armaments initially included four Hispano Mk V cannons mounted in the nose. Tests showed the Meteor to have improved performance when matched against the propeller-driven Hawker Tempest Mk V, which was also in production at this time.

Operations

GREAT BRITAIN

No.616 Squadron RAF was the first squadron to be equipped with the Meteor, with the first aircraft delivered to them in early July 1944 at RAF Culmhead in Somerset.

A couple of months earlier a new Tactical Flight ('T-Flight') had been formed at Farnborough to prepare pilots for the change to flying jet aircraft, due to the substantial differences in flying a jet aircraft to a piston-engine aircraft. After receiving the first Meteors the pilots of 616 Squadron familiarised themselves with their new aircraft through various training exercises, including flying with large formations of USAAF bombers and fighters to allow American crews to gain experience and develop tactics when facing jet engine aircraft. The Meteor was deemed so technologically secret that pilots did not operate over enemy territory for fear of the aircraft being shot down and recovered by the Germans, so the first Meteors were used in the defence of Britain as the new threat of the V-1 Flying Bomb emerged in the summer of 1944.

The Meteor accounted for a small number of V-1s being destroyed, mostly by 'tipping' the wing of the V-1 and sending it crashing out of control. As the V-1 threat subsided, the RAF was finally able to send Meteors to Europe in January 1945, based in Belgium and flying reconnaissance and ground attack missions. But continuing limitations on flying over German-held territory meant the Gloster Meteor never faced its German contemporary, the Me 262, in aerial combat. As a result of this lack of a jet dogfight, the debate over which wartime jet was better continues for many to this day.

Post-war development would see the Gloster Meteor break an air-speed record in 1946, flying at 606 mph. Despite its limited wartime record it would go on to be the principal post-war RAF fighter until more advanced jet aircraft would take over. The Gloster Meteor signalled the dawn of a new aviation era and, despite its limited impact on the outcome of World War II, the jet age had arrived.

ABOVE: Maintenance crew at work on a Gloster Meteor F.3. On the left, an armourer is using a cleaning rod on one of the four 20-mm cannon housed in the aircraft's nose.

RIGHT: A Gloster Meteor F.3 of No.616 Squadron takes off from Belgium. Pilots found that flying Meteors was far less noisy in the cockpit than propeller aircraft they had previously flown.

115

#20
Grumman F4F Wildcat

The Grumman F4F Wildcat was an American single-seat carrier-based fighter aircraft, which also saw service with the Royal Navy in Britain as the 'Martlet'.

Its sturdy design would allow it to survive heavy enemy fire, but it was inferior to the main Japanese fighter in the Pacific, the A6M Zero, in performance and combat. The innovative tactics of American naval pilots allowed it to score success against its more superior enemy, and it helped to curtail the Japanese in the early years of the Pacific war before being replaced by more powerful aircraft.

Origins and Operations

The Wildcat was originally conceived as a biplane with a fixed landing gear when it was proposed for the US Navy, but as the prototype evolved from 1936 it became a mid-wing monoplane with retractable wheels.

Despite its inferior performance next to the superior handling of the Brewster Buffalo aircraft, the US Navy persisted with the development. The French Navy placed an order for the Wildcat before the fall of France in 1940

A Grumman Wildcat in flight, displaying the stripes carried by aircraft of the Allied Expeditionary Force during the Normandy landings. The Wildcat was named 'Martlet' whilst in service with the British.

Grumman Wildcat fighter aircraft on the flight deck of HMS *Formidable*. The folding 'Sto-Wing' in later versions allowed for more aircraft to be stored in carriers.

led to the French order being sold and diverted to the British Royal Navy.

Production of the Wildcat saw it enter service from 1940 after modifications, including a more powerful supercharged Pratt & Whitney Twin Wasp engine, and trials of a new Grumman-patented 'Sto-Wing' folding wing led to the F4F-4, the version that saw most combat in the early war years. The 'Sto-Wing' developed by Grumman allowed for more aircraft to be stored on an aircraft carrier and is still used to this day on Grumman carrier-based aircraft.

Although the speed of the Wildcat was inferior to other fighters, it first saw combat in British hands when land-based Martlets shot down a Junkers Ju 88 German aircraft over the Royal Navy base at Scapa Flow in Orkney. The Wildcat/Martlet would see further service in Europe, including during the American landings in North Africa in 1943.

In the Pacific, following Pearl Harbor, the Wildcat would put up stubborn resistance to the Japanese Zeros, even with its inferior speed and manoeuvrability. In part, despite experienced American pilots disliking the F4F-4 due to diminished firepower being spread over more guns than earlier versions, the self-sealing fuel tanks of the Wildcat allowed it to withstand more enemy fire when in combat with lighter Japanese fighters. Innovative tactics also helped the Wildcat take the fight to the Japanese at the Battles of the Coral Sea and Midway. One such tactic was called 'Thach Weave', named after one of the leading American pilots who devised it. This allowed formations of Wildcats to collectively defend against diving attacks, whilst an ambush dive from altitude on enemy fighters was also used by Wildcat pilots, especially during the Battle of Guadalcanal.

Overall, just under 8,000 of this sturdy and stubborn American aircraft were produced. Whilst it lacked performance ability, in the hands of its skilled pilots it would do 'enough' to keep the Japanese from dominating American forces in the air war in the Pacific in the early war years.

#21
Grumman F6F Hellcat

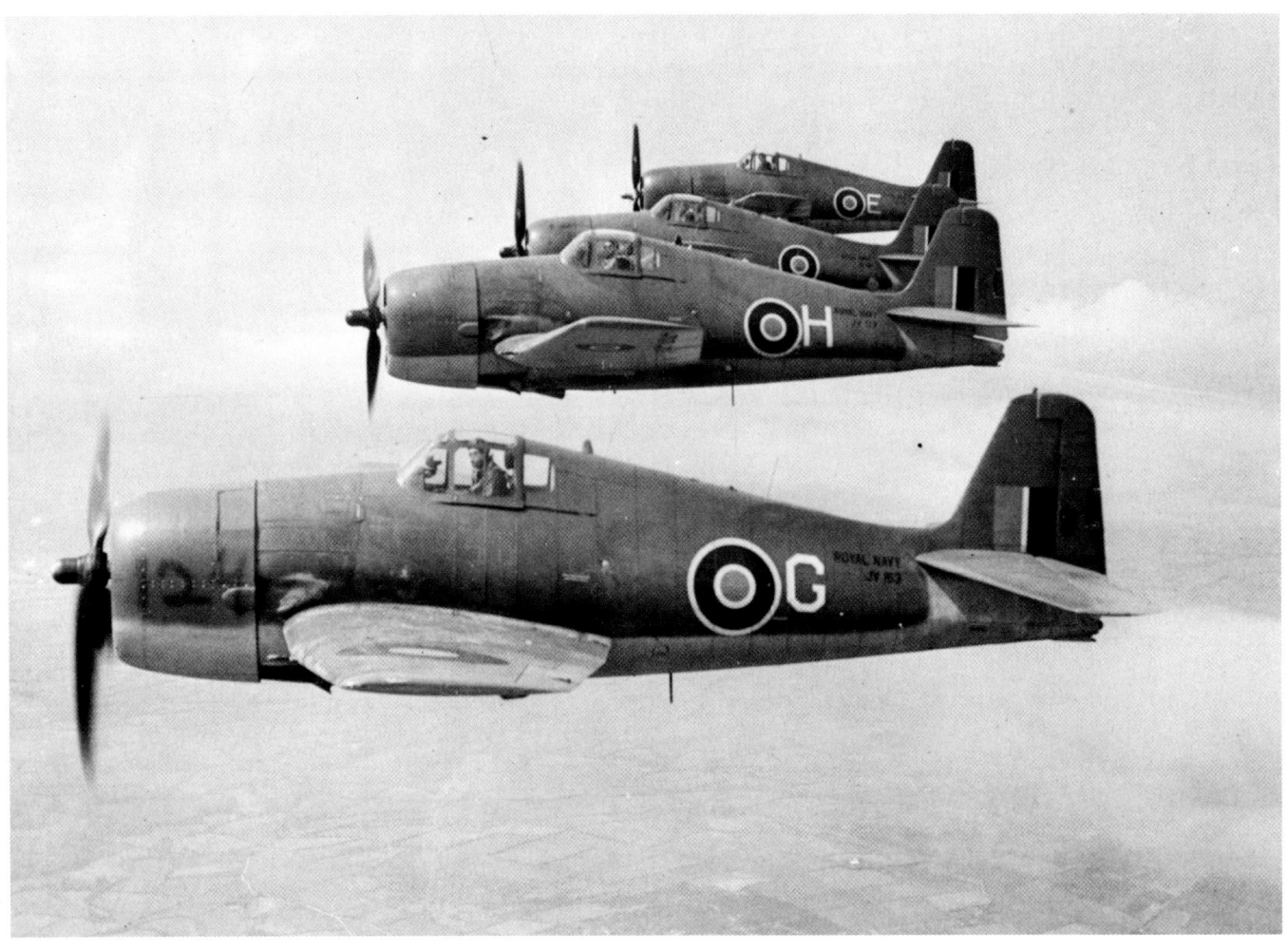

The Grumman F6F Hellcat was an American single-seat fighter that would become the principal carrier-based fighter of the US Navy in the Pacific in World War II.

It was destined to be a success from its conception, based on its predecessor the Grumman F4F Wildcat and lessons learnt from both the European air war and early clashes in the Pacific. This sturdy and robust aircraft, if not the most sleek or glamourous of aircraft like its competitor the Vought Corsair, would gain air superiority over the principal Japanese aircraft in the Pacific, the Mitsubishi A6M Zero, when it rose to challenge it for the first time in the summer of 1943, ensuring its place in aviation history.

ABOVE: A formation flown by Dutch pilots in Grumman Hellcats in service with the British. The Royal Navy Fleet Air Arm would also operate around 1,200 Hellcats from 1943 to 1945 as part of the Lend-Lease deal.

Origins

The Hellcat was designed as a replacement for the smaller F4F Wildcat, which was struggling to match the Japanese A6M Zero, and the US Navy placed an order in June 1941 for a new prototype with Grumman Aircraft Engineering Corporation.

Grumman had already been working on a successor design. Lessons learnt from earlier combat saw the basic design altered to move the wing to a lower mid position than the Wildcat, an improved all-metal skin and wider undercarriage. The aircraft was fitted with improved armour around the cockpit and early combat showed the need for more guns, so the Hellcat was fitted with six machine guns, giving enough firepower to down enemy aircraft. Extra fuel tanks mounted under the Hellcat would also extend its range, much needed over the large Pacific Ocean.

The adoption of the Pratt & Whitney R-2800 Double Wasp engine was the real key to the success of the Hellcat, as it was the engine that was also used in the Corsair and Thunderbolt, and it delivered the power needed to push this sturdy and robustly designed aircraft. The engine was added and the aircraft's frame was strengthened to take the new engine. The prototype XF6F-3 flew in the summer of 1942 before quickly going into production and being delivered by the summer of 1943 to front-line American units in the Pacific.

Operations

UNITED STATES

Although the Hellcat was slightly slower than its main competitor the Corsair, it was quickly introduced to US carrier operations in the Pacific, as due to its sturdy design it made landing the Hellcat at sea easier for pilots than the Corsair.

The Hellcat made its combat debut in the Pacific in August 1943 and proved to be a match against the Japanese Zero. Its main success was during the Battle of the Philippine Sea in June 1944, when Japanese aircraft from nine enemy carriers attacked the American Task Force 58. The Hellcat was at the forefront of the battle; by the end so many Japanese aircraft had been shot down that the battle in the skies earned the nickname the 'Great Marianas Turkey Shoot'. Simultaneously, Hellcats flying from British escort carriers were providing air cover to the Normandy D-Day landings in Europe. The Grumman Hellcat has assured its place in aviation history as the aircraft that turned the tide in the Pacific campaign and was one of the most successful naval fighters of World War II.

A Hellcat from a US aircraft carrier flying off the Japanese coast. The use of drop tanks extended the range of the Hellcat.

#22
Grumman TBF Avenger

The Grumman TBF Avenger was an American torpedo bomber that was developed to replace an earlier bomber, the Douglas TBD Devastator, and would go on to play a considerable role in the war, especially in the Pacific.

The Avenger would be designed with the Grumman-patented 'Sto-Wing' folding wing, which was intended to maximise space available on aircraft carriers.

Origins

The Avenger was ordered as a prototype in 1941 by the US Navy and would carry a crew of three: pilot, turret gunner and a radio/bombardier/gunner. It could carry one torpedo of 2,000 lb in its large bomb bay and had an array of machine guns, including initially a .30 calibre in the nose and .50 gun in the electrically operated rear turret.

Another gun mounted under the aircraft could be used by the radio operator to shoot at enemy fighters attacking from below. It could also carry up to four 500-lb bombs.

The aircraft was designed with a good sturdy airframe and fitted with a Wright Twin Cyclone engine, giving a maximum speed of 257 mph and a range of just over 1,000 miles, ideal for long-range patrols over the Pacific. The Avenger was also manufactured from 1943 by General Motors and these aircraft were designated TBM, as Grumman moved over to producing the Hellcat fighter. Overall production of the Avenger would be just short of 10,000 and it remained in service until the end of the war.

An Avenger displaying D-Day markings.

UNITED STATES

Operations

As starts to combat service go, the Avenger's went badly.

A delivery of them was sent to Pearl Harbor in June 1942, but arrived too late to join the American carriers heading out to meet the Japanese at what would become the Battle of Midway. However, a small squadron of six Avengers had arrived on the island of Midway; once the battle started these were all but destroyed along with the more obsolete Devastators flying from the USS *Hornet*. The success of the Americans was down to the bombs dropped from dive bombers and not torpedo bombers at Midway. Despite this start, as the Avenger arrived in numbers it grew into being the principal American torpedo bomber in the Pacific, seeing action in the Solomon Islands, where it sank a Japanese battleship in late 1942 during Guadalcanal. Late in the war in 1945, Avengers sank two large 'super' battleships of the Japanese: *Musashi* and *Yamato*. The Avenger also counted a future US President amongst its pilots: George H.W. Bush flew in them before being shot down over the Pacific in 1944 when he took part in an attack on a radio station at Chichijima, part of the Bonin Islands located 600 miles

A line of Avengers at a jungle-fringed station.

UNITED STATES

A Grumman Avenger of Fleet Air Arm lands on HMS *Trumpeter* and is captured by the arrestor wire.

southwest of Japan. Bush was the sole survivor of the aircraft shot down during the raid and was rescued by the US submarine *Finback*, which surfaced offshore to rescue any downed aircrew. He would spend the next 30 days on board the submarine before returning to Hawaii.

The Avenger also flew with the Royal Navy Fleet Air Arm, where it was initially called 'Tarpon', but went back to being called Avenger as the British adopted American aircraft names. British Avengers saw service in Europe, including attacks on German U-boats in Norway and later in the Pacific. The Avenger undoubtedly proved to be one of the key torpedo bombers of the war, contributing greatly to the destruction of Japanese naval power. They were also at the centre of one of the most famous mysteries associated with the Bermuda Triangle when a post-war flight of five Avengers disappeared in December 1945 on a training mission in the 'triangle' and were never found.

#23
Handley Page Halifax

The Handley Page Halifax was a British heavy bomber that was built to the same Air Ministry specification as the Avro Lancaster.

Along with the Lancaster it formed the backbone of RAF Bomber Command force throughout World War II. It performed admirably and demonstrated great flexibility in the type of missions it could fly. Even so, the Halifax was deemed inferior to the Lancaster and suffered from this poor comparison, even though later models were able to match the performance of the other British bomber.

Origins

The Halifax was originally intended to be a twin-engine medium bomber, but like the Lancaster's predecessor, the Avro Manchester, two engines were not thought to be powerful enough, and the decision was made to switch the Halifax to a four-engine aircraft powered by Rolls-Royce Merlin engines.

The prototype H.P.57 flew in 1939 and it entered service in late 1940, named 'Halifax' due to the practice of naming bombers after British towns.

Handley Page Halifax Mk I L7245, the second prototype aircraft, in flight in 1940. It was deemed inferior to the Lancaster despite its solid performance during the war.

A row of Halifax bombers being assembled at the Handley Page factory at Cricklewood in northwest London, although production was split between several companies to aid the speed of delivery.

The aircraft had a straightforward design as a mid-wing monoplane with an all-metal alloy skin covering most of the structure. Its bomb bay was 22 ft long and it had a range of around 2,000 miles. It carried a crew of seven and had a number of turrets for defensive armaments. In later types, from the Mk III introduced in 1943, the nose became more streamlined and was made of glass Perspex.

The Mk III, which entered service in 1943, was fitted with the more powerful Bristol Hercules engine, negating some of the performance issues from earlier types. It suited the aircraft and improved the performance of the Halifax to perform more like the Avro Lancaster. Unfairly, comparisons to the Lancaster were to remain negative despite statistics showing the loss rate of the Halifax had improved with the new Mk III. Over 6,000 Halifaxes were built during the war, requiring production to be spread over several aviation companies, including English Electric and Fairey Aviation. New manufacturing techniques were introduced, with the Halifax being assembled from pre-assembled sections.

Engineers at work in the wind tunnel at the Handley Page factory, 1940.

A Handley Page Halifax flies over a smoke-obscured target during a daylight raid on the oil refinery at Wanne-Eickel in the Ruhr, 12 October 1944.

Operations

The Halifax entered service in late 1940 and began to be used for RAF bombing raids from 1941, including against the German battleship *Scharnhorst* that was at that time moored on the French Atlantic coast.

With increasing German fighter attacks, the Halifax was removed from daylight bombing at the end of 1941. In 1942, the Halifax was used in the formation of a Pathfinder Force to identify and 'mark' bomb targets. This led to the Halifax becoming an integral part of Bomber Command pathfinder operations, including successful daylight raids on oil facilities in Germany in 1944.

The biggest issue for early types of Halifax was that the Merlin engines provided insufficient power when operated at higher altitude, making it more susceptible to attack by German fighters. This was improved when the Mk III was developed with the Bristol Hercules engines, which gave it a superior performance to protect it against German fighters. From 1943, the Halifax was eclipsed by further deliveries of the Avro Lancaster, but the Halifax remained in production, even though new factories were primarily focusing on manufacturing the Lancaster.

As the Luftwaffe became stretched in 1944 and was unable to send up large numbers of fighters to oppose the Allies, the Halifax continued in its bombing role. It took part in daylight bombing raids, hitting the German coastal defences along the 'Atlantic Wall', as well as V-1 Flying Bomb sites, with some accuracy. By early 1945, as Allied air superiority was ensured, Halifax squadrons bombed cities deep within Germany, particularly targeting infrastructure such as railways, and these raids were often devastating. Despite the improved later Halifax versions, with the Bristol Hercules engine having a lower loss rate and better crew survival than the Lancaster, the Halifax continued to operate in the shadow of the favoured Avro Lancaster until the end of the war.

GREAT BRITAIN

The interior of the fuselage of Handley Page Halifax B Mk II, showing some of the many holes caused by splinters from an anti-aircraft rocket that hit the aircraft during an early pathfinder operation over central Europe.

Special Operations

The earlier Mk II versions of the Halifax had a good flying range for supporting resistance across Europe.

Several 'Special' versions were made to assist the British SOE (Special Operations Executive) in dropping supplies to resistance groups in occupied Europe and parachuting in their special agents. It was also used by RAF Coastal Command and used to mine enemy ports, as well as conducting anti-submarine and reconnaissance patrols. As a glider tug it had a better tow weight than the Lancaster, which allowed it to tow into the air the British glider, the Hamilcar, used by airborne forces to transport a light tank, and used by the Allies in their attempt to cross the Rhine at Arnhem during Operation Market Garden. The Halifax was also used in transport roles during the war, with later Mks VI and VII being 'tropicalised' to be used in Asia, but the war ended before they could be used there.

The Halifax continued to be used in the post-war period, but this adaptable and highly capable aircraft never received the recognition of the Avro Lancaster, despite its bombing record and delivering a significant contribution to the Allied war effort in the air.

A Halifax Mk II Series I flying over the English countryside.

Fleet Air Arm Hawker Sea Hurricanes flying in formation. The Hawker Hurricane was modified for use by the Royal Navy as the 'Sea' Hurricane, in maritime protection roles.

#24

Hawker Hurricane

The Hawker Hurricane was a British single-seat fighter aircraft, which played a pivotal role during the Battle of Britain in 1940.

The Battle of Britain has given the Hurricane a prominent place in British national wartime history, even though it does not always attract the same level of fame or recognition as the Supermarine Spitfire. It was cheaper and easier to produce than its contemporary, and pilots found it was easy to fly. It could be repaired quickly and for the first few years of the war was the workhorse of RAF Fighter Command, holding its own against Luftwaffe enemy fighters that were causing havoc and destruction during the German occupation of Europe.

Origins

The Hurricane was designed by Hawker Aircraft Limited's chief designer, Sir Sydney Camm.

It was based on an earlier Hawker aircraft biplane, the Hawker Fury, with it being given an early nickname, 'Fury Monoplane'. Whilst the British Air Ministry in the 1930s was still commissioning biplane aircraft, the advent of the monoplane fighter required a British single-seater fighter that could match fighters being developed in Germany, such as the Messerschmitt Bf 109. As a result, various Air Ministry specifications in the early 1930s looked to acquire a new 'generation' fighter for the RAF, capable of speeds over 300 mph. Camm's design evolved to include characteristics that would serve the Hurricane well in the coming conflict.

GREAT BRITAIN

A Coles Crane is used to haul the fuselage of a damaged Hawker Hurricane Mk IIB onto a 'Queen Mary' trailer in the Western Desert. This highlights the ability of basic repairs being conducted in the field for the 'simple' Hurricane structure.

By 1935, agreement was reached between the Air Ministry and Hawker for a prototype to be built, with several modifications being considered for the new specification F.36/34. The main change in this specification was for the fighter to be armed with eight machine guns, capable of firing 8,000 rounds per minute, or 400 rounds per three seconds. This followed armament research in 1934, which showed a need for this level of firepower to be able to shoot down modern fighters. The first prototype Hurricane, K5083, flew for the first time in November 1935, with one RAF test pilot, Sammy Wroath, describing it as 'simple and easy to fly with no apparent vices'.

Based on initial flight tests, and with a belief from Camm and the Hawker design team of its worth, the board at Hawker took a commercial gamble in 1936 to start to develop a production line for the manufacture of the Hurricane even before an official order had been placed. This faith in the aircraft design was well placed, as an order for 600 Hurricanes arrived in June 1936 and the aircraft was officially named 'Hurricane' by King Edward VIII.

Design and Production

The Hawker Hurricane was a traditionally built low-wing monoplane, where the wing sat low against the fuselage of the aircraft.

Its traditional construction method, more like biplanes from an earlier era, saw it gain a reputation for ruggedness that could quickly be repaired after battle. But when compared to other contemporary all-metal alloy-skinned aircraft, such as the Supermarine Spitfire, it was outdated.

The manufacture of the Hurricane could be described as a mixture of 'ancient and modern'. First, the ancient: the aircraft structure was built of metal steel tubes with a wooden secondary structure built over the top. Over this Irish linen was placed, strengthened with 'dope' to seal the linen and form a rigid skin for the aircraft. The Hurricane had a strong and lightweight structure as a result of this fabric covering, which extended to the wings. In later versions, fabric-covered wings were replaced with metal-skinned wings, which were more robust, though wing types were interchangeable, should metal-skinned ones be unavailable.

The advantages of this more traditional type of build would help with the amount of damage a Hurricane could sustain in combat. Often shells or bullets from the enemy would pass through the structure and out through the other side without exploding and causing more severe damage to the fuselage. The other advantage was that linen could be replaced and repaired easily by ground crew, whilst its basic structure allowed it to be shipped in crates and assembled near to the front line with little specialist equipment. However, despite the Hurricane being one of the first RAF fighters capable of going over 300 mph, this structure meant it lacked speed and manoeuvrability when placed against sleek metal-skinned aircraft such as the Spitfire.

The Hurricane had some key features that added to its flying appeal; the ease of landing being one. Getting back on the ground after a gruelling air battle or patrol was a key consideration for pilots, and the design of the Hurricane's wheels and undercarriage helped. A hydraulic undercarriage that opened the landing wheels from the inside to out (compared to a Spitfire where the wheels moved from outside to in, in the opposite direction) gave it a wide and stable wheel 'track', which gave the Hurricane great stability landing and when on the ground. Pilots described how they could be 'ham fisted' when landing the Hurricane. Another modern advantage that the Hurricane had was the use of the now famous Rolls-Royce Merlin engine, which became a priority in the early years of the war under Lord Beaverbrook at the Ministry of Aircraft Production. The introduction of eight Browning machine guns was another reason the wings of the Hurricane had been altered to an all-metal alloy skin, and this increase in firepower offset any speed deficiencies. Over 14,000 Hurricanes were built until 1944 in Britain, at Hawker, Gloster and Austin Motors, and in Canada by the Canadian Car and Foundry Co., the other Allied country to manufacture the Hurricane.

Following the Munich Crisis of 1938, Hawker and the British government had seen the need to increase production. The designs were sent to Canada, where the first Canadian-built Hurricane came off the production line in February 1940, just in time for these to take part in the Battle of Britain later in that year. Production in Canada was overseen by Elizabeth 'Elsie' MacGill, a pioneering female aeronautical engineer. Her job was to ensure rapid production and she devised solutions for the Hurricane such as de-icing controls, which earned her the nickname in Canada of the 'Queen of the Hurricanes'.

TOP: Mechanics feeding ammunition into the Browning gun of a Hawker Hurricane. The change to eight machine guns in its design phase during the 1930s proved critical when the Hurricane went up against German aircraft during the Battle of Britain.

BOTTOM: A Hurricane Mk I undergoing maintenance in April 1940. The Hurricane was able to be maintained easily in the field, including adding the 'Shilling' restrictor valve that helped resolve issues with stalling engines in negative G-force dives.

OPPOSITE TOP: A section of Hawker Hurricanes. Hurricanes were the highest number of fighter aircraft available to RAF Fighter Command at the outset of the war.

OPPOSITE BOTTOM: Sergeant G. 'Sammy' Allard being congratulated on his return to Lille-Seclin in France on the evening of 10 May 1940 after shooting down the second of two Heinkel He 111s. Behind him ground crew are busy refuelling and rearming his Hawker Hurricane Mk I.

Operations

The Hurricane Mk I entered service with RAF Fighter Command in 1937.

It was the first modern fighter to enter RAF service and one of the most advanced in the world at the time. At the outbreak of the war in 1939, the RAF's largest number of fighters was the Hurricane and squadrons of the aircraft were sent to France in support of the British Expeditionary Force (BEF). Despite skirmishes during the 'Phoney War' from 1939 until spring 1940, Hurricanes would see limited action. However, early sorties against Luftwaffe fighters like the Messerschmitt Bf 109, and later during the Battle for France, showed that the Hurricane and its stablemate the Spitfire both had a key vulnerability in aerial dogfights.

The Rolls-Royce Merlin engine that was fitted in both aircraft would stall in a nose-down dive. This resulted in negative G-forces, as the engines would flood the carburettor, a problem that German aircraft with fuel-injection engines did not suffer from. This advantage allowed the German fighters to go into a negative G-force dive and the Hurricane, despite being able to turn in a tighter circle than the German fighter, was unable to follow. Fortunately for the Allies, a female British engineer who worked at the Royal Aircraft Establishment, Beatrice Shilling, devised a brass restrictor with a small hole in it. It was officially known as the RAE restrictor, but commonly known as 'Miss Shilling's orifice' amongst other names. This tiny metal piece limited the full amount of fuel that could flood the engine and could quickly be retrofitted into the engines of Hurricanes and Spitfires, which reduced, if not fully solved, the problem.

The Battle of France began in May 1940 with the German blitzkrieg on France and the Low Countries. The Hurricane was at the forefront of the Allies' response with ten squadrons operating in France, but it suffered considerable losses in its attempt to halt the German 'blitzkrieg'. After one week of action, the number of operational squadrons had dropped to three and on 20 May 1940 the Hurricanes were ordered to abandon bases in France and return to Britain. Hundreds of Hurricanes were left at airfields such as Abbeville. Despite the brave actions of their crews, the front-line Hurricanes were unable to halt the German onslaught. As the French and British Expeditionary Forces retreated to the port of Dunkirk, Hurricanes provided air cover operating from airfields in Britain. As British and French forces were evacuated from France at Dunkirk during Operation Dynamo, several Hurricane pilots became 'aces' during the operation. These air battles with the Luftwaffe had demonstrated that the Hurricane was a robust, steady aircraft that could turn tightly, but its performance suffered with its two-blade propeller as it struggled to catch German bombers and fighters. Modifications to the Rolls-Royce Merlin at the time gave it an engine boost with a supercharger that could add a further 30 mph to its top speed, whilst a three-blade propeller further improved its performance.

Battle of Britain

With the departure of British forces from France in the summer of 1940, new Prime Minister Winston Churchill advised the world that the Battle of Britain was 'about to begin'.

In RAF Fighter Command, just over half of its squadrons were equipped with Hawker Hurricanes. Though they had shot down many enemy aircraft in the preceding months, the performance of the Hurricane was still inferior to the German Bf 109.

The Battle of Britain lasted from July to October 1940, but the main aerial fighting took place from 8 August to 21 September 1940. Using the 'Dowding' home defence system of both radar and the Royal Observer Corps to plot incoming German aircraft, RAF Fighter Command Spitfires and Hurricanes would be 'scrambled' to intercept and attack the enemy formations. The superior performance of the Spitfire meant its main task was to attack the escorting enemy fighters, whilst the Hurricanes were tasked with engaging the enemy bomber formations. As a result of these tactics, the Hurricane secured its place in history by accounting for over 50 per cent of German aircraft losses during the battle, with Polish No.303 Squadron claiming the highest ratio of aircraft shot down.

There were many acts of great bravery by pilots in the summer of 1940, none more so than the recipient of the only Victoria Cross, Britain's highest honour, during the battle: Flight Lieutenant James Nicolson. On 16 August 1940, his Hurricane was attacked by three Bf 110 fighters, which saw his engine hit by cannon shells and catching fire. Another weakness that had become apparent during combat for the Hurricane had been the position of the petrol tank, which was just in front of the cockpit. If set on fire, the flames would blow into the pilot who was attempting to bail out, resulting in many RAF pilots sustaining burns.

This was very much the case for Nicolson, whose petrol tank was alight, but as he fought the flames and attempted to bail out, he noticed one of the enemy fighters in front of his Hurricane. Feeling the intense heat burning him in the cockpit, he remained and fired on the enemy even as it was trying to escape him. He could now do no more. With burns searing his flesh to the bone, he managed to escape the plane before landing in a field and was rushed to hospital. His injuries and burns took a while to heal but it encapsulated the rugged spirit of both the pilot and his sturdy Hurricane. Due to concerns over the fuel tank position, many Hurricanes had their engines fitted with a rubber coating which helped to 'self-seal' the petrol tank if it was set on fire.

American pilots of No.71 'Eagle' Squadron demonstrate a 'scramble' to their Hurricanes.

OPPOSITE TOP: Troops and civilians pose with Junkers Ju 88A-1, which belly-landed on the evening of 21 August 1940 having been intercepted by No.17 Squadron Hurricanes during an attack.

OPPOSITE BOTTOM: Three Hawker Hurricane Mk Is simulate an attack. During the Battle of Britain, Hurricanes were tasked with intercepting enemy bomber formations, which they did with great accuracy.

BOTTOM RIGHT: Two men of the Royal Observer Corps on a cliff top. Once the enemy was detected, the 'Dowding System' allowed RAF Fighter Command to scramble quickly to meet their formations during the Battle of Britain.

The Big Wing

During the Battle of Britain, maverick British pilot Douglas Bader, one of the leading Hurricane aces, proposed the concept of multiple squadrons of aircraft, including the Hurricane, converging together to form a 'big wing' to attack enemy bomber formations.

This would provide a show of force to the enemy and a counterattack to the enemy raid. Bader was based at RAF, now Imperial War Museum, Duxford, and his area was concerned with protecting the north of London and the industrial Midlands. But he was itching to get into the fight and he had senior commanders who supported his theory of a 'big wing'.

The controversy over its effectiveness continues to this day, as once the Luftwaffe changed its tactics to bombing London in September 1940, it enabled RAF fighters north of London to engage the enemy, but it took too long to coordinate large numbers of Hurricanes. The 'Dowding System' was designed to maximise the aircraft available and direct them to the enemy quickly, but the 'big wing' was more suitable for large formations of aircraft supporting ground operations when the Allies had control of the air, which during the Battle of Britain had at that time not yet been fully 'won'. Many Hurricanes in a 'big wing' served a psychological purpose even if, tactically, it proved less effective during the Battle of Britain.

Advocate of the 'big wing', Squadron Leader Douglas Bader seated on the cockpit of his Hurricane at Duxford, 26 September 1940.

Sea Hurricanes

GREAT BRITAIN

The Hurricane entered service with the Royal Navy in 1941 and was used to protect maritime convoys, as later types had been adapted to carry additional weapons, including bombs.

The Sea Hurricane proved an effective weapon in the air war at sea, supporting the relief of Malta and protecting convoys in the Atlantic. Initially, Sea Hurricanes were 'fired' from merchant ships using catapult rockets, but the pilot would eventually have to find land if near the coast or ditch into the sea to be retrieved, which inevitably led to many pilot losses. Later Sea Hurricanes flew from converted merchant ships that had a flight deck installed.

The Hurricane was withdrawn from day-fighter roles after the Battle of Britain and became a successful night fighter for a period of the war, first during the Blitz and later attacking bombers over France. During the desert campaign in North Africa, the Hurricane demonstrated its worth as a fighter bomber when it supported the Allies as part of the Desert Air Force. In Asia, Hurricanes were at the front line in attempts to stop the Japanese advance, operating from Singapore and in Southeast Asia.

The Hawker Hurricane also saw combat with the Soviet Union on the Eastern Front, as the first Allied Lend-Lease aircraft to be supplied to the Soviets. It became the most-used British aircraft in Soviet service. The use of Hurricanes over the Soviet Union amply demonstrates the robust workhorse nature of the aircraft.

Although production of the Hurricane ended in 1944, this relatively 'unglamorous' aircraft was the backbone of RAF Fighter Command in the early years of the war. Its contribution to the Allied victory is measured in its combat victories during the dark days of the Battle of Britain, when the balance of the war hung by a slender thread. Those who piloted the Hurricane at that time were to earn their place, and that of the Hurricane, in aviation history as being part of Winston Churchill's 'gallant few'.

A Hawker Sea Hurricane being catapulted from the Catapult Armed Merchant (CAM) ship at Greenock in Scotland. The long flame comes from the rocket assistors.

Hawker Hurricane Mk IIDs rolling out soon after noon on 6 April 1943 for a tank-busting raid.

A Hawker Hurricane Mk IID demonstrates the effect of its firepower on an abandoned enemy tank in Tunisia.

Hurricane Mk IIC.

GREAT BRITAIN

137

#25
Hawker Tempest

The Hawker Tempest evolved from the Hawker Typhoon, and was originally called the Typhoon II.

But significant changes to its wing and further improvements to rectify some of the issues that plagued the Typhoon led to it becoming one of the most powerful and fastest propeller-powered fighters operated by the RAF during the war.

Tempest Mk V, EJ743, on a test flight.

Origins

GREAT BRITAIN

During development of the Hawker Typhoon in 1940, it had become clear to Sydney Camm and the Hawker designers that the thickness of the wing of the Typhoon was causing issues with drag and hindering its speed at higher altitudes.

This limited its ability to fulfil what was to be its primary role as an all-altitude fighter to intercept enemy aircraft to ensure air superiority for the Allies. To improve on the Typhoon design, three areas were looked at: a redesigned wing, improved cockpit visibility and increased fuel loads to improve the flying range of the aircraft.

The redesigned wing was semi-elliptical, significantly reduced in its ratio of thickness, and of metal laminar flow construction, further reducing drag with recessed rivets, a technique also used on the P-51 Mustang. This 'thin wing Typhoon' required further design because of this wing: the fuselage was lengthened to accommodate fuel tanks that could no longer be stored in the wings; the cockpit moved further down the body with a one-piece sliding 'bubble' canopy to give better pilot visibility; a larger tail fin improved stability; and new Hispano Mk V cannons allowed for enough ammunition to fit into the new wings. Further modifications included a new slimmer undercarriage and wheels. A large four-blade propeller also significantly improved the aircraft's speed.

The ongoing wartime issue of engine development also had a significant impact on the design of the Tempest. Camm wanted to install Napier Sabre IV engines, with the aim to remove the bulbous 'chin' of the Typhoon, placing air vents in the wing. The Typhoon II went into prototype production in 1941 with five variants. Mk I and Mk V were to be powered by the Napier Sabre IV and II engines, Mk II was to use the Bristol Centaurus radial engine, and Mk III and Mk IV were to use Rolls-Royce Griffon engines.

The first Mk I flew on 2 September 1942. However, problems with the Napier Sabre Mk IV engine saw the engine development cancelled, delays to the Bristol Centaurus radial engine, and the Rolls-Royce Griffons going into the development of later Spitfires confusingly meant the Mk V with a Napier Sabre II engine would become the only operational version during the war. Perception of the new aircraft was also of some importance following negative reactions to the Typhoon, and the changes and fresh look were deemed significant enough to rename the aircraft 'Tempest' in August 1942, prior to the first test flight the following month.

Profile of a Tempest Mk V. The thin semi-elliptical wing, 'bubble' canopy and large tail fin all contributed to its improved performance.

Operations

The Tempest entered operational service with the No.3 Squadron RAF and No.486 Squadron Royal New Zealand Air Force in April 1944, initially flying cross-Channel missions in the build-up to the D-Day campaign.

It scored its first victories against Bf 109s on 8 June 1944. However, the air speed of the Tempest, at 440 mph in level flight, was vital in a decision that saw it being pulled back from Normandy to assist with a new threat that was just emerging over the skies of Britain in the summer of 1944.

V-1 Flying Bomb

On 13 June 1944, one week after D-Day, a Fieseler Fi 103 unmanned aircraft was fired towards London, partly in response to the Allied landing in Normandy.

It landed in Grove Road, Mile End in London, exploding and killing eight civilians. This early version of what could be described as a guided missile became known as a V-1 Flying Bomb, nicknamed 'doodlebug'. The V-1 was the first of Germany's vengeance weapons and at its peak over 100 a day were being fired at London and the south of England. Now in 1944, it brought a new wave of destruction to Britain.

To counter this new threat and to prevent the V-1s from reaching their targets, the Hawker Tempest was deployed for its exceptional speed at low/medium altitude. It was fast enough to catch the rocket-propelled missiles and could shoot them down with its cannons. This ensured the chasing Tempest did not get caught in the blast, or use the aircraft itself to divert the missile off course by using air flow over the Tempest's wing, which would disrupt the V-1 autopilot and send it into an out-of-control dive. However, to begin with there were only a handful of Tempests available to combat this new weapon and it was not until September 1944 when further Tempests entered service that V-1s could be brought down in significant numbers.

The Tempest would continue to serve in Europe until May 1945, flying in support of the operation at Arnhem and as the Allies advanced into Germany. It was also credited with shooting down Me 262 jets, often when the jets were slowing down to land and at their most vulnerable. The Tempest II eventually arrived with its Centaurus engine and without a defined air vent 'chin'. It was prepared for service in Asia but could not be deployed before the war ended. The Tempest proved to be an excellent aircraft and, although it entered service from 1944, was a decisive aircraft in the eventual victory of the Allies in Europe.

GREAT BRITAIN

OPPOSITE TOP: Hawker Tempest Mk Vs undergoing servicing at Newchurch, Kent.

OPPOSITE BOTTOM: Flight Sergeant Morris Rose points out the essential characteristics of the V-1 Flying Bomb, 23 June 1944. The pilot had downed his first 'doodlebug' on 16 June. A V-1 Flying Bomb carried a warhead of nearly 2,000 lb and was guided to its target by an autopilot. It had an average speed of 340 mph.

RIGHT: *Tempests Attacking Flying Bombs*, by artist Walter Thomas Monnington.

BOTTOM: Hawker Tempest Mk II aircraft lined up beside the runway at the Hawker Aircraft Limited factory, showing the removal of the prominent 'chin' on the earlier Tempest with air vents now situated in the wing.

#26
Hawker Typhoon

The British Hawker Typhoon was developed by Sydney Camm, the designer of the Hurricane, in response to Air Ministry Specification F.18/37.

Camm produced a fighter capable of exceeding 400 mph at 15,000 ft and taking on heavily armed escorting fighters. The Typhoon did eventually meet the Air Ministry requirement, but its construction and engine would lead to many early questions over its performance. This ultimately led to the plane almost being cancelled, before modifications saw it adapted into a fighter bomber that would secure its place as one of the most famed and feared Allied aircraft of World War II.

Origins

The Typhoon was designed in early 1937 in response to early questions Camm had posed to the Air Ministry about what type of aircraft Hawker should be working on after the Hurricane.

The resulting requirements gave Camm and his team at Hawker a head start on other manufacturers. As the design evolved, the Typhoon was to be similar but become much larger than the Hurricane. This enabled Hawker to work within existing manufacturing tooling, greatly helping to reduce manufacturing assembly costs.

A Typhoon Mk IB in flight.

The design of the Typhoon was to be a hybrid of existing methods of construction combined with emerging modern technologies. The front section of the Typhoon, from the engine to behind the cockpit, used the more traditional method of construction at Hawker, using metal tubes bolted and welded together and covered in metal panels. The rear section of the aircraft would be a 'stressed skin' or semi-monocoque construction, where the strength of the structure is in the all-metal skin of the aircraft.

The Typhoon's engine was to be critical in fulfilling the requirement to intercept the enemy at over 400 mph. The choice was between the Rolls-Royce Vulture engine and the Napier Sabre engine. As both engines developed, the design of the Typhoon was split between the two engines, with the Vulture engine prototypes known as 'Tornado' (Type R) and the Napier engine prototypes known as 'Typhoon' (Type N). When the Vulture engine programme was cancelled, the Typhoon continued to be developed with the Napier Sabre engine, but this was just the start of its initial performance problems.

The Typhoon had a 'thick' wing compared to contemporary aircraft made of a strong two-spar structure, with a slightly cantilevered 'gull wing' appearance. This robustness, whilst providing a strong and stable platform for weapons and fuel tanks, prevented it from reaching maximum speeds at higher altitudes. Combined with the Napier Sabre engine's initial unreliability, the Typhoon had a poorer rate of climb than the German Focke-Wulf Fw 190. There were other vulnerabilities too, including poor rear vision, carbon monoxide seeping into the cockpit and, most worryingly, issues with the rear part of the fuselage breaking away.

Between 1941 and 1942 some of these problems were resolved. These included pilots wearing oxygen masks to help with carbon monoxide (though despite some fixes it persisted at lower levels throughout its service history); external strengthening plates and internal supports added to the join between the front and rear fuselage parts; and a 'bubble' canopy, which greatly improved visibility. An infamous exchange took place between Camm and an RAF pilot complaining about the poor rear vision, to which Camm is said to have replied that the Typhoon was 'so fast that you will not need to look behind you'.

Sydney Camm, chief designer at Hawker Aircraft Limited and designer of the Hurricane and Typhoon.

The Typhoon had a bulbous air inlet under the propeller, which aided engine oil cooling. Visible in the centre is an inlet for the supercharger, forcing more air into the engine to produce greater power.

Operations

The Typhoon did not enter operational service until late in 1941 with No.56 Squadron at RAF Duxford, to combat the new threat from the German Fw 190.

However, losses due to the rear fuselage structural issues meant that the Typhoon did not become more dependable until late 1942, with the possibility of it even being cancelled in favour of the American P-47 Thunderbolt. But through modifications it began to demonstrate its ability as a good low-level fighter, fast enough to catch and shoot down the Fw 190A-4, which the Luftwaffe had engaged in nuisance 'Tip and Run' fighter-bomber raids over the south of England between 1942 and 1943.

By 1943, the low-level performance, powerful engine and stable capabilities of the Typhoon marked it as an outstanding candidate to support the British and Canadians in the upcoming invasion and campaign in Europe with the Second Tactical Air Force (TAF): Typhoons were fitted with up to two 1,000-lb bombs or four 60-lb rockets under each wing, leading to the nicknames 'Bombphoons' and 'Rocketphoons'. Most of the squadrons of Typhoons developed as either rocket or bomb-carrying squadrons, to allow pilots to develop greater skill with each designated type of weapon. The Typhoon's evolution to a ground attack fighter bomber in support of Allied soldiers was about to be unleashed with devastating effect upon German-occupied Europe.

Armourers fit two extra 60-lb rocket projectiles to the wing rails of a Hawker Typhoon Mk IB. The ability of the Typhoon to carry rocket projectiles was crucial to its success as a fighter bomber in the Normandy campaign.

D-Day

The Typhoon gained a 'war-winning' reputation in 1944 with the D-Day campaign, Operation Overlord.

The Second TAF and RAF squadrons of Typhoons played a significant part in destroying enemy radar capability in advance of the Allied landings, whilst the plan to 'seal' off the landing area with attacks on key infrastructure targets in the peripheral areas near to the landing zone was to pave the way for a successful Allied landing.

The rocket-firing Typhoons proved extremely effective against railway locomotives, hindering Germany's ability to build up troops and respond to the Allies' advance from the landing beaches.

As the Allies gained a foothold in Normandy, Typhoons began to operate just behind the front lines. Forward Aircraft Controllers (FACs) with radios were able to call upon Typhoons to attack ground targets using a 'cab rank' system. Typhoons would be up in the air circling with pre-planned targets and could be called from the 'rank' to help troops on the ground if needed. Any aircraft not called would then continue to attack their pre-planned targets. The effect of the rocket attacks on German troops was often devastating and the enemy soldiers soon feared the Allied 'Jabos', short for '*Jagdbombers*', meaning 'fighter' or 'hunter' bombers.

Whilst the deployment of Typhoons close to the battle was effective in supporting troops, it soon became apparent that the conditions for maintaining the aircraft were far from ideal during the summer of 1944. Dust from the propellers was blown into the engines; as it contained abrasive material it caused damage and it was estimated that the Typhoons would be limited to only a small number of missions. As a result, and after some attempts to rectify the issue, air filters were fitted to cut down on the impact of this abrasive dust.

The filter changes were needed as the encircled Germans in Normandy attempted a counterattack to break out around Falaise. On 8 August 1944, at Mortain, the Germans struck, and Typhoons were credited by the Supreme Allied Commander, Dwight D. Eisenhower, with slowing the German counterattack sufficiently for the Allies to recover the situation. Reports after the defeat of the German armies at Falaise from the battlefield suggested that the number of enemy tanks destroyed by rocket-firing Typhoons was as low as four per cent in Normandy, but the psychological impact of the 'Jabos' Typhoons on the enemy was to continue until the final victory in Europe in 1945.

The final years of the war were to see the Typhoon disrupt the Germans with attacks on key headquarters throughout northwest Europe, and final actions by Typhoons in May 1945 included the sinking of large passenger ships in the Baltic. Over 3,000 Typhoons were built during the war, and the devastating firepower of the aircraft and the innovative use of rocket projectiles would secure its place as one of the leading fighter bombers of World War II.

A Hawker Typhoon of No.181 Squadron RAF showing a rocket projectile fired towards German motor transport trying to escape through the Argentan-Falaise gap, Normandy 1944.

A pilot scrambles to his waiting Hawker Typhoon Mk IB following a call from the Group Control Centre ordering an air strike.

#27
Lockheed Hudson

The Lockheed Hudson was an American light bomber based on a commercial airliner from the 1930s, which found considerable success as a coastal reconnaissance and maritime aircraft during the war, primarily with the RAF.

It would also play a part in dropping agents into occupied France. Despite being replaced over the Atlantic by larger aircraft later in the war, it continued to serve in the Mediterranean and Southeast Asia until the war ended.

An RAF Lockheed Hudson Mk VI over the pyramids of Egypt. The aircraft, based on a commercial airliner, would serve the Allies throughout the war.

UNITED STATES

RAF fitters change the engine of a Lockheed Hudson aircraft at a West African base.

Origins

The Hudson was developed as a military version of the Lockheed Model 14 Super Electra commercial airliner, which was used by many airlines in the late 1930s.

It was used to transport British Prime Minister Neville Chamberlain back from the Munich conference with Hitler in 1938, when on his arrival in London he proclaimed 'peace for our time'. Plans for a military version began in late 1937 when drawings were published. The British Purchasing Commission ordered the Hudson to replace the ageing Avro Anson, to be used primarily in a maritime reconnaissance role. The Hudson, as based on an existing aircraft, was delivered quickly, arriving in Britain by May 1939.

The aircraft could carry a crew of up to six, had machine guns fixed in the upper part of its nose, as well as a turret gun mounted at the top of the fuselage towards the rear. It had a range of just under 2,000 miles and could carry up to 1,000 lb in bombs, with later versions fitted with Air to Surface Vessel radar. Although initially purchased by the British, later types, including the Mk VI version with a more powerful Pratt & Whitney Twin Wasp engine, would be supplied under the American Lend-Lease deal with Britain.

Operations

As war erupted in Europe in 1939, the Hudson was pushed straight into action with RAF Coastal Command.

A Hudson became the first RAF aircraft operating from Britain to shoot down a German aircraft when a Do 18 seaplane was shot down at Jutland. During 1940, Hudsons patrolled the Norwegian coast, over the evacuation of the British and French forces from Dunkirk in May 1940, and over the captured Atlantic ports in France. In Malaya in 1941, Hudsons participated in attacks on invading Japanese forces landing at Kota Bahru, whilst Australian Hudsons also operated against the Japanese in Sumatra and Java. A rumour persisted in Southeast Asia at that time that the Japanese were using captured Hudsons to drop paratroopers, but these were in fact Kawasaki Ki 56 transport aircraft that had also been originally developed from the Lockheed 14.

The Hudson was used successfully in the Atlantic. It served with US naval forces and was responsible for the first sinking of a U-boat by the US Navy. This workhorse would prove to be an often overlooked yet versatile aircraft that would serve the Allies well, especially in its role as a maritime patrol aircraft.

A Lockheed Hudson approaches Dunkirk during the evacuation of the British and Allied troops in May–June 1940.

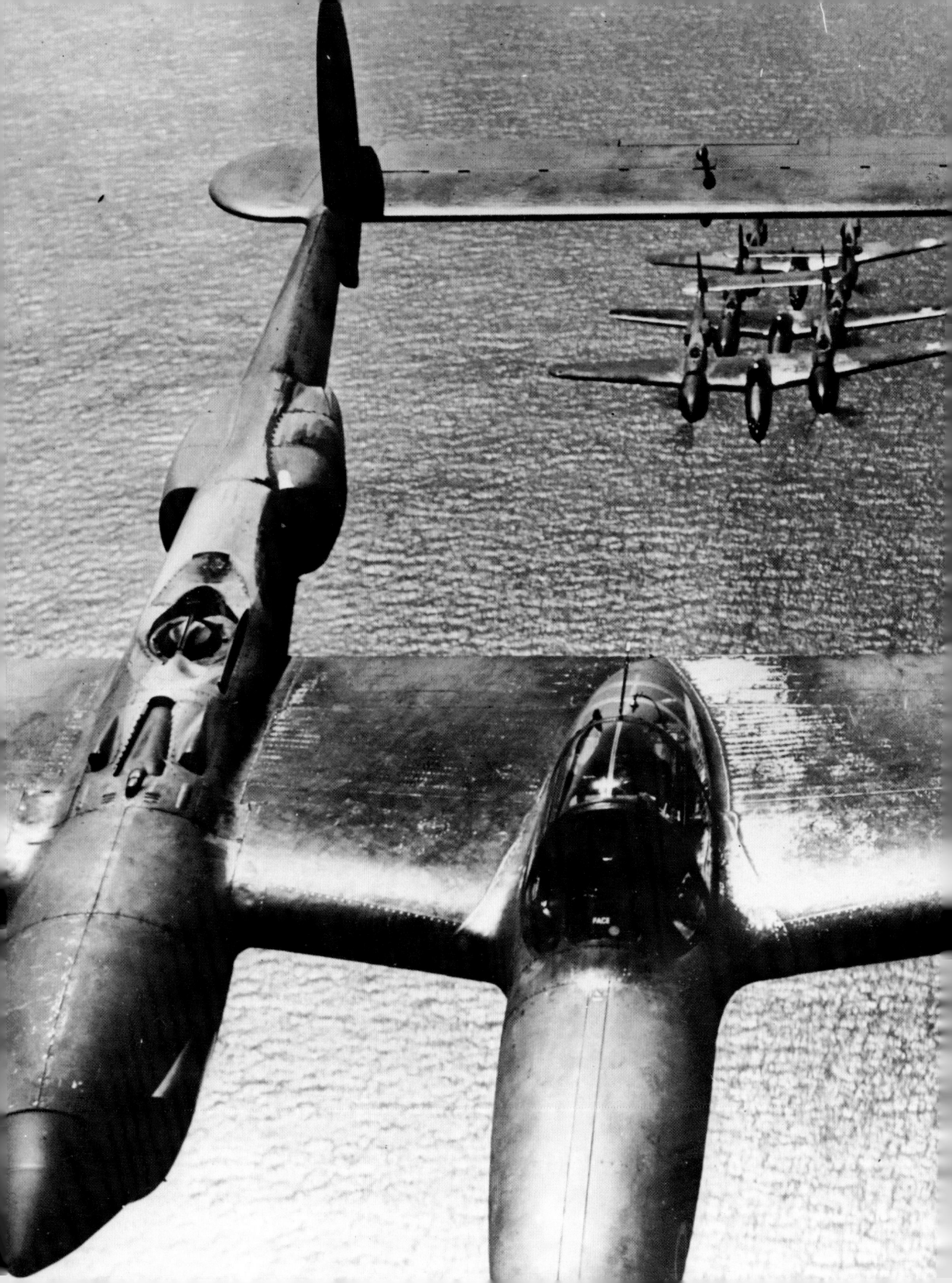

#28

Lockheed P-38 Lightning

UNITED STATES

The Lockheed P-38 Lightning was one of the most distinctive aircraft of the war.

An American twin-engine fighter, the radical design of the Lightning with its twin-boom tail and powerful concentrated nose armament meant that it would see considerable service throughout the war as the most advanced fighter then available to the Americans, following the Japanese attack on Pearl Harbor in 1941.

It served in Europe, the Mediterranean and North Africa, and in the Pacific where it was most suited to combat with its long range and twin engines. It would claim one of the most famous and significant Japanese combat losses, when P-38 Lightnings shot down the architect of Pearl Harbor, Admiral Yamamoto. A direct ancestor of today's modern multi-role fighters, the Lightning would secure its place in history as the main front-line fighter of the Americans in the early years of World War II.

A formation of P-38Es in flight off the coast of California in early 1941. The Lightning was the most modern fighter aircraft available to American aviators at the start of the war and played a significant role, especially in the Pacific. After the Japanese attack on Pearl Harbor in December 1941, the P-38 was the aircraft that shot down and killed the main architect of that attack, Admiral Yamamoto, in 1943.

Origins

The Lightning originated from Lockheed's response to a 1937 US Army Air Corps requirement for a long-range interceptor fighter.

The new aircraft would have to fly at over 360 mph over 20,000 ft, which no aircraft at the time or in development could meet. Lockheed were keen to offer a design to break into the lucrative high-performance military aircraft market in the United States in the late 1930s. The company set up an offshoot special engineering section to complete the design, which later gained fame in the post-war period as the 'Skunk Works'. The team, led by Hall Hibbard and Clarence 'Kelly' Johnson, quickly realised that two engines would be needed for the new fighter to give the performance required to meet the specifications.

The prototype XP-38, with its radical 'futuristic' design of a 52-ft wing and twin engines, situated in two long 'booms' joined at the tail, with the cockpit positioned in a central nacelle section, first flew in January 1939. The P-38 was fitted with the Allison V-1710 engine, which was also used by its contemporary, the P-40, and had an all-metal skin that had flush rivets, a first on an American fighter. Production throughout the war would total just over 10,000 aircraft of different variants. The main production models, E, F, H, J and L, saw increases in engine power, especially the use of turbochargers, that brought air into the engine to boost speed, giving the P-38 a maximum speed of 414 mph by the time of the 'J' version.

However, the unique design of the P-38 did not come without its faults. It initially suffered from control locks when at high speeds, especially in dives, which led to the tail becoming unstable. Although this issue was reduced, the P-38 also had engine issues throughout its service. The British, who gave it the name 'Lightning', which was adopted by the Americans, found in tests that it did not fight at a higher speed than the German Fw 190 and Bf 109. In Europe, although seeing considerable combat, the P-38 began to be replaced by the P-51 Mustang. Despite these issues, the P-38 Lightning still proved to be an exceptional modern fighter for the Allies.

The nose guns on a P-38 Lightning. The concentrated firepower of four machine guns and a cannon gave the P-38 a considerable advantage when in aerial combat or strafing targets on the ground, carrying an additional bomb load of up to 4,000 lb.

A pilot of the 20th Fighter Group in the cockpit of his P-38 Lightning.

Operations

At the start of the war in the Pacific from the end of 1941 and into 1942, the P-38 began to be used extensively.

Although it struggled to out-turn the principal Japanese fighter, the A6M Zero, its superior speed and rate of climb gave it a highly effective combat edge over the Japanese when using basic air manoeuvre tactics. Initially the P-38 in the Pacific began escorting bombers and successfully took part in the Battle of the Bismarck Sea in March 1943, which disrupted Japanese attempts to move troops to New Guinea in the South West Pacific. The most famous action in the Pacific by the P-38 Lightning was in April 1943, after American code breakers discovered that Admiral Yamamoto, planner of the Japanese attack on Pearl Harbor in 1941, was due to fly to Bougainville Island in the New Guinea islands to view troops. With its long range and devastating firepower, the P-38 was chosen to intercept the flight of Yamamoto. For the loss of one P-38, the Mitsubishi G4M 'Betty' transporting Yamamoto crashed into the jungle. Recovering his body from the wreckage delivered a significant psychological blow to the Japanese Navy and a boost to American forces in scoring such an important public propaganda victory.

In Europe, the P-38 first saw combat in North Africa and the Mediterranean where it met the Luftwaffe with mixed results. Some P-38 pilots scored victories against German opposition, whilst others were easily knocked out. It was alleged that the Germans gave the P-38 its nickname, 'Fork-tailed Devil', on initial skirmishes, although this was reported in a *Life* magazine article and could have been created more for the aircraft's public relations image. The P-38 saw much combat across Europe: attacking the Ploesti oil fields in Romania supplying the German war machine; during the D-Day landings in 1944 on fighter-bomber missions; and it was the first fighter used to escort US bombers of the USAAF Eighth Air Force to Berlin, before being later replaced by the P-51 Mustang in this role.

Overall, the combat results of the P-38 were significant in the war, with many aces flying the aircraft in the Pacific, where it was particularly suited to conditions. Despite a more mixed success over Europe, the radical design of the 'Fork-tailed Devil' would secure its place in aviation history.

#29
Martin B-26 Marauder

The Martin B-26 Marauder was an American medium bomber.

It initially had a number of issues when it first entered operational service, but would go on to become a leading medium bomber aircraft in both Europe and the Pacific theatres of war. Despite the early controversies, it would become safer to fly and be attributed as having the fewest combat losses of any aircraft flying with the USAAF, becoming one of the most important tactical bomber aircraft the Allies would have at their disposal.

Origins

The B-26 Marauder was developed by the Martin Company in response to Circular Proposal 39-340, a US Army Air Corps specification for a new medium bomber.

In a similar vein to de Havilland in Britain with the Mosquito, the designer, Peyton M. Magruder, favoured speed. The Marauder was developed with two powerful Pratt & Whitney radial engines, a smooth rounded 'torpedo-like' fuselage with a tricycle undercarriage and the ability to carry up to 5,000 lb of bombs. The all-metal modern design was so impressive that an order was placed even before the first prototype flew.

The Marauder had a crew of seven: pilot, co-pilot, bombardier/gunner, navigator, radio operator, and gunners in the tail and on top of the fuselage in a turret. The wing mounting was high on the sleek fuselage body at the 'shoulder', but after the first prototype flew in November 1940 it emerged, as units began to receive the new bomber in 1941, that the wing was not large enough for the weight of the aircraft. This led directly to a higher landing speed than other contemporary bombers, and this combination saw inexperienced pilots in training suffer a high rate of accidents, coining the aircraft's nickname at this time of 'Widowmaker'. Other pilot complaints were the inability of the B-26 to fly on one engine, but this was quickly disproved by more experienced pilots.

To make the aircraft safer, modifications were made to the next major production model, the B-26B. A new extended wingspan and taller tail fin helped the aircraft become safer, but it would take a further modification with the B-26F of where the angle at which the wing joined the fuselage before the accident rate would fall further. By the end of the war just under 5,000 had been built by Martin in Baltimore and Nebraska, serving not only with the USAAF but also with other Allied air forces, including the RAF and South African Air Force (SAAF).

UNITED STATES

B-26 Marauders fly in formation during a mission.

Operations

Pacific

The Marauder entered service in February 1941 with the 22nd Bombardment Group conducting anti-submarine roles on the west coast of the United States. After the Japanese attack on Pearl Harbor in December that year, the group was moved to Australia, becoming part of the Fifth Air Force.

Despite the initial difficult handling and issues with the weight of the aircraft in relation to the wing, it proved to be a match for the Japanese in service, carrying out raids on Rabaul in New Britain and New Guinea in early 1942, and during the Battle of Midway, attacking the Japanese fleet using torpedoes. The B-26 began to be phased out in the South West Pacific by 1944, eclipsed by the B-25 Mitchell, but its role in the battles in the Pacific showed it was a fast and efficient bomber in the Pacific theatre.

A B-26 Marauder of the 322nd Bomb Group strafes a factory at Montabaur, Germany during a mission, 22 February 1945.

UNITED STATES

Europe

The Marauder entered the European air war in March 1943 with the USAAF 322nd Bomb Group arriving in England.

Training for low-level missions, the first raids in May 1943 did not go well. A low-level attack with fighter support on a power station at IJmuiden in the Netherlands with 11 Marauders suffered badly at the hands of the Luftwaffe and enemy flak, with the loss of all 11 aircraft. Consequently, the B-26 Marauder was switched to its medium-bombing role at altitudes of 10,000–15,000 ft with the Ninth Air Force, usually with fighter cover, which suited the aircraft. It went on to perform devastating raids in the lead up to D-Day against infrastructure targets before moving to bases on the European continent. The last raid by a Marauder for the USAAF in Europe took place in May 1945, by which time the aircraft had proved its accuracy and become a potent medium bomber. Ironically for an aircraft that suffered crashes in its early development, the Ninth Air Force would claim the B-26 had the fewest losses of any American bomber in Europe.

Mediterranean

In the Mediterranean, the B-26 operated throughout the Allied advance up through Sicily and Italy, having first supported the American landings in North Africa.

With the RAF, the Marauder I was used by the British to drop torpedoes to sink merchant ships and shoot down German and Italian aircraft flying between Italy and North Africa.

The longer-winged B-26C (Marauder II) served with the South Africans taking part in bombing missions in the Eastern Mediterranean and supporting the partisans of Tito in former Yugoslavia. In the hands of the Free French Air Force, the B-26 took part in operations over Italy and in support of the Allied landing in southern France in 1944.

Although the Marauder came into service with a poor reputation for crashing, by the end of the war this sleek and fast medium-sized bomber, in the hands of experienced pilots, would prove to be a significant weapon for the Allies across Europe, the Mediterranean and the Pacific. For any enemy forces caught by one of its raids, it really would become the ultimate 'Widowmaker'.

The underside of a B-26 Marauder of the 320th Bomb Group in flight.

#30

North American B-25 Mitchell

The North American B-25 Mitchell was the most-produced American medium bomber of the war and played a significant role in all theatres, having been used by many Allied air forces.

There were many adaptions to the original design, partly because of combat experience where, in the Pacific, it was found to be deadly at low-level anti-shipping and 'jungle' strafing missions. Nearly 10,000 of all types were built by the North American Aviation company, who were also manufacturing the P-51 Mustang at the same time. This rugged and dependable medium bomber would prove to be one of the best strategic bombers available to the Allies in the war.

Origins and Variants

The Mitchell, named after General William 'Billy' Mitchell, an American World War I pilot who was regarded as the father of American air forces, was started in 1938 when North American Aviation believed the US Army Air Corps would require a new modern bomber.

The prototype, NA-62, was put forward when such a proposal was issued by the US Army Air Corps in 1939 and it was accepted, alongside the Marauder B-26 medium bomber, to be designated B-25.

The design initially had some issues with the wing, which caused stability problems, but changing an angle of the outer wing solved this. Early versions, the B-25A and B-25B, were delivered to the USAAF, with the B-25B becoming operational in 1942 and seizing the headlines due to its use in a daring raid. Later versions would see changes to gun placements and different engines. The B-25C became the first mass-produced type, whilst the B-25G was notable as it was developed for use in the Pacific as an anti-shipping bomber, using an M4 cannon in its nose, producing considerable firepower for firing down onto ships. The last factory production series was the B-25J, with just over 4,000 being built. The B-25 Mitchell was built at North American factories in Inglewood, California and Kansas City, Missouri.

UNITED STATES

A B-25C Mitchell of the 7th Photographic Reconnaissance Group. The versatility of the bomber saw it excel in many wartime roles.

Operations

Pacific and Asia

The B-25 Mitchell became one of the most famous bombers of the war when the 'Doolittle Raid' led by 'Jimmy' Doolittle took place on 16 April 1942.

Sixteen B-25Bs were launched 668 miles from Tokyo from the US aircraft carrier USS *Hornet* to deliver the first American bombing raid on the Japanese home islands, in response to the earlier Japanese attack on Pearl Harbor in December 1941. All the B-25 crews bombed their targets in Japan, including the capital Tokyo and four other cities, and despite limited damage to the Japanese, the psychological effect of the raid was significant. For the Japanese, the raid showed that their home islands could be reached by American aircraft, leading to the Imperial Japanese Navy's plan to extend the outer perimeter of Japanese territory in the Pacific. This led to a catastrophic defeat for the Japanese at the Battle of Midway in June 1942. The effect on American morale was that it was given a great boost when it was engaged in early battles trying to halt the Japanese in the South West Pacific. The effect of the raid for the 80 B-25 crew who took part was more profound, with many bailing out or ditching as they tried to reach China. Ten crew were killed, though most of the 80 eventually made it home.

The potential for the B-25 to be a ground attack aircraft in addition to being a medium-altitude bomber was to emerge in campaigns where the B-25 Mitchell flew in Pacific islands, including Papua New Guinea, the Solomon Islands and New Britain. The dense jungle on these islands prevented useful medium-altitude bombing raids, so with its increasingly powerful forward-firing guns, it took on successful ground-strafing missions. These were adopted using the modified B-25G variant, with a nose that would see a cannon added for extra firepower while attacking ground targets. There were also successful operations attacking enemy ships throughout the Pacific, with naval groups set up by the US Marine Corps operating the B-25 in anti-shipping raids. In Asia the B-25 flew missions against the Japanese in Burma, including helping to resupply Allied troops fighting at Imphal in 1944, as well as offering close air support in fighting with the Chinese against the Japanese Army in China.

Europe and Middle East

The RAF received around 900 Mitchells under the Lend-Lease deal.

These, along with B-25 Mitchells of the USAAF, would support operations from 1942 with the campaign in North Africa, through Sicily and Italy and were used to great effect before and during the D-Day landings. With the longer range of the B-25 compared to the Douglas Havoc/Boston, it could fly further into occupied Europe on bombing missions.

As the Allies landed in Europe and troops pushed towards Germany, B-25 Mitchells were based in France and Belgium with the RAF. The aircraft would also serve with a variety of air forces, including the Australian, Canadian and Dutch. The Soviet Union also received 862 B-25 Mitchells, again under the Lend-Lease deal.

The B-25 Mitchell was a dependable and deadly medium bomber. It proved especially effective in the Pacific campaign when flying ground- or ship-attack missions on targets and played an integral role with many Allied air forces throughout the war.

A B-25 bomber of the USAAF, piloted by then Lieutenant Colonel James Doolittle, takes off from USS *Hornet*, bound for a raid on Tokyo and other Japanese military centres on 18 April 1942.

UNITED STATES

Ground staff of No.98 Squadron RAF paint the 102nd bomb symbol onto its tally of operations, 14 August 1944.

North American Mitchell flying over the Colombelles steelworks near Caen in Normandy during an attack on 22 June 1944.

#31
North American P-51 Mustang

The North American Aviation Mustang was an American single-seat fighter that operated as a fighter and fighter bomber during World War II.

It is famed for its long flying range due to its fuel capacity, enabling it to fly to 'Berlin and back' in support of daylight bombing raids by the USAAF. This reduced American bomber losses, which greatly helped to establish Allied control of the skies over Europe towards the end of the war. It was widely regarded as one of the finest aircraft in Allied service and due to its origins has occasionally been referred to as the 'American Spitfire'. Its design and performance have placed it amongst the truly iconic aircraft that emerged during the war.

ABOVE: Lieutenant Vernon R. Richards of the 361st Fighter Group flying his P-51 Mustang. The development of the Mustang was an Anglo-American success, eventually producing one of the finest aircraft of the war. British pilots who first flew the Mustang were impressed by its space compared to other fighters, which would become an important 'comfort' when flying long missions deep into Germany later in the war.

OPPOSITE: A close-up of the nose of a P-51 Mustang.

Origins

In 1940, British aircraft companies were struggling to meet the demands of the RAF to stem the tide of the war, which was going in Nazi Germany's favour, and so the British Purchasing Commission (BPC) approached North American Aviation to help fill the gaps in British aircraft manufacturing. Britain produced an RAF requirement for a fast and heavily armed fighter that could operate effectively over 20,000 ft, and they needed it quickly.

The BPC, which had an office in the United States based in New York, initially sought to buy the P-40 fighter from the Curtiss company, but Curtiss were themselves running at capacity, so the P-40 was in short supply. Staff at the BPC instead approached the North American Aviation company with the idea to produce the P-40 under licence. However, the P-40 as an aircraft was not without some faults, notably its Allison V12 engine. Whilst being good at lower altitudes, it did not perform as well at higher altitudes, where initial combat experience by the British suggested the air war in Europe would be fought.

The North American Aviation President, James Howard Kindelberger, was not overly interested in producing another company's design. Instead he suggested that a new fighter design from his company would be quicker to set up for mass manufacturing and could take to the air faster than producing a licenced P-40. A prototype aircraft, NA-73X, designed by Edgar Schmued and powered by an Allison V12 engine, took to the air by October 1940. It included several new features that would ensure the success of the Mustang and place it at the centre of the war in the skies. These features were evident in the initial prototype.

The P-51 Mustang's sleek lines were complemented by a unique laminar air-flow wing. Laminar flow is based on fluid dynamics and in aircraft it works in relation to the flow of air over the wing. In the Mustang, the laminar foil wing reduced drag, and when combined with a smooth and sleek fuselage created with recessed rivets, a 'low drag' airframe was created that improved the aircraft's speed and performance when the engine power was added. In the Mustang, the thickest part of the wing was two-thirds of the way down the wing towards the tip, which aided the reduced drag and made the P-51 faster than a Spitfire.

Another key feature was the radiator, which had a cooling duct located under the fuselage, giving the Mustang a distinguishing identifiable feature. The single air duct brought in air to cool the large radiator and the oil cooler, but it was also later found that the design of the duct could aid the aircraft by taking advantage of the 'Meredith effect', named after a British engineer. This was an effect that would offset the drag, caused by the cooling radiator duct under the fuselage, by using the duct to expel heated air to produce some extra thrust. A final important feature was that the aircraft was divided into five main sections, all fitted with necessary pipes and wires before assembly, which would aid mass production.

Initial evaluation of the aircraft by the British AFDU (Air Fighting Development Unit) and RAF test pilots showed the fighter to be an excellent aircraft to fly. It had reliable performance but struggled at higher altitude, as the Allison V12 did not work as well in the thinner air found at higher altitudes. However, it was excellent at lower altitudes so the initial order was delivered to the British in 1941. It was to enter service with the Army Cooperation Command to be used as a fast fighter bomber, designated the Mustang Mk I; only later, when new variants of the Mustang came into service with the USAAF, would it be designated the P-51.

At this stage, and late in the day, the USAAF began to evaluate the Mustang Mk I. As it had been born from British specifications, but built by an American aircraft company, it was suggested that American officials were slow to champion the aircraft. This would have later repercussions for the Allies in the air war over Europe, and especially the USAAF daylight bombing raids over Europe that began from 1943.

An early production P-51 Mustang. It clearly shows the early variant of the Mustang with the more restrictive viewing cockpit canopy, replaced with the 'bubble' canopy for the P-51D. The introduction of the Merlin engine enhanced the speed and performance at altitude of the Mustang.

Engines and Variants

The P-51 Mustang, whilst initially performing well, would reach its full potential with the adoption of a new engine.

Following evaluation by the RAF, the British suggested to North American Aviation that a switch to a Rolls-Royce Merlin engine would enhance the speed and performance at altitude of the Mustang I. The Merlin was a V12 two-speed and two-stage cooled supercharged engine, which at that time was also being fitted to Spitfire Mk IX variants. The Merlin engine was fitted to the Mustang X prototype, as they were called by the British, increasing the maximum speed of the aircraft from 390 mph to 441 mph. Representatives from North America, including the designer Edgar Schmued, visited Britain to evaluate the Merlin Mustang with the British AFDU and Rolls Royce, where the tests looked very promising.

Following the tests in Britain, North American Aviation began to manufacture Merlin-powered Mustangs in 1943, based on a prototype, XP-51B. The car manufacturer Packard had been granted a licence to build the Merlin engine, which became the Packard V-1650 engine, fitted to older Mustang P-51As and in the new P-51Bs and Cs that were just coming into production. The North American Aviation factory at Inglewood in California would manufacture over 1,900 P-51Bs, whilst at a new factory in Dallas, Texas over 1,700 P-51Cs were built, but modifications were required with the wing moving slightly forward and a four-blade propeller added. Delivery of these aircraft to the USAAF and RAF began from winter 1943 into early 1944, as early combat experiences of the USAAF led them to direct manufacturers to maximise internal fuel tanks to improve its fighter escort flight range. In the Mustang, an additional 85-US-gallon tank was fitted into the fuselage behind the pilot, enhancing the range over earlier Mustang versions, when working in tandem with extra drop fuel tanks fitted under the Mustang.

The RAF would also receive P-51B/C Mustangs, that were designated Mustang III, and the P-51D, which was Mustang IV under the Lend-Lease arrangement with the

Warrant Officer Cecil Broxton hefts above his head an empty pressed-paper composite wing-mounted auxiliary fuel tank used by P-51 Mustangs. It demonstrates the lightness of a wing auxiliary tank used by P-51 Mustang fighters. They were made from pressed paper and when empty were discarded. Sometimes when full they were dropped by the Mustangs on targets and then set alight when firing with incendiary bullets at the fuel tank.

United States. However, pilot visibility from the cockpit had been an issue for the RAF, so a new 'bubble' canopy offering greater all-round visibility and increased size and comfort in the cockpit was fitted to some RAF Mustangs. This included some operated by the USAAF, and which, after North American Aviation had also fitted a one-piece sliding canopy to P-51Bs, became the standard cockpit configuration for the next and most widely produced version, the P-51D Mustang.

Around 8,000 P-51D Mustangs were built in California and Dallas. This version also had a strengthened wing with increased calibre .50 Browning air-cooled machine guns, and other armament options saw rocket launchers mounted under each wing. The final variant to be built in any large quantity was the P-51K, which was remarkably like the P-51D except for a different manufacturer's propeller. The success of the Mustang for the RAF and the USAAF ensured it would continue to fly in the post-war years, including in the early part of the Korean War.

Operations

RAF

As the Mustang had been based on a British specification with the British Purchasing Commission, the first Mustangs to see combat were with the RAF when they entered service in early 1942.

Due to its excellent performance, this new aircraft allowed the RAF to transition from a defensive war against the Luftwaffe to more offensive operations. The longer range of the Mustang, and its lesser performance in the earlier versions at higher altitudes, meant it was suited for 'Rhubarb' raids by the RAF. These were 'nuisance raids' by RAF fighters attacking enemy targets on the ground in France, and took place on cloudier days and at low altitude.

Mustangs also covered the ill-fated Allied amphibious

attempted landing at Dieppe in 1942, and destroyed large numbers of locomotives and other infrastructure, before turning attention to V-1 sites during 1943–4. John Tilson from 610 Squadron RAF recalled: 'It was a delight to fly. It trimmed beautifully, it manoeuvred beautifully. I almost looked upon it as the American Spitfire.' Despite the success of the early Mustang Is in RAF service in a ground attack role, it would take the introduction by the RAF of the more powerful Merlin engine to enhance the Mustang and allow it to become the premium Allied bomber escort fighter in the latter years of the war.

USAAF

The United States Army Air Forces had been slow to see the potential of the P-51 Mustang, in part due to the pre-war doctrine that heavily armed bombers, such as the B-17, would always be able to fight their way through to a target.

Following the start of the Allied Combined Bomber Offensive in 1943, the USAAF experiences with the Eighth Air Force in the skies over Europe, carrying out daylight raids, would severely dent this theory. By October 1943, after missions deep into Germany to Schweinfurt and Regensburg, some of these missions were seeing the loss of nearly a quarter of all attacking B-17 bombers. Despite the vast arsenal of aircraft being made in American factories, the losses were unsustainable and B-17 missions were postponed at the end of 1943 until a long-range fighter was available to support the bombers.

Fortunately for the USAAF, the P-51 Mustang was beginning to arrive in increasing numbers in the European theatre of operations from the end of 1943. With a large internal fuel tank and external mounted fuel tanks made from compressed paper, the range of the Mustang was sufficient enough to escort the bombers to Berlin and back.

When the Combined Bomber Offensive resumed in 1944, the new leadership of Major General James Doolittle unshackled the P-51D Mustang from its bomber escort role. This change in tactics allowed the growing numbers of Mustang groups to fly in advance of the main bomber streams. Mustangs were tasked with finding and attacking the Luftwaffe on the ground or in the air, with the bombers as bait, to gain Allied air supremacy in Europe in advance of the Allied invasion.

P-51 Mustangs of the 361st Fighter Group fly in formation above the clouds. The introduction of the P-51D Mustang to the European theatre in 1943/44 would protect the Allied bombers and go some considerable way to winning the air war in Europe.

The Luftwaffe would struggle with the new P-51 Mustang. The Focke-Wulf Fw 190 was unable to take on the Mustang when laden with weapons designed to take on the bombers at high altitude. Whilst the Messerschmitt Bf 109 could match the Mustang at the altitude of the bombers, additional weapons again saw it fail to match the nimbler thoroughbred at altitude, which was the Mustang. The Luftwaffe tried a new tactic of sending large groups of aircraft up to meet the Mustang and American bombers. The Bf 109 took on the Mustangs and the Fw 190A attacked the bombers. Whilst there was some successes for the Luftwaffe, the German groups took time to assemble, a similar problem faced by the British 'big wing' earlier in 1940. But the superior numbers of Mustangs and the superior quality, as German pilots were lost, of the American pilots, meant the Allies were coming out on top by the spring of 1944.

By spring 1944, attacks on Luftwaffe airfields by the USAAF began to subside as targets were identified for the upcoming invasion of Europe, and for the fact that the number of German fighters was dwindling. Targets included rail infrastructure for the Mustangs in the run-up to D-Day in 1944. A new threat to the dominance of the Mustang began to emerge, however, as the Luftwaffe began to operate its new jet fighter, the Messerschmitt Me 262, in September 1944. Although the Me 262 was faster than the Mustang, the Allies using Mustangs and other types of piston-powered aircraft quickly learnt that German pilots were at their most vulnerable when taking off or landing in the Me 262. This proved to be a nullifying tactic when facing the jet-powered Me 262. As the Germans threw more rocket-powered weapons at the Allies, including the V-1 Flying Bomb, the Mustang could catch the V-1 missiles and, alongside Spitfires and Tempests, could lessen the threat from these 'V' weapons. By the end of the war in 1945, the Mustang had claimed about half of all aircraft shot down by the USAAF. But irrespective of the numbers, the Mustang was the aircraft that most helped the Allies secure air supremacy in Europe, as they were supporting the vast bomber streams decimating the German Reich, whilst attacking the Luftwaffe wherever German aircraft could be found.

In the Pacific and Southeast Asia, the Mustang arrived relatively late to play as significant a role as in Europe. But early versions such as the P-51C would perform adequately in missions over Burma, whilst by spring 1945, flying from bases located on the captured Japanese islands of Iwo Jima and Okinawa, the Mustangs fought and supported the

A pilot of the 339th Fighter Group wearing the runway control officer's uniform of striped 'pyjama' jacket and white baseball cap, on the runway. Mustangs would take off from the grass runway in pairs. Once assembled they would head for the rendezvous with the bombers they were assigned to escort. To save time and fuel, the 339th used an experienced fighter pilot who would stand beside the runway signalling to each new pair of aircraft that it was safe to take off. The colourful striped jacket and white baseball cap helped pilots to see him.

An aviator with an inflatable decoy P-51 Mustang.

A P-51 Mustang returning from an escort mission over Germany in 1945. In the Pacific, flying from captured islands, the P-51 would also escort B-29 bombers on missions over Japan.

UNITED STATES

USAAF B-29 bombers attacking the main Japanese home islands. Like the role it played in Europe, the Mustang was also used to attack Japanese air forces and their bases. As the war was to continue on into the summer of 1945, it succeeded in diminishing the Japanese fighter threat. As the Japanese surrendered in 1945, following the use of atomic bombs on the cities of Hiroshima and Nagasaki, the Mustang's wartime operations would come to an end, even though it would serve in many air forces, including during the early part of the Korean War in 1950.

The North American P-51 Mustang was one of the pre-eminent aircraft of World War II. Designed and manufactured by an American company in vast quantities, with the adaption of the Rolls-Royce/Packard Merlin engines based on combat experiences of the British in the skies of Europe, it would belatedly deliver an aircraft that can simply be described as 'war winning'. For the pilots who flew it, the later P-51D was the epitome of piston-powered flight. With its unique streamlined airframe, 'bubble' canopy providing 'roomy' space for the pilot flying long missions to Berlin and the fuel capacity to get the pilot back to base, it was a superlative and powerful machine. If the 'American Spitfire' did not have the same handling as an actual Spitfire, this Anglo-American success story would at least be able to get you back to base in Britain after duelling with the Luftwaffe over Berlin. Few aircraft during the war could claim such an accolade.

Personnel of the 55th Fighter Group look at aircraft contrails from the wings of a P-51 Mustang, 11 December 1944.

#32
Northrop P-61 Black Widow

The P-61 Black Widow, named after a North American poisonous spider, was the first aircraft of the war designed specifically as a night fighter, supported by the airborne radar mounted in its nose. It went on to see combat in all theatres of the war from 1944.

Although it flew during the war, a lack of power from its engines made the aircraft a 'good' night fighter but one that never really eclipsed the successes of other Allied aircraft, like the de Havilland Mosquito, with some competitions set up between the two aircraft by the Allies to see which was the more effective twin-engine aircraft. The P-61 was produced in limited numbers compared to other fighter aircraft, with just over 700 being built, but its distinctive design and elongated nose marks it out as one of the most unique aircraft developed in the war.

Origins

The P-61 had its origins in the Luftwaffe's nightly Blitz on London in 1940, when US Army Air Corps officers witnessed first-hand the threat of night bombing on cities.

Developments by the British of Airborne Interceptor (AI) radar, based around a cavity magnetron, demonstrated the potential of mounting radar in aircraft directly. This enhanced a night fighter's attempts to shoot down enemy bombers in the night skies.

As a result of an urgent need to combat the threat of night bombing, the British issued a specification for a radar-equipped night fighter that could stay in the air over a city at night for a long period of time. The British

UNITED STATES

Ground crew members of the 425th Night Fighter Squadron pack ammunition near a P-61 Black Widow nicknamed 'Dangerous Dan'.

Purchasing Commission, with offices based in the United States, put forward the specification for consideration by all leading aircraft manufacturers. Northrop began to design a twin-engine fighter, which would have AI radar and a crew of two, but before a prototype could be built for the British, the US Army Air Corps would effectively take over the project. It was supported by the British Technical and Scientific Mission to the United States in 1940 (more commonly known as the 'Tizard Mission' after one of the leading British scientists on it). The mission brought with it the cavity magnetron, a vacuum tube used in early radar, which meant AI-manufactured radar could now be built in the US.

OPPOSITE: A P-61 Black Widow (serial number 41-2670) night fighter in flight. Although specifically designed as a night fighter, it was also used in ground attack roles due to its extensive cannon armament.

Operations

After the first prototype flew in May 1942, the P-61 finally arrived in the war in both the Pacific and Europe in the spring of 1944.

It had significant armament of four 20-mm cannons placed on its underside and four machine guns on the top of its fuselage, plus the SCR-270 AI radar mounted in its elongated nose. The P-61 supported the US forces in the D-Day landings in June 1944 with patrols. It was also used in the support of American troops as a ground attack aircraft during the Battle of the Bulge, and it was used in flying missions until the end of the war in Europe. In the Pacific, the P-61 often struggled to find targets but still proved effective as a night intruder against Japanese naval ships and over land targets.

The P-61 proved to be an effective night fighter in the war, and performed adequately against those German and Japanese aircraft it came up against. But a lack of top speed from its Wasp R-2800 engines, only rectified by a later 'C' version, meant it never had enough power to be a truly great aircraft of the war, though it would be the largest pursuit 'P' fighter used by the Americans during World War II.

#33
Republic P-47 Thunderbolt

The Republic P-47 Thunderbolt was an American fighter, the largest and heaviest fighter of the war, which was designed and built around its powerful engine.

It would significantly improve the protection given to USAAF bombers participating in daylight raids in Europe when it arrived from 1943. It would excel in a role as a fighter bomber, using its larger than standard bomb load for a fighter, and later rockets, along with its fearsome array of eight machine guns. The 'Jug', as it was affectionately nicknamed, was loved by most of the pilots who flew it, due to its power, speed when diving, performance at high altitude and ability to withstand enemy fire. It would become one of the most powerful and feared Allied aircraft in all theatres of war during World War II.

Origins

The origins of the Republic P-47 Thunderbolt can be traced to the Seversky P-35 and the P-43 Lancer.

It evolved from these aircraft when the chief designer at Republic Aviation Corporation in the US, Alexander Kartveli, a Georgian aeronautical engineer who had fled to America via France to escape from the Bolsheviks, developed two new prototypes. These were the AP-4, using a large Pratt & Whitney radial engine, and the AP-10, using a more traditional liquid-cooled engine. Following assessment of air combat in Europe in 1940, the US Army Air Corps changed its specification from a 'lightweight' fighter to a design that could perform at higher altitudes. Kartveli realised the liquid-cooled Allison engine would

OPPOSITE: A ground crew servicing the Republic P-47 Thunderbolt, showing the 'paddle blade' propeller that improved the Thunderbolt's performance. The size and power of the P-47 Thunderbolt would ensure its legacy as the largest single-seat fighter and one of the most successful American fighters of the war.

UNITED STATES

not suffice and he redesigned his prototype to use the most powerful engine available, a Pratt & Whitney Double Wasp radial engine, powerful enough to produce 2,000 horsepower, and the XP-47B prototype was born.

The XP-47B was an all-metal construction with a slightly swept back elliptical wing that was straight on the front wing edge. It first flew in May 1941. It was a large and roomy aircraft with an air-conditioned cockpit and a relatively 'comfy' chair for the pilot. Initial tests were promising and, despite some initial problems that were ironed out in testing, the monstrously large XP-47B was ordered by the new USAAF, giving it the designation P-47, with the first variants being delivered in December 1941. With eight .50 calibre Browning machine guns and the early production types being fitted with the Pratt & Whitney R-2800 radial engine, the fast development of the P-47 would see it reach combat theatres as early as 1943.

Variants

The first variants of the P-47 Thunderbolt to enter service were the P-47B and C models, fitted with the Curtiss four-blade propeller.

The Thunderbolt became the first American fighter to receive a four-blade propeller. Due to the large engine, nose and 12½ ft propeller, it was fitted with telescopic landing gear to ensure the underside of the aircraft could clear the ground on take-off and landing. It weighed approximately 13,200 lb without bombs fitted, making it considerably larger when compared to a Mk V Spitfire. The early versions of the P-47 were built in their hundreds before the main production variant emerged: the P-47D Thunderbolt.

The P-47D was widely produced, with around 13,000 being built. It served with the USAAF, and the RAF also received 'D' type aircraft being designated by the RAF as Thunderbolt Mk I and II. About half of the P-47D aircraft had a framed 'razorback-style' sliding cockpit canopy, which was also found on the earlier variants; although it offered some protection to the pilot, it did hinder visibility. The later P-47D variant was changed to a new 'bubble' canopy, which sat on top of the large fuselage and gave much greater visibility for the pilot.

The air-cooled engine, bringing in air through 'gills' at the rear of the engine cover or cowling, had advantages to the liquid-cooled engines and this became apparent when the P-47 entered service. Unlike the liquid-cooled Merlin engine found in Spitfires that could be seriously damaged if the coolant or radiator was hit, the air-cooled engines of the P-47 could suffer more enemy fire as the engine could still be cooled. This gave the P-47 a reputation of being able to withstand enemy attacks, tolerate more damage and still make it back to base.

The armament of the P-47 types was also significant. Along with its eight Browning machine guns, for its fighter-bomber role the P-47 could carry 2,500 lb of bombs, and later rocket projectiles. Also, the addition of fuel through mounted drop tanks, like the P-51 Mustang, increased the operational range of the Thunderbolt from short to medium range, so that it could escort bombers further into Germany. As Mike Titre, a Thunderbolt pilot with the 405th Fighter Group recalled: 'No other air force had an airplane equivalent to the P-47 with eight .50 calibres, which is the best firepower that any fighter had. And the bomb carrying capability. We never fired anything but two guns in training. So, the first time I fired the guns on a combat mission, there was a kick to it. We were told that straight level, if all eight guns are fired, it would slow the airplane [by] 35 miles an hour.'

Later variants of the P-47 included the P-47M, which had engine modifications including a supercharger and improved propeller. The aim was to increase speed to take on the new threats from V-1 Flying Bombs and Luftwaffe jet fighters towards the end of the war in Europe. However, despite some fighter groups changing to P-51 Mustangs, pilots remained loyal to the performance and firepower of the 'Jug', some say so-named after the resemblance of its large round nose and fuselage to a milk jug, others that because of its size it was a 'juggernaut'. Several of these formidable aircraft are restored and remain flying today.

A stockpile of drop fuel tanks. The light-grey pile in the foreground were made of sheet steel. The silver-finished tanks in the background were made from a paper and plastic composition. The fitting of drop tanks to the underside of a P-47 Thunderbolt's fuselage provided sufficient fuel for increasing fighter support on longer-range bomber escort duties.

Operations

Europe

The first production of P-47s rolled off the factory floor were sent to Europe by the end of 1942 to serve with the 56th Fighter Group of the Eighth Air Force of the USAAF based in England.

By spring 1943, the P-47 Thunderbolt would encounter the Luftwaffe in the skies for the first time while conducting fighter 'sweeps' across the Channel and escorting the B-17 and B-24 bombers on their daylight bombing raids. But initial skirmishes were not promising. The P-47 lacked range to accompany the bombers all the way on missions. In combat with Luftwaffe aircraft its slow rate of climb, and a lack of manoeuvrability when compared to the lighter and more agile German aircraft, meant experienced German pilots could escape the powerful P-47 and its armament by climbing quickly out of its way.

However, a combination of technical modification and evolving tactics based on combat experience would soon improve the performance of the Thunderbolt. Due to the size of the aircraft (prompting RAF pilots to joke that the best way to escape an enemy fighter in the Thunderbolt

Captain Frederick J. Christensen of the 56th Fighter Group with his P-47 Thunderbolt. He was an ace in the 'Zemke Wolf Pack', the top-scoring US fighter group in England.

was to simply hide somewhere in the large aircraft fuselage itself, as it could be so easily outmanoeuvred) the addition of a new Curtiss 'paddle blade' in early 1944 helped the P-47 increase its rate of climb at lower altitudes. An additional modification included the injection of water into the engine to increase speed. As Gerald Johnson, a pilot with the 56th Fighter Group explained: 'So they eventually, but this was not until after we'd been in combat for about six months, they'd add what was called "paddle blade propeller", plus water injection to the engine. And water injection to the engine, when you shot the water to the engine that increased your horsepower by about a third.'

Tactical innovation would also help the P-47 Thunderbolt adapt to the air war in Europe. One such early proponent of the P-47 would be Major Hubert Zemke, who was not initially impressed with the performance of the aircraft. But he concentrated the 56th Fighter Group on the positives of the Thunderbolt, rather than the more negative issues of slow rate of acceleration and climb, and focused his pilots on the strengths, developing the 'dive and fire' tactic before using the aircraft's good roll rate to recover its position. His tactics would prove to be a turning point in Europe for the P-47, with several pilots of the 56th Fighter Group becoming aces in Thunderbolts.

The large, powerful, heavily armed and rugged P-47, with the improved performance and tactics, could now match anything the Luftwaffe could fly. With the extra fuel drop tanks it would now escort bombers, alongside the newly arriving P-51 Mustang, deep into Germany. The arrival of the new 'bubbletop' canopy versions in Europe in early 1944 saw the fighter provide a significant contribution to the Allies during the invasion of Europe on D-Day in June 1944. It was also used, alongside the British Hawker Typhoon, as flying 'artillery' to support troops on the ground, using bombs, rockets and machine guns to nullify threats from the Germans on the ground during the Battle for Normandy. The use of forward air controllers, able to call on patrolling Typhoons and Thunderbolts, proved to be a significant psychological boost to Allied troops, as well as a significant disruption to the German army trying to respond to the Allied advance in Normandy. By the end of the war the Thunderbolt had been credited with destroying 9,000 locomotive trains, 86,000 train wagons and 6,000 armoured vehicles. The contribution of the P-47 Thunderbolt to the Allied victory in the air in Europe by 1945 was ensured.

Pacific and Other Theatres

By mid-1943 the P-47 Thunderbolt would also be delivered to the Pacific theatre, serving in all operational USAAF theatres by 1944.

The improvements in fuel capacity would help the P-47 over the Pacific, where distances could be greater than in Europe. It proved to be a successful partner to the Spitfire in Burma against the Japanese, when it began to replace Hurricanes in the RAF Southeast Asia Command. The ground attack capability of the Thunderbolt was used in one of the final battles of the war. This was when the Japanese attempted to break out through Allied forces' lines at Sittang, before Thunderbolts and Spitfires carrying their bombs could inflict heavy damage on the Japanese attack.

The P-47 Thunderbolt was a supremely large and well-armed Allied fighter aircraft, which from 1943 played a significant role in the Allies' eventual victory against Germany and Japan. Despite its flaws, the pilots who flew it honed it into a supreme weapon that was to guarantee it would become one of the iconic aircraft of the war.

With guns poised for action, Republic P-47 Thunderbolts of the US 12th Air Force fly over the snow-covered Italian Alps as escort for North American B-25 Mitchells headed for German targets in northern Italy. The innovative tactics in Europe, focusing on the P-47's strengths of high-speed dives and firepower, would see the aircraft begin improving its performance against the Luftwaffe.

#34
Short Stirling

The Short Stirling was a British four-engine heavy bomber, the first to enter service with RAF Bomber Command, before the Avro Lancaster and Handley Page Halifax bombers.

Although it took part in many early Bomber Command raids, limitations with its design meant that its relatively low maximum altitude when fully laden made it vulnerable to air defences. As a result they were withdrawn from British bombing raids but went on to take up other roles, including as glider tugs during D-Day and further transport roles towards the end of the war.

Sixteen 250-lb bombs are checked by ground crew before being loaded into a Short Stirling bomber. The large undercarriage and landing gear gave it a pronounced nose and pointing-up profile when on the ground, whilst a central bomb bay strut would limit the size of bombs it could carry.

Origins

The Short Stirling was designed by Short Brothers, an aircraft manufacturer based in Belfast and commonly referred to as 'Short' or 'Shorts'.

It was proposed in response to Air Ministry Specification B.12/36 for a long-range bomber that could transport troops to the corners of the British Empire and then support them with bombing operations. The desire was for the aircraft to fit pre-war hangar sizes and be able to be broken up into sections to be transported by train, with the added benefit that this would also help to simplify production. Shorts were sent the specification due to, at the time, developing and manufacturing four-engine flying-boat aircraft. The Stirling prototype S.29 was developed based on the Short Sunderland aircraft, with the lower boat half removed.

A view of the instrument panel and controls in the cockpit of a Short Stirling Mk I, which had two pilots.

In 1936, this prototype aircraft was selected as a 'back up' but modifications were requested by the Air Ministry, including reducing the wing length to 100 ft to fit into existing pre-war designed aircraft hangars, even though hangar widths were slightly larger at that time. The length of the wing would have a profound impact on the aircraft's performance when it entered service with the RAF during the war.

The modified S.29 flew for the first time in 1939 and received its service name 'Stirling'. It was produced in Shorts factories in Belfast and Rochester as well as in 'shadow factories', motor factories designated in the 1930s by the British government to aid with aircraft manufacture in the English Midlands. The production of the aircraft was disrupted by Luftwaffe attacks early in the war, especially at the facility in Rochester in Kent during the Battle of Britain. The bomber was eventually delivered to RAF units in 1940 (and entered operational service in 1941), despite the Air Ministry rejecting further modifications from Shorts, that would have improved the aircraft's performance.

The Stirling was powered by four Bristol Hercules engines and carried a crew of seven, including two pilots seated in a fully glazed cockpit. It had a long fuselage and a large but relatively shallow bomb bay, although unlike its contemporaries, the Halifax and Lancaster, the bomb bay had a central spar running the bay's length, limiting the size and width of the bombs it could carry. On entering service it could carry the largest bomb load in Bomber Command, until other heavy bombers had entered service. Crews generally found the Stirling to be easy and manoeuvrable to handle once in the air, and it could out-turn night fighters due to the rigid thickness of its wing. But its limited wingspan, for the size of the plane, meant its maximum altitude of 12,000 ft when fully loaded was disappointing and it became extremely vulnerable to air defences at this low altitude.

Operations

The Stirling entered service with the RAF in 1941 and was the initial spearhead of the bomber campaign by the RAF, forming part of the 1,000 bomber raid on the German city of Cologne in May 1942.

The Stirling also helped equip the Pathfinder squadrons tasked with marking bombing targets for the following RAF bombers. But flying at low altitude when laden with bombs meant the Luftwaffe pilots began to concentrate on the lower flying Stirlings, and the number of aircraft being shot down began to grow. As Bomber Command began to use larger bombs and specially designed bombs on missions, the restrictions of the design of the Stirling bomb bay also meant it began to be superseded by the Avro Lancaster and it was relegated to lesser roles.

By the end of December 1943, the Short Stirling was removed from service as a front-line bomber. But a requirement for 'tug' aircraft to tow gliders for the upcoming invasion of Europe, set for 1944, saw the Stirling selected for the task. Mk III Stirlings were converted to the Mk IV without nose or rear turrets to assist with this operation, whilst a smaller number were tasked with dropping small strips of aluminium called

A bomb train of 16 250-lb bombs arriving to be loaded into Short Stirling bomber N6101. The Stirling was at the forefront of the bomber force early in the war.

'Window' to disrupt German radar and provide misleading readings of a decoy Allied fleet approaching France. The Stirling was also used to drop supplies to resistance groups in Europe by the SOE.

Overall, the aircraft proved adequate to the tasks it was given, but its design based on pre-war requirements for a shorter wing would hinder its success as a bomber in the war and the required altitude it would need. This led to it being quickly eclipsed by the more famous Lancaster and Halifax bombers.

The crew of a Short Stirling B Mark III report their experiences to an intelligence officer after returning from the major raid on Berlin of 22/23 November 1943.

A flight of Short Stirling aircraft.

#35
Short Sunderland

A Short Sunderland Mk I about to take off from Oban Bay in Scotland. The sheer size of the aircraft, taller than a London double decker bus, was an impressive sight. A large float under each wing helped to deliver buoyancy and stability on water.

GREAT BRITAIN

The Short Sunderland was a British flying boat that was used extensively during World War II in a patrol and anti-submarine role.

It had a significant impact on the Battle of the Atlantic, countering the threat of German U-boat submarines on Allied shipping convoys delivering vital resources, troops and military equipment to Britain. It was one of the most powerful flying boats used by the Allies in the war. Capable of conducting long-range missions for hours, with its extensive number of gun positions and armament sticking out from the aircraft, it quickly developed the nickname the 'Flying Porcupine', as coined by German fighter crews who encountered the aircraft in the skies.

Origins

Short developed the Sunderland in response to Air Ministry Specification R.2/33, which called for a long-range flying boat for maritime patrol and reconnaissance duties.

Designed in parallel with the Short Empire flying boat for civilian use, the Sunderland first took to the skies in October 1937. Powered by four Bristol Pegasus X radial engines, it had an optimum cruising speed of around 150 mph, which gave it the ability to fly for up to 18 hours and cover over 1,700 miles. The Sunderland Mk I entered service in June 1938, both in Britain and in Singapore, and by the start of the war in 1939 some 90 Mk Is were in service.

The Sunderland was a large aircraft with two decks and a crew of ten or more, depending on the type of mission flown. The crews found it spacious when compared to other large aircraft of the time. Its roomy interior allowed the crew to stand up in places. Its lower deck offered a wardroom for up to six bunks (beds), a galley with a stove for the preparation of food, a flushing porcelain toilet and a small workshop for any in-flight repairs. The Sunderland also had a bomb storage room with winches that could attach bombs to bomb racks, which were then manoeuvred out onto the underside of the wings for release. The cockpit for two pilots was found on the upper deck, where the navigator was also positioned.

A Short S23 C Class Empire flying boat, on which the Short Sunderland design was based.

A view of a Sunderland Mk III. The aircraft's top surfaces are faded and weathered from months of duty over the Atlantic.

A low-level photograph taken from a Short Sunderland Mk III while attacking a German submarine, U-625, in the Atlantic Ocean.

The nautical theme continued with many space-saving design features, more commonly found on yachts, for neatly storing equipment. The crew were trained in naval navigation for safely operating on water and the aircraft had features designed to keep it watertight, including internal doors to compartments. It was also fitted with 'beaching' gear, wheels that allowed it to be pulled out of the water.

Armaments included a bomb bay which could carry just under 5,000 lb of bombs or mines, and it was found that depth charges were a more successful anti-submarine weapon for the Sunderland to carry. Defensively, there were up to 16 machine guns as the various types of the aircraft developed. These were found at the rear turret, front nose and along the side of the fuselage just behind the wings and, later, fixed machine guns that could be operated by the pilot either side of the aircraft bow. The introduction of on-board radar, initially using Air to Surface Vessel (ASV) Mk II radar, allowed the Sunderland to attack surfacing U-boats. This prompted a technological 'cat and mouse' game, as U-boats developed measures to counter this threat.

Operations

At the outbreak of the war, the Sunderland Mk I was to see action early on when, in September 1939, a Sunderland rescued the entire crew of a torpedoed merchant ship.

Early tussles with German fighters during the Norway campaign in 1940 saw the Sunderland able to defend itself successfully due to the aircraft's impressive armament. It also operated in the Mediterranean on reconnaissance missions before the British attack on the Italian fleet at Taranto. Production switched to a Mk II version that was fitted with radar. But increasing equipment also led to increased weight, with an upgrade to the Pegasus engines and a more streamlined 'hull', which then went on to form the Mk III from December 1941. This became the largest number of the types in service during the war.

The Sunderland's ongoing battle with U-boats during the Battle of the Atlantic saw the aircraft modified further, based on previous combat action. Radar had allowed the Sunderland aircraft to successfully attack U-boats on the surface, but the Germans responded by installing a radar detection warning system, before a switch to newer Air

The rear fuselage interior of a Short Sunderland Mk I with a tail gunner leaving his turret. Crew were able to walk upright inside and found the interior to be very spacious compared to other bombers in the war.

to Surface vessel Mk III radar swung the radar battle back in favour of the Allies. Further German changes saw the introduction of flak guns on U-boats for greater protection from Sunderland air attacks. The Royal Australian Air Force was one of the most innovative users of the Sunderland; its crews fitted four machine guns into the nose, allowing pilots to fire as they dived down onto U-boats, and this became a common modification.

In 1940, with the Battle of the Atlantic developing, it became apparent that bombs were proving ineffective for sinking German U-boats, so the principal explosive weapon shifted to the depth charge. These charges would be dropped on or near the submarine and explode just below the surface and at a certain predefined depth. But early depth charges were unreliable and often broke up when they landed on the sea's surface. This was greatly improved as a weapon with the introduction of a new type of explosive, Torpex, which was more powerful than previous TNT explosives used. These new depth charges would be used by Short Sunderlands in sets of six, when they were released at a low height of around 50 ft.

Short Sunderlands continued to patrol in the Atlantic throughout the rest of the war. As radar continued to improve they took part in night attacks on U-boats and were at the forefront in the rescuing of aircrew shot down over the Atlantic. A later version of the Sunderland was the Mk V, which entered service towards the end of the war. This version was again modified after a request by crews to increase the engine power, with Pratt & Whitney engines being used. These were already being fitted to other RAF aircraft, so this also helped with ongoing maintenance and parts.

Despite the long hours on patrols, crew were to remember the Short Sunderland as an aircraft with the addition of some home comforts. It provided a crucial maritime reconnaissance and rescue role throughout the war. It was used for convoy protection patrols and, with modifications to its weapons, proved formidable in anti-submarine warfare, whilst its 'prickly' defensive array of guns and sheer size meant that it was a difficult aircraft for enemy fighters to shoot down. British Prime Minister Winston Churchill wrote later after the war that his only real fear had been the U-boat 'peril' and the Sunderland went some way in combatting this threat. It played a significant role in helping the Allies win the vital Battle of the Atlantic and protect the precious material that would be needed to win the war.

An original colour photograph of a Spitfire Mk VB based at North Weald, Essex.

#36

Supermarine Spitfire

The Supermarine Spitfire was a British single-seater fighter aircraft, operated by the RAF and other Allies, and to begin with it was fitted with the Rolls-Royce Merlin engine.

It is without doubt the most famous aircraft of World War II and was the only aircraft to remain in continuous production before, during and after the war. Over 20,000 Spitfires were built and a further 2,000 naval versions called 'Seafire'.

Today, it continues to grace the skies with restored versions flying at air shows, where it provides an awe-inspiring spectacle. But despite going through numerous developments and versions, and serving throughout all combat areas of the war, it was, at times, not always the most dominant fighter in the war. Some versions suffered from performance issues or a lack of firepower, and these are often forgotten when looking back and objectively reviewing the wartime career of the aircraft. This is not unsurprising, however, when even as early as 1939, on the eve of war, a journalist was to describe the Supermarine Spitfire as a 'poem of speed and precision'.

Origins

GREAT BRITAIN

The Supermarine Spitfire had its origins in the racing sea aircraft of the 1920s that competed for the Schneider Trophy.

The trophy had been announced in 1912, by a French financier, to help with aircraft development, but it would later become purely about an aircraft's speed during races. The race ran 12 times from 1913, when it was 'won' by Great Britain and retained indefinitely after an uncontested race in 1931. Supermarine Aviation Works, which had become a subsidiary of Vickers-Armstrong, developed seaplanes in the pre-war years to compete in the races under the guidance of their chief designer, Reginald Joseph Mitchell.

Mitchell began working at Supermarine in 1916, during World War I. It was recognised that, as a mathematician, he was able to look at designs creatively, going on to become the chief designer for Supermarine in 1919 at the age of just 19. Mitchell was responsible for developing racing seaplanes that took part in the trophy races until 1931. The sleek designs of these aircraft, culminating in the SB.6 seaplane, were the embodiment of fast and powerful aircraft of the time, and his seaplanes helped place Mitchell at the forefront of aviation design.

In 1931, the British Air Ministry issued specification F.7/30 calling for a modern all-metal day and night fighter that would be capable of flying at speeds over 250 mph. Various aviation companies submitted several designs to the specification, including Mitchell at Supermarine who put forward his Type 224 aircraft. This design was that of an inverted 'gull wing' monoplane, which used the Rolls-Royce Goshawk engine. However, when it first flew in 1934 it performed poorly. The aircraft did not fly over the required 245 mph top speed, so it was not selected by the Air Ministry. Mitchell proposed significant changes that would improve the performance, including a new wing, tailplane and engine. But by this time, the Air Ministry required any aircraft to be fitted with eight machine guns, as research had shown this number was needed to shoot down modern fighters, so the Type 224 aircraft would be scrapped in favour of a new Mitchell design: the Type 300.

A Supermarine S.5 seaplane at Calshot, near Southampton, for the 1929 Schneider Trophy competition. The seaplanes developed by R. J. Mitchell for Supermarine were to place him at the forefront of aviation design throughout the 1920s and 1930s.

The Type 300 was a vastly improved design compared to its predecessor. Features included a retractable undercarriage, enclosed cockpit with oxygen for the pilots and, more importantly, it would use the improved and more powerful Rolls-Royce V-12 engine, later known as the 'Merlin' engine, named by Rolls Royce after a bird of prey. The Merlin was a 12-cylinder piston engine, with two groups of six cylinders arranged in a 'V' formation around a central crankshaft that powered the propeller blades. The first production V-12 engines emerged from the factory in 1936 and went on to become one of the best engines of the entire war. The design of the Spitfire, along with its contemporary the Hawker Hurricane, had been based on the use of this new engine, which gave the Spitfire an initial starting 1,000 horsepower, and the first Mk I Spitfires a considerable top speed of 355 mph.

But the engine alone was not the sole reason for the success of the Spitfire. Mitchell and his design team, in the quest for speed, now gave the Type 300 prototype its most prominent and defining feature that still resonates with generations of aircraft enthusiasts: an elliptical shaped wing. Mitchell had previously used this shape wing in an earlier seaplane, the Supermarine S.4 in the 1920s, and remained a key advocate for the wing type. Its benefits were that it gave superior lift and reduced drag, which helped to achieve great speed, and it was thin and strong enough to not twist or break at high speeds when used in a semi-elliptical design, where the wing tips curved at the ends. But it also had disadvantages as the wing still had to mount guns and have a retractable undercarriage, a challenge in such a thin aerodynamic wing.

Mitchell and his team were aware of the German development of this wing shape in the 1930s, primarily by Heinkel. But working with aerodynamicist Beverley Shenstone, Mitchell was keen for the Spitfire to use a semi-elliptical shaped wing that would provide a thin, strong and aerodynamically 'perfect' shape, which would give the Spitfire great speed. A thicker span closer to the fuselage would give the best performance, whilst still allowing for the undercarriage and guns to be fitted. As Shenstone was later to note, it also 'looked nice'.

But the semi-elliptical wing, despite its sleek lines, came with some compromises. The undercarriage retracted from outside back into the fuselage, which, unlike the Hurricane where this happened in the opposite direction, gave it a narrow landing track for the wheels, making it hard for pilots to master during landing and take-off in the Spitfire. The four Browning .303 machine guns mounted in each wing also had to be put on to their side due to the thickness of the wing. This was fine for firing at lower altitudes but could cause them to jam when operating in higher altitudes due to the cold, or in high-G manoeuvres during dogfights. As a result, the gun holes were covered with a piece of 'doped' fabric to protect them from cold or from dirt entering the barrels before they were first fired. Another solution saw warm air pumped from the engines through the gun settings.

Ground crew working on the Merlin engine of a Supermarine Spitfire in southern Italy, January 1944.

A Spitfire Mk VB. This clearly shows the Spitfire's famous semi-elliptical wing shape that was incorporated into the original Spitfire design, and which gave it both its iconic shape, and its excellent flying and handling performance.

Prototype to Production

By March 1936, following funding from the Air Ministry, the first prototype, K5054, took off from Eastleigh aerodrome, now Southampton Airport, for its first flight.

Following further test flights by Supermarine test pilots, including Jeffrey Quill, a new propeller was fitted. This increased the top speed to 350 mph and, despite some initial handling sensitivities, the test pilots were impressed with the prototype Spitfire, seeing it as a truly exceptional aircraft to fly.

Sadly, prototype K5054 would be the only Spitfire chief designer Mitchell would see fly. In 1933 he was diagnosed with cancer and although it was treated, it returned in 1936. This time treatment was not effective; he died in June 1937, aged just 42. In his obituary he was described as 'one of the leading designers in the world' who had the 'capacity to grasp essentials'. Following his death, one of his team at Supermarine, Joseph Smith, would become chief designer in 1939 and take the Spitfire from production to the last versions of the Spitfire at the very end of the war.

An order for 310 Spitfires was initially placed in 1936, but due in part to the relatively small scale of Supermarine at its plant in Woolston, near Southampton, combined with problems encountered manufacturing the all-metal alloy skin of the Spitfire, the first production did not roll off the factory floor until 1938. This in part prompted the British government, with war looming, to establish a 'shadow factory' plan for using motor car factories to manufacture aircraft. To help speed the production of the Spitfire, a new factory was started at Castle Bromwich, Birmingham, to be managed by Morris Motors. But despite Spitfires coming out of the factory here by the summer of 1940, teething problems meant it was eventually taken over by Vickers-Armstrong. By the end of the war, however, over 12,000 Spitfires had been built at Castle Bromwich Aircraft Factory, making it the largest Spitfire factory of the war.

By the end of the war in 1945, over 22,000 types of Spitfires and Seafires had been built. But the aircraft was complex and could be slow to produce, with issues such as the skill and precision engineering required to develop all-metal skin and, initially, the labour force needing retraining to accomplish this task. Additionally, the iconic semi-elliptical wing took three times the hours to build than the wing of the mass-produced German fighter, the Messerschmitt Bf 109. During the Battle of Britain, the Luftwaffe also targeted production of the Spitfire. The destruction of Supermarine factories in the Southampton area, following bombing in September 1940, saw production being dispersed to several smaller facilities across the south of England, before the Castle Bromwich Aircraft Factory began to increase its Spitfire production in 1940.

Under the guidance of Joseph Smith, the Spitfire would evolve from the pre-war Mk I to its final incarnation as the Mk 24. In that time the power of the engine and length of the fuselage massively increased, armaments were altered and even the famous wing design was to evolve. But the airframe designed by Mitchell and his team was able to support this evolution, allowing the Spitfire to respond to new threats that emerged throughout the war. As Alex Henshaw, test pilot at Castle Bromwich, noted, the Mk I was a highly manoeuvrable and fine flying aircraft, and although later versions were equally impressive, the development of more powerful engines were to lessen the handling of the Spitfire compared to the original Mk I. This would be the variant used so successfully during the Battle of Britain, where British victory would ensure the Spitfire's legendary status.

TOP: Supermarine Spitfire prototype K5054. Sadly, it was the only Spitfire its chief designer, R.J. Mitchell, would see fly before his death.

BOTTOM: Prime Minister Winston Churchill observes a female riveter working on a Supermarine Spitfire at the Castle Bromwich factory in Birmingham on 28 September 1941.

GREAT BRITAIN

Spitfire Types and Variants

The Spitfire evolved from early pre-war production Mk I aircraft to later versions up to the Mk 24, and there were other sub-variants of some.

But not every version ended up being put fully into production; for instance, the early Mk I and IIs effectively jumped to Mk V for the next large production version. Joseph Smith, who took over from R. J. Mitchell, was to be the driving force for the ongoing wartime evolution and development of the different versions of the Spitfire at Supermarine.

Spitfire Mk I/II

The Mk I was the first version of the Spitfire based on the prototype K5054.

The first Mk I Spitfires came into operational service in August 1938, and were based at RAF Duxford, now Imperial War Museum Duxford. This can claim with some justification to be the spiritual 'operational home' of the Spitfire and now has the largest collection of Spitfires in the world, including IWM collection aircraft and privately owned Spitfires, where these numerous examples can still be seen flying today. RAF 19 Squadron, which received the Spitfire Mk Is at Duxford in 1938, were impressed with the new aircraft in comparison to the Gloucester Gauntlet biplanes they were flying before the Spitfire. RAF pilot John Banham said, 'We each of us flew for about half an hour in the thing. Oh, it was a tremendous thrill.'

But the early Mk Is were not perfect: the machine guns were prone to freezing at high altitude or during high-G force manoeuvres, the engine could overheat due to a lack of coolant and it had a short flying range. The long, powerful nose section housing the Rolls-Royce Merlin engine gave pilots limited visibility to the ground, and pilots had to operate the retractable undercarriage manually in the early Mk Is using a handle to the right of the pilot's seat to bring the wheels up. This often led to inexperienced Spitfire pilots 'porpoising' or bouncing on take-off as they controlled the aircraft with the left hand on the column stick and pumped the handle with the right hand, leading to a bouncing motion. Some pilots on the early Mk I struggled with this, as pilot Gordon Sinclair recalled: 'I must admit I didn't terribly like the Spitfire to begin with, but then I had a reason not to, because the first flight I ever did in one I turned it upside down on the aerodrome landing. And I suppose it gave me an inborn fear of it. It took me quite a lot of hours to get over that.'

The Mk I equipped a number of front-line RAF squadrons when war broke out in September 1939, but were not as numerous as the mass-produced Hawker Hurricane. One officer at RAF Duxford shopped in Cambridge for rear-view car mirrors to adapt their Mk Is to allow the pilots to see what was behind them, this proving to be an important modification when the Battle of Britain erupted

in the summer of 1940. There were just over 1,500 Mk Is produced in total between 1938 and 1941, when the Mk II with a more powerful Merlin XII engine began to emerge. The Spitfire Mk II also saw adaptations to try to increase the firepower of the Spitfire, with the addition of two 20-mm Hispano cannon firing armour-piercing shells into the aircraft. But due to the size of the ammunition drums having to be mounted sideways in the 'slim' wing, these often didn't work under G-force stresses on the wing, to such an extent that experiments with cannon would cease for a time during the Battle of Britain.

For many pilots the early Mk I Spitfire with its sensitive handling was a true pilot's aircraft. As pilot Cyril Bamberger recalled: 'The Spitfire was nothing like I'd flown in before and oddly enough I've never flown anything like it since. It was a wonderful aircraft to fly, and you were part of the aircraft. Some aircraft you sit in them, and you fly them. Well after not a lot of experience of a Spitfire, you became part of the aircraft and you felt you could do anything in it.'

Spitfire Mk V

The Mk V Spitfire was a hurriedly rushed version of the Spitfire in response to the emergence of enemy fighters that now outperformed the original Mk I and II Spitfires.

The improved Messerschmitt Bf 109F and a new fighter, the Focke-Wulf Fw 190, tipped the balance of fighter supremacy during 1941 in favour of the German Luftwaffe. A Mk III Spitfire was proving too slow to build, so the Mk V was rushed into production to meet the threat from the enemy fighters. This version took the fuselage of a Mk I/II and fitted a more powerful Merlin 45 engine. Another adaption was the 'clipping' of the end of the Spitfire wing to give it a squared appearance. Although this was not as aesthetically beautiful as the original elliptical wing, it allowed the Mk V to move more easily out of the way of the better-performing Fw 190. 'Clipped' wings also went on to feature in other later types of Spitfires.

The issue of sufficient armament was again reviewed in the Mk V versions, with three types of wings being used. The 'A' wing could carry eight browning .303 machine guns, but this was proving to be lacking in 'punch' when trying to knock out enemy fighters, so a 'B' wing was developed, which could carry two .303 machine guns and one 20-mm cannon in each wing. The 'C' wing or universal wing allowed for a variety of combination of guns, with 'C' wings able to carry two .303 machine guns and two 20-mm cannon in each wing.

Even though the Mk V was rushed into service to combat these new aerial threats, it proved so successful, serving in many theatres including North Africa and the Mediterranean, that nearly 6,500 were built as it bore the brunt of front-line fighter service for the RAF between 1941 and 1943.

OPPOSITE: A Spitfire Mk I in flight, May 1940.

RIGHT: A need for increased firepower to match German fighters led to the fitting of cannons to later Spitfire versions.

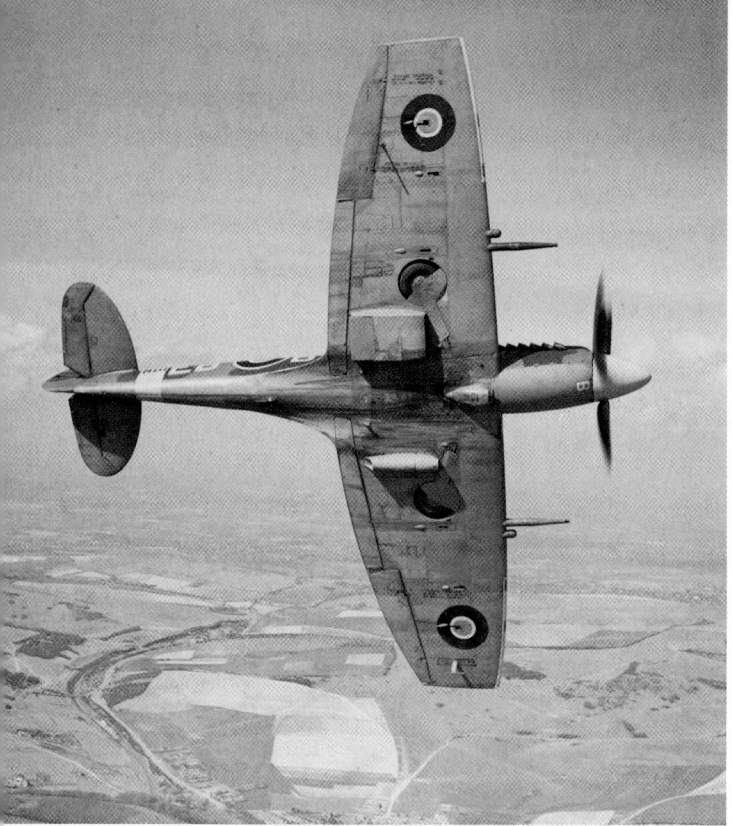

A Spitfire Mk XII, showing the 'clipped' wings that first appeared in the Spitfire Mk V variant to help pilots escape the new Fw 190 German fighter.

Spitfire Mk IX

Throughout 1941–2, the Mk V Spitfire suffered at the hands of the Luftwaffe's Fw 190A.

An updated version was needed to restore the Spitfire's aerial superiority and to counter 'nuisance raids' being conducted by German fighters fitted with bombs, which attacked targets over the south of England. The Mk IX was intended as another stopgap using a Mk V airframe slightly modified to fit an upgraded Merlin 61 engine. The key to the success of this version lay in a two-stage/two-speed supercharger in the Merlin 61, which gave increased power to the aircraft at medium and high altitudes, and a four-blade propeller. Two radiators were now positioned to allow for improved engine cooling, giving the Mk IX 1,650–1,700 horsepower. The more powerful supercharger now allowed the Mk IX to operate more effectively at the thinner higher altitudes where dogfights with the Luftwaffe were occurring, and it tipped the balance of power back in favour of the Spitfire. Despite its temporary nature, the Mk IX was popular with pilots, and over 5,000 were built, with later upgrades switching to the Merlin 63 engine. This type served in many theatres, including over Italy, and the Spitfire became once again a dominant fighter for the Allies.

Supermarine Spitfire Mk VCs flying in loose-line astern formation over the Adriatic Sea while on a bombing mission. The 'C' wing is visible, with two cannons alongside two machine guns in each wing.

Between sorties, Wing Commander J. E. Johnson, a leading Spitfire ace in the war, rests on the wing of his Supermarine Spitfire Mk IX with his Labrador retriever, Sally, in Normandy, 1944.

Spitfire Mk XII/XIV/XVI

The Spitfire Mk XII was the first variant to use the new Rolls-Royce Griffon engine, named after another bird of prey, the Griffon Vulture.

The Griffon was only slightly larger than the Merlin engine but its capacity was up to one third greater, meaning it could deliver higher levels of horsepower than the Merlin, and it could be fitted with a five-blade propeller to harness this extra power. However, the engine also used more fuel, so range was limited. This was a common trait throughout the various types of Spitfires, but it was pressed into service against the Fw 190 for the air defence of Britain, with the Mk XII entering service in 1943 and shooting down the first Fw 190 for the type in April 1943. Only 100 were built, though, being quickly superseded by the Mk XIV variant.

The Mk XIV was the first Griffon-powered Spitfire to go into large-scale production. Using the Griffon 65/66 engines, it had a top speed of 448 mph. Whilst it was heavier than earlier types to compensate for the engine weight, it had almost too much power for the airframe; some pilots struggled with take-off, reporting that the aircraft felt like it would 'rotate' around the propeller. Even considering this lack of pilot experience, the aircraft was a formidable weapon. When it entered service in late 1943 to early 1944, it had enough straight-line speed to counter the threat of the V-1 Flying Bombs that appeared over the skies of southern England in 1944, outpacing other Allied planes such as the Tempest V in pursuit of these guided bombs.

The Mk XVI was used primarily in a ground attack role, which by 1944 was a clear example of how good the original Spitfire design had been. It had been designated as a new variant as it carried a US-built Packard-Merlin 266 engine, and this type began to appear from late 1944. The performance of the engine gave it great speed at low levels and it became a lethal fighter bomber, which would support the advancing Allied armies as they fought their way into Germany in 1945.

Seafire

GREAT BRITAIN

The Spitfire developed for the Royal Navy was the Seafire.

However, it took until 1942 for the Seafire version to be delivered to the Royal Navy, as some of the issues that afflicted ground-based RAF Spitfires, such as a narrow landing gear, meant it was not the most suitable aircraft for use on short aircraft carriers and their deck runways. As the Spitfire was deemed the most modern fighter at the time, the Seafire entered service with few modifications to RAF Spitfires. Due to the long nose of the Spitfire/Seafire, pilots were trained to land on carriers with their heads looking out and over the side of the Seafire to aid with landing it on the deck.

The first Seafires were ex-RAF Mk VBs, modified with a strengthened undercarriage and a hook for landing, becoming the Seafire Mk IB. The most numerous types were the Mk III Seafire, which finally had modifications more suitable for carrier operations, including folding wings. This entered service in 1943 and remained in production until 1945, with over 2,000 of this type being built. The Seafire gave the Royal Navy modern fighter capability, serving from the Mediterranean to the Normandy beaches and into Asia.

A Supermarine Seafire with its nose resting on the flight deck of HMS *Smiter* after a heavy landing during exercises. There were some difficulties adapting and operating Seafires on carriers, but it finally gave the Royal Navy a capable modern fighter.

Operations

The Spitfire served throughout the war across numerous geographical areas using its diverse types, but its 'finest hour', as coined by British Prime Minister Winston Churchill, came during the Battle of Britain in 1940.

Battle of Britain

The Spitfire entered service in time for the start of the war in 1939 and fought the Luftwaffe in the skies as the Germans swept to victory during the defeat of France in May 1940. Though not credited at the time by the troops trapped on the beaches, the Spitfire helped the BEFs to escape at Dunkirk by holding off the Luftwaffe. One such Mk I Spitfire at Dunkirk was N3200, which was shot down and crashed on Sangatte beach in France. It was excavated from the sand in 1986 and restored to full flying status; it is now part of the collection of Imperial War Museums and flies at IWM Duxford. But losses were high over France, and as the Spitfire was a longer and more complex machine to manufacture, British Air Chief Marshal Sir Hugh Dowding wanted to pull them back to British bases, fearing the Nazi onslaught on Britain that was imminent following the fall of France.

The RAF and its air defences used a coordinated defence system, the 'Dowding System'. This used radar and spotters on the ground to feed information to control stations that could 'scramble' fighters to meet the enemy aircraft approaching. This helped save time and directed the Spitfires and Hurricanes to intercept the enemy

A pilot of No.64 Squadron running towards his Spitfire during a squadron 'scramble' at RAF Kenley, on the outskirts of London, 15 August 1940.

efficiently, useful with the Spitfire's limited fuel range.

During the Battle of Britain, the Hurricane was the most numerous British fighter aircraft of the RAF. But the superior performance of the Spitfire meant the RAF lost fewer of them, and it had a higher victory ratio, which gave the aircraft its legendary status after the battle. Working with the Hurricane, Spitfire pilots would engage the accompanying enemy Bf 109 fighters, whilst the more numerous Hurricanes would attack the bomber formations. As the Germans switched tactics in September 1940, from attacking airfields and infrastructure to bombing London directly, the tide of the battle turned in favour of the Allies. Control of the air over Britain remained with the RAF, which prompted the cancellation of the German invasion of Britain in 1940.

Pilots of No.19 Squadron confer at Fowlmere in Cambridgeshire, 21 September 1940. The strain of battle is evident on the face of Squadron Leader Brian 'Sandy' Lane (centre), the Squadron Commanding Officer.

GREAT BRITAIN

Flight Lieutenant Walter 'Farmer' Lawson, photographed in his flying kit in 1940. He wears a Type B flying helmet, Mk II goggles and a Type D constant-flow oxygen mask.

Soldiers and police inspect a Messerschmitt Bf 109E-4, which force-landed at East Langdon in Kent, 24 August 1940. Spitfires were tasked with engaging enemy fighters during the Battle of Britain.

Mediterranean and Italy

The Spitfire Mk V was the first variant to serve outside of France and Britain, fighting against the Italians and Germans over North Africa and the Mediterranean. The Spitfire stopped the Italian and German Air Forces from attacks on Malta, and supported the Allies during the invasion of both Sicily and Italy in 1943. The Spitfire was adapted for operation in the desert as the Mk V was 'tropicalised' by adding an air filter to the aircraft.

Supermarine Spitfire Mk Vs of the Royal Canadian Air Force in loose formation over the Tunisian desert. The red propeller spinner was a marking for day-flying Allied aircraft in that combat area.

The Spitfire was also shipped as part of the Lend-Lease initiatives to the Soviet Union and used on the Eastern Front, with the last shipment arriving in 1945. In the Pacific the Spitfire struggled against the Japanese Zero fighter, which could out-turn the Spitfire. To counter this, pilots developed tactics using the better diving speed of the Spitfire to attack the Zero. Once the Mk V was replaced with Mk VIII the Allies gained air superiority, though the Pacific and Southeast Asian combat areas were deemed less of a priority for the Spitfire than Europe. Even so, it was used to defend the north of Australia and the port of Darwin by the Royal Australian Air Force and saw action in Burma.

Variants of the Spitfire were adapted without armaments to conduct photo reconnaissance missions, and Photographic Reconnaissance Unit (PRU) Spitfires were fitted with extra fuel tanks to allow for longer missions. They confirmed the existence of German V weapon sites. Flying at all levels of altitude, the PRU Spitfires were a constant source of vital intelligence throughout the war for the Allies.

The Spitfire is an icon of the war. The original design by R. J. Mitchell, which went on to be constantly adapted by Joseph Smith, provided many variants that performed admirably in various roles throughout the war. Its performance during the Battle of Britain, though often over-stated, was to secure its status as the most famous aircraft to serve in the war and can evoke a feeling of overwhelming nostalgia when witnessing the surviving aircraft, powered by the Merlin engine, still flying today. Those Spitfires still flying are a memorial to the many pilots who flew in them, and to Churchill's 'few'. It is an aircraft that will always seem like a 'poem of speed and precision'.

Three Supermarine Spitfire Mk VBs flying in 'vic' formation over the Essex countryside.

GREAT BRITAIN

#37
Vickers Wellington

The Vickers Wellington was a British medium bomber that held the accolade of being the most-produced British bomber of World War II and the only British bomber in service for the entirety of the war.

Although designed in the 1930s, its unique geodetic airframe gave it a unique strength to withstand anti-aircraft defences. It was switched to night-bombing missions early in the war before it was given other roles when the British four-engine heavy bombers superseded it in operations. A stalwart of the RAF throughout the war, its sometimes-unsung status saw it form the backbone of the RAF in the fight against Nazi Germany.

Origins

The Wellington was developed by Vickers in response to an Air Ministry requirement in 1932, B.9/32, for a twin-engine day bomber that could outperform any aircraft at that time.

The chief designer at Vickers, Rex Peirson, worked with Barnes Wallis (the structure chief at Vickers who later was to develop the famous 'bouncing bomb') to use Wallis' geodetic airframe. This construction method had previously been used in airships and Wallis developed it further into aircraft airframes. Its key feature was the interlocking metal lattice weave work, made from

GREAT BRITAIN

duralumin metal alloy, which produced a strong yet light fuselage and wing. This could then be covered in treated fabric, which was useful when intending to mass produce large numbers.

The fabric covering of the Wellington would also, in theory, allow it to survive a large amount of machine-gun fire. This was fitted to most of the fighters in development at the time as bullets would pass through the fabric, then the geodetic airframe, and exit out the other side of the fabric fuselage covering, still maintaining the strength of the aircraft's airframe.

A protype was commissioned, once tests of the airframe proved its strength, and Type 271 went into production, flying for the first time in 1936 at Brooklands in Surrey. Originally named 'Crecy', its name was changed to Wellington as Vickers had named previous aircraft after the famous British duke and this also fitted with the Air Ministry's practice of naming bombers after towns. The first Wellington Mk I aircraft flew in 1937, with RAF Bomber Command squadrons receiving Wellingtons in 1938.

The Wellington had a crew of five. It was initially powered by Bristol Pegasus engines, whilst later versions would use the more reliable Bristol Hercules and Rolls-Royce Merlin engines. It could carry an impressive bomb load in relation to its total weight, and with modification became the first RAF bomber to carry the 4,000-lb

OPPOSITE: RAF ground crew push a 4,000-lb 'cookie' bomb towards the bay of a Vickers Wellington bomber.

TOP: The geodetic framework of a Vickers Wellington bomber being welded together at the Vickers-Armstrong factory in Chester, 1942.

BOTTOM: A Vickers Wellington Mk IV, having lost most of its rear fuselage fabric through battle damage in September 1942 when raiding Bremen, Germany. Despite the damage, the pilot and crew managed to return, highlighting the strength of the geodetic airframe.

'cookie' bomb, which had enough explosive power to destroy a whole street. It had defensive gun turrets front and rear, and as turrets developed into specialised equipment to keep up with the speed of fighters, these changed to power-operated Nash & Thompson turrets. Overall, crews reported that the Wellington was easy to fly, and the aircraft was used by RAF training units, training crews who would go on to operate other RAF 'heavies' like the Lancaster bomber.

Successes of the geodetic construction for the Wellington were that it could be adapted to carry larger bombs like the 'Blockbuster', it could store long-range fuel tanks and be modified to carry torpedoes. But for the crews, the survivability of the Wellington after sustaining heavy damage from air defences was a key success of the geodetic construction, with crews managing to return even with parts of the metal lattice construction missing, proving the great strength of the frame. A morale-boosting event for the Wellington occurred in 1943 when workers at the factory at Broughton, near Chester, built a Wellington bomber in just under 24 hours, beating the record set in the United States. The achievement was filmed by the Ministry of Information for a British propaganda film.

Operations

At the outbreak of the war, the RAF had six squadrons flying Wellingtons.

They were quickly in action with early raids against German shipping, before raids in December 1939 against the German fleet in the Heligoland Bight proved to be disastrous, with nearly half the attacking force of Wellingtons being lost to fighters and flak. The aircraft proved vulnerable to air defences, lacking sufficient defence for daylight bombing, and this led to the bomber being switched to night bombing. It took part in the first British bombing raid on Berlin in August 1940, during the Battle of Britain. The bombing of Berlin that summer is believed to have persuaded Hitler and the Luftwaffe to change tactics during the Battle of Britain, switching to bombing London and other towns. This relieved pressure on RAF Fighter Command airfields in the south of England that had been under sustained attack. This allowed the RAF stations to recover and was seen as a turning point in the eventual British victory in the Battle of Britain.

Vickers Wellington Mk Is in flight, 1939. The geodetic airframe is just visible through the fuselage and above the top of the wing and engine.

In May 1942, Wellingtons made up 66 per cent of the bomber force that formed the first 1,000-strong bomber raid on Cologne. But just like the Wellington itself, its crews were also made of strong stuff. One notable example was New Zealander James Ward, a sergeant pilot on a Wellington returning from a raid in July 1941 that was attacked by a Messerschmitt Bf 110 night fighter. This caused a fire to break out in one of the engines. Efforts to put out the fire using extinguishers pumped through a hole in the fuselage failed and with the fire looking likely to engulf the whole wing, the crew were preparing to bail out. Instead, Ward suggested he climb out to try to extinguish the fire using an engine cover. Fitted with a parachute and secured with a rope, the aircraft slowed slightly, and Ward climbed out, moving along the wing cutting holes in the fabric covering for his hands and feet with an axe. He managed to successfully smother the fire with the cover, stuffing it into a hole in a damaged fuel line, and made it back inside despite being buffeted by high winds. The aircraft managed to limp back and made an emergency landing, with the crew surviving. For his actions, Ward received the highest British military honour, the Victoria Cross, but sadly he was lost just months later, shot down on a raid to Hamburg.

With the introduction of Bomber Command's four-engine heavy bombers, the Wellington began to be removed from front-line night-bombing raids, although it continued to operate in a bombing role in the Mediterranean, and later in India and Asia. The versatility of the Wellington saw further specialist adaptions, including the bizarre-looking DWI variant, which was fitted with a large magnetised ring that was used to explode magnetic mines dropped by the Germans at sea. Few were produced but it was successful in this specialist role, helping to minimise this threat to Allied ships.

RAF Coastal Command also made significant use of the Wellington, with adaptions allowing it to drop torpedoes used in the Mediterranean, whilst the addition of a powerful 'Leigh' searchlight allowed it to attack submarines during the Battle of the Atlantic. By 1944, radar-equipped Wellingtons were also used to guide other aircraft to intercept and destroy V-1 Flying Bombs.

Over 11,000 Wellingtons were built and the 'Wimpy' (nicknamed after a character from *Popeye*) would prove to be a pivotal aircraft in service with the RAF throughout the war. Its unique construction allowed for great versatility and for use in many roles. It was a battle-hardened veteran of the conflict, as tough as an old 'wellington boot'. For those that were to fly in it during the war, this versatile aircraft would mean many more crews would go on to survive World War II.

A train of 18 250-lb HE (high explosive) bombs is prepared for loading into a Vickers Wellington III at Mildenhall in Suffolk, January 1942. The bomber was to spearhead RAF night bombing in the early years of the war.

Close-up of a Vickers Wellington DWI Mk II with the 48-ft diameter electromagnetic ring, for exploding magnetic sea mines, suspended from the wings and fuselage of the aircraft.

#38
Vought F4U Corsair

UNITED STATES

The Vought F4U Corsair was an American single-seat fighter bomber, originally conceived primarily as a fighter operating from aircraft carriers.

But it would prove to be a considerable opponent for the Japanese in the Pacific, where it was initially used by American Marine pilots flying from land-based airstrips, successfully supporting the Marine Corps as they pushed the Japanese out from occupied Pacific islands. Built around the same powerful Pratt & Whitney Double Wasp engine as the P-47 Thunderbolt and F6F Hellcat, its bent inverted 'gull wing' design needed to accommodate the largest propeller of any fighter at the time, and this would be its main recognisable feature.

US Marine Corps F4U Corsairs on Tarawa Atoll in the central Pacific. Although originally intended as a carrier-based fighter, delays by the US Navy operating the Corsair from carriers meant the US Marine Corps flew them from land in support of the Marines in their battles to drive out the Japanese from Pacific islands.

Origins

The F4U Corsair was designed in response to a request from the United States Navy Bureau of Aeronautics for a proposal for a single-engine fighter with a range of at least 1,000 miles.

Chance Vought, a division of United Aircraft, responded with the XF4U-1, designation V-166B. Fitted with a prototype of the Pratt & Whitney R-2800 Double Wasp engine, the XF4U-1 flew for the first time in May 1940.

To maximise the speed from the experimental Wasp engine, the largest propeller mounted on a fighter in development was a 13-ft propeller built by Hamilton Standard. The sheer size of this propeller would, however, cause issues that would affect the design of the XF4U-1 prototype. To ensure that there was enough space for the large propeller to clear the ground, an inverted or bent 'gull wing' design was developed that would become the Corsair's main identifying feature. This would allow for standard-size struts for the undercarriage and wheels, and enable the Corsair to have a folding wing, necessary for operating from the confines of a short deck on aircraft carriers. Although this helped with the production, the bent wing would be heavier and take longer to build, but the engine and propeller configuration offered little other option. Assessment of the air war in Europe also showed that two guns in either wing would not provide enough firepower to shoot down enemy aircraft, so the design changed to three .50 calibre machine guns in each wing, improving its capability. By 1941, the US Navy placed an order for the Corsair, named after another Vought aircraft, a biplane from the 1920s. The new Corsair would look vastly different.

A Chance-Vought Corsair fighter of the Fleet Air Arm cruises above the clouds over its American base in New England during a training mission.

UNITED STATES

Operations

UNITED STATES

At an early stage in the US Navy taking delivery of the Corsair, problems were encountered that hindered its ability to land on aircraft carriers.

Although it could fly slowly enough to attempt a landing on a carrier, the Navy noticed issues, including its left wing which could drop rapidly, leading to stalls, and the undercarriage could bounce the aircraft as it landed. In addition, visibility for the pilot was difficult when landing at sea: the size of the nose and propeller, and location of the cockpit, meant it was hard for pilots to see the deck. As a result of these trials, the F6F Hellcat, which was also entering service at the same time as the Corsair, was favoured by the US Navy as it delivered slower speed than the Corsair and was deemed a simpler aircraft for novice pilots to land on a ship's deck.

The US Marine Corps, battling the Japanese in the Pacific, required a replacement for the F4F Wildcat fighter. They were happy to embrace the Corsair, as the Marine Corps was operating from air strips that were on land, which presented fewer issues than carrier landings. In 1943, the Marines began operating Corsairs from Guadalcanal and other bases in the Solomon Islands. One pilot, Lieutenant Bob Hanson, shot down 20 Japanese Zero fighters in a Marine Corsair, whilst defending Rabaul, in New Britain, part of Papua New Guinea, which was under attack over 17 days of combat flights in 1944.

The British Royal Navy also took deliveries of the new F4U Corsair, to serve with the Fleet Air Arm and to replace ageing carrier fighters such as the Fairey Fulmar. In November 1943, the first aircraft were delivered, and new Royal Navy squadrons were formed and trained with the aircraft on the east coast of the United States before crossing the Atlantic. The British put the Corsair straight to work on its carriers and, despite crashes, persevered with carrier operations out of a necessity for more modern carrier fighters. Modifications were made by the Fleet Air Arm to air carrier landing, including raising the pilot seat by seven inches to help pilot visibility, which resulted in the British Navy operating Corsairs from carriers long before the US Navy. The Corsair served with the British in Europe and the Pacific. In Europe, it took part in attacks in 1944 against the German battleship *Tirpitz*, whilst with the British Pacific Fleet it took part in raids in Southeast Asia, and at the end of the war in 1945 against the Japanese home islands.

The Corsair was eventually passed for US Navy carrier operations in spring 1944, helped by the British experiences and a reinforced landing strut, which reduced bouncing on carrier landing. It went on to perform well against Japanese fighters, becoming the principal aircraft for fighter bomber missions in the Pacific. Such a distinctively shaped and powerful Allied aircraft would go on to serve in the post-war period, including in the Korean War in 1950, a testament to one of the last great piston-engine aircraft of World War II.

ABOVE: A Vought F4U-5 Corsair in VMF-312 markings from during the Korean War, flying over Oshkosh, Wisconsin.

LEFT: A Chance-Vought Corsair landing on HMS *Vengeance*. The British Fleet Air Arm would modify the Corsair to aid with carrier landings.

SOVIET UNION

#39

Yakovlev Yak-9

The Yakovlev Yak-9 was the principal Soviet single-seat multi-role fighter that served with the Soviet forces in the final years of the war and was based on a series of aircraft that stretched back to the original Yak-1 fighter.

As the Yak-9 entered service it proved to be a match for the Bf 109 and Fw 190 Luftwaffe fighters, and helped to increase Soviet air superiority on the Eastern Front, serving into the post-war period in Korea. It was the most-produced Soviet fighter of World War II, playing a significant role in the defeat of Nazi Germany on the Eastern Front.

Soviet Yak-9 interceptors in flight.

Origins and Operations

The Yak-9 originated from the previous Yak-1/7 aircraft versions of the Yak series, which were designed by Soviet aeronautical engineer Alexander Sergeyevich Yakovlev, and would become one of the most advanced modern Soviet fighters of the war.

The original Yaks had been designed and built based on a 1938 Soviet requirement for a front-line fighter, and this led to Yakovlev's 1-26 design winning the race to become the Yak-1. The original Yak-1 design had been a mix of plywood and metal construction, and was available to Soviet forces when the German invasion began in 1941.

The Yak-7 was similar to the Yak-1 but was initially conceived as a two-seater training aircraft. However, it was more lightweight and easier to construct, and so went into service as the Yak-7B fighter, with a Klimov M-105PF engine and a top speed of 372 mph. This robust fighter led to the Yak-9, which in 1942 developed the Yak-7 aerodynamically to include a clear, unobstructed cockpit canopy and a more lightweight duralumin aluminium metal skin replacing the plywood covering of the Yak-7. The engine used was the Klimov M-105PF, before a later version, the Yak-9U, used an even more powerful Klimov VK 107A engine. The Yak-9 also had powerful armament, with a mixture that usually included a 20-mm cannon firing through the nose hub and two 12.7-mm machine guns. It was capable of carrying 441 lb of bombs under its wings.

The Yak-9 would use different wing types, engines and armament set ups, as the basic airframe design could be adapted to combat needs. The Yak-9 first entered combat in 1942. It was used on the Eastern Front as an anti-tank, light bomber and, due to its long flying range of 870 miles, for reconnaissance missions, as well as a front-line fighter. Initial poor training for Soviet pilots on the aircraft meant it had limited success, but this improved by the Battle of Stalingrad in 1942–3. It went on to match the Luftwaffe in the Battle of Smolensk in 1943, before the Yak-9U entered service from 1944.

Overall, the Yak-9 made a significant contribution to the Soviet victory on the Eastern Front and went on to serve for a time in the post-war period, earning a NATO nickname of 'Frank'. Just over 14,500 were built during the war, the most of any Soviet fighter, before production finally ended in 1948.

SOVIET UNION

Yakovlev Yak-9D fighters lined up on an airfield where the squadron guards the new US bases for aircraft landing in the Soviet Union.

AXIS POWERS

Axis Aircraft

The aircraft used throughout World War II by the Axis powers, primarily Germany and Japan, were technically advanced and, initially, dominant across the world. But it did not stay that way. As the Allies' vast manufacturing power and industrial output increased, the sheer numbers and quality of Allied aircraft would eventually overwhelm the Axis forces, and lead to the defeat of both Germany and Japan.

Germany started the war with its invasion of Poland in 1939, with a relatively new air force, the Luftwaffe. It had expanded rapidly in the 1930s, and gained experience in tactics and its aircrafts' performance supporting Spanish Nationalist fascist forces during the Spanish Civil War. This experience placed much emphasis on German aircraft development and the ability to 'dive bomb', eventually hindering the development of any long-range German bombers needed for a global war, for flying over the vast Atlantic Ocean, where most of the Allies' vital equipment would be shipped. However, this strategic blunder had been unthinkable as the superb Messerschmitt Bf 109 fighter won many victories at the outbreak of war as German armies swept all before them. It was followed by another exceptional aircraft, the Focke Wulf Fw 190, and, later still, the first operational jet-powered fighter aircraft of the war, the Messerschmitt Me 262. It would also operate an aircraft that would be forever associated with the terror of World War II, the Junkers Ju 87 Stuka dive bomber, with its wailing air siren, an emblem of Germany's 'blitzkrieg' (lightning war).

Yet despite these aircraft, the Germans were unable to defeat the British RAF in 1940, occupy vast lands of the Soviet Union, hold on to their conquests in Europe or protect their homeland Reich from waves of Allied bombers. These would eventually reduce parts of Germany to rubble and played a significant role in contributing to its final defeat.

In Japan, the vast expanse of the Pacific Ocean would lead to the development of the most famous fighter of the Pacific war, the Mitsubishi A6M Zero, which would prove unstoppable following the infamous attack on American forces at Pearl Harbor in Hawaii. But as the limits of Japanese conquest receded in the Pacific and Asia, the use of valuable aircraft for kamikaze suicide attacks would become a poignant sign of both the futile nature of war and sheer barbaric waste of Japanese pilots' lives. Basking in early war successes, Japanese fighter development would be unable to keep pace with Allied aircraft, leaving the Japanese home islands vulnerable when the most expensive aircraft of the war, the US Boeing B-29 Superfortress, would arrive to deliver destruction to Japan on an unbelievable scale.

Although they experienced early success in the war, the Axis air forces would suffer from a lack of ongoing wartime development. They were unable to develop aircraft required for the rapidly evolving conflict, industries were unable to out-produce the Allies and they suffered further delays due to Allied strategic bombing targeting vital factories. This combination, despite operating some exceptional aircraft during the war, would lead to the final defeat of the Axis powers in 1945.

A Dornier Do 17Z-10 2 used in the night-intruder role during 1940–1.

#40

Dornier Do 17

The Dornier Do 17 was a German twin-engine light bomber, which saw extensive service with the Luftwaffe at the start of the war, making up the main German bomber force alongside the Heinkel He 111.

It had initial successes during the Spanish Civil War in 1936, fighting for the fascist Nationalists of General Franco. However, when World War II began with the German attack on Poland in 1939, the Do 17 suffered at the hands of the RAF with their modern fighters during the Battle of Britain in 1940. This led to the 'Flying Pencil', as it was often known, being withdrawn from manufacture by 1942.

Two German Dornier Do 17 bombers over London during a raid on the first day of the Blitz, 7 September 1940.

Origins and Operations

GERMANY

The Dornier Do 17 evolved from a high-speed mail carrier aircraft that first flew in 1934.

However, the cramped cabin for a crew of six meant it was not deemed to be suitable by Lufthansa, but the Reich Aviation Ministry *(Reichsluftfahrtministerium)* designated it Do 17 and felt it could be adapted into a bomber. They ordered a prototype with the addition of a bomb bay, an 'H' tail configuration and defensive machine guns. It gained the nickname of 'Flying Pencil' due to its long, slender fuselage.

The Do 17 served with the Condor Legion in Spain in 1936. Experience from this combat had shown that it was vulnerable from an attack from below, so the next main and most-produced variant, the Do 17-Z, would feature a downward-firing machine gun and an adapted glazed 'stepped' cockpit. It was able to carry a bomb load of just over 2,000 lb, but fully loaded its range was limited to just 205 miles. The Do 17-Z had success in 1939 in Poland, but would soon be tested during the Battle of Britain when facing the Spitfires and Hurricanes of the RAF. Production of the Do 17 ended when it proved unable to withstand the onslaught of these modern fighters; it was removed from front-line service, only being used later in the war as a glider tug with the Luftwaffe.

The Dornier Do 17 took part in the invasion of Poland where it could hold off slow Polish fighters. It was quick at low altitudes, but when it was to face the RAF over France and during the Battle of Britain in the summer of 1940, its lack of armament and defensive weakness, combined with a limited bomb load and flying range, saw an estimated 150 Do 17s being shot down. This included eight alone on 18 August 1940 during an attack on RAF Kenley, just south of London.

The Do 17 was virtually obsolete by the time it was to play its role in the Battle of Britain, and this distinctive aircraft would soon be relegated to a support role by the Luftwaffe.

An RAF guard points out bullet holes in the fuselage of a crashed Dornier Do 17, 1940.

#41
Focke-Wulf Fw 190

The Focke-Wulf Fw 190 'Würger' was a single-seater monoplane German fighter. It first appeared in combat in March 1941 and would go on to be one of the best piston fighters of the war, posing a constant and significant problem for Allied air forces.

It would excel in a variety of roles for the Luftwaffe, including as a fighter bomber in a ground attack role as the 'Butcher Bird', and would gain air superiority for a time for the Luftwaffe in Western Europe, until later versions of the Spitfire and Mustang restored Allied control. Serving in all German theatres of war, the defeat of Nazi Germany ended further development of this remarkable fighter.

GERMANY

Origins

The Focke-Wulf Fw 190 had its origins in the late 1930s. In 1938, the Reich Aviation Ministry, concerned that rapid aviation development may overtake the principal Luftwaffe fighter of the time, the Messerschmitt Bf 109, asked Focke-Wulf to work on a supplementary fighter to support it.

The chief designer at Focke-Wulf, Kurt Waldemar Tank, would go on to design one of the best piston aircraft of the war, helped in part by his own experiences in World War I.

Tank had served in the cavalry during that conflict, despite wanting to join the fledgling German air service. Based on his experience he realised that he needed a stable 'workhorse' aircraft to complement the 'thoroughbred' aircraft that was the Messerschmitt Bf 109. He developed an aircraft design that would be easy to maintain and could absorb battle damage – as he had witnessed that equipment had to work harder during war – and that could operate from rudimentary airstrips close to the front line. The basic design would also need to be able to be constantly adapted as there would inevitably be technological developments during the conflict.

To fulfil these aims, Tank's design would use some key features to make it stand out from other aircraft being developed. The engine chosen by Tank was an air-cooled radial engine, which differed from the liquid-cooled engines of its contemporaries, primarily meaning it would not have to compete with the Messerschmitt Bf 109 for engines then being manufactured in Germany. The other advantage to using this type of engine was that it was more resilient in battle, as bullets could more easily ignite the cooling liquid of an 'inline' engine, but it was thought to be less aerodynamic, as the air flowing into the engine to cool it needed a larger opening that would increase drag and slow the aircraft down, especially on a small aircraft like a fighter. Development by the US Navy in the late 1930s resolved some of this problem by introducing a shaped ring in the cowling of the engine to increase the air flow, but reducing the size of the opening required to do so. Tank adapted this further, encompassing the BMW 801C air-cooled engine into a cylindrical drum in the nose, which gave early Fw 190 versions an acceptable top speed of 388 mph.

Further design features also helped Tank to achieve his aims with the Fw 190. These included a wide-track landing gear, like the British Hawker Hurricane, which opened

A Focke-Wulf Fw 190A-3 after landing by mistake in Britain, June 1942. Introduced in 1941 to supplement the Bf 109, the Fw 190 was Germany's best piston-engine fighter.

217

inwards, and a wide spacing between each forward landing wheel that gave stability and strength on the ground. This meant it could operate from unmaintained airstrips, and was easier for pilots to land and take off. To allow for easy maintenance, Tank's team used solid rods to work the controls, rather than cables and pulleys that were more liable to stretching and therefore required more maintenance. Equipment was also electrically powered rather than hydraulic, which was used by most aircraft manufacturers, with Tank believing electric wiring would be less susceptible to damage from enemy gunfire.

The first prototype flew on 1 June 1939 and delivery of the Fw 190A-0 to front-line units began in March 1941.

One of the early criticisms of the Fw 190 was the lack of armament, despite early variants having four 0.31-inch MG 17 machine guns, two in the nose and two in the wings, so two 20-mm cannons were fitted into the wing roots where the wing met the fuselage. As the 'A' variant developed, this increased to four wing 20-mm cannons and two nose machine guns, which was a significant amount of firepower.

As was common with Focke-Wulf aircraft, the Fw 190 was named after a bird: the '*Würger*'. In English this is a shrike, a small bird similar in size to a sparrow. Some shrikes impale their prey on thorns and leave it hanging like a butcher would, so it developed the nickname 'Butcher Bird'. This became an appropriate moniker for

A group of Focke-Wulf Fw 190 fighters at Flensburg airfield in Germany, awaiting disposal.

the aircraft when it first appeared in combat over the English Channel.

As the Fw 190 began to show its capability in combat as a fighter, it was quickly adapted to a ground attack role. It was modified to carry up to 2,205 lb of bombs, with bomb racks under the fuselage and wings. With the advent of the Allied bombing campaign in Europe from 1943, the Luftwaffe required the Fw 190 to be able to fight and perform at higher altitudes (where the bombers and accompanying fighters were flying) than it had been able to do so far with the earlier 'A' series of the aircraft. Development from 1942 onwards, for higher altitude versions, eventually led to the '*Langnasen-Dora*' ('Long-nosed Dora') entering service in August 1944.

GERMANY

Using an 'inline' Jumo 213 engine, and employing a water/methanol engine booster, the 'Dora' was to have a fast rate of climb and a top speed of 426 mph, crucial for defending the skies above Germany where long-range Allied fighters roamed at higher altitudes. Overall, there were just under 20,000 Fw 190s built during the war. It proved so successful as a 'back up' to the Messerschmitt Bf 109 that Kurt Tank was granted the honour of naming any subsequent Focke-Wulf designs with the prefix 'Ta' (based on his surname), although only two aircraft, the Ta 152 and Ta 154, were to fly with this designation before the war ended.

Operations

The Focke-Wulf Fw 190 entered service in October 1941.

Its first role was supporting with air cover the German Navy's 'Channel Dash' operation, where two battlecruisers and a heavy cruiser sailed through the Channel from Brest in France to Germany, much to the humiliation of the British Royal Navy. It wouldn't be until the following year that the RAF became more fully aware of this new, powerfully armed and highly manoeuvrable Luftwaffe fighter. This happened when Fw 190s began to attack targets along the south coast of England, and 15 Spitfires were attacked and shot down near to Bruges in Belgium over two days, for no German losses. It became clear to the Allies that the new fighter was a match for any aircraft then available to them. The aircraft was also deployed to the Eastern Front in 1942, to the *Jagdwaffe* (fighter force) JG 51 and JG 5, where it would operate as a fighter bomber and again prove to be a match for anything the Soviets could deploy against it.

In the spring of 1942, the RAF was genuinely concerned by the performance of this new German fighter that was able to master the existing Spitfire Mk V variant. In desperation to evaluate the new aircraft, an interesting operation was hatched to steal a working Fw 190. 'Operation Airthief' was conceived by a British commando, Captain Phillip Pinckney, to go to France and steal the Fw 190 and help the RAF more quickly evaluate it.

The plan involved Pinckney and a pilot. He proposed he and his friend, chief Spitfire pilot Jeffrey Quill, would be dropped just offshore from occupied France by a fast MTB (Motor Torpedo Boat), before canoeing to land and hiding near an Fw 190 base. The following day, as ground crew arrived to work on the aircraft and run the engines, they would attack the crew, with Quill jumping in the Fw 190 and flying it back to England, whilst Pinckney would escape and rendezvous with the boat to return. Fortunately for both men the plan was never put into action as in June 1942 an Fw 190A-3 based in Brittany took part in a dogfight over the Channel with Spitfires of Czech 310 Squadron. The pilot became disorientated in combat and flew north rather than south back to his base; landing at RAF Pembrey in South Wales instead, he was quickly captured. The RAF now had a working Fw 190 to evaluate.

As the Spitfire Mk IX entered service and USAAF bombers began to arrive in numbers to take part in the daylight bombing raids as part of the Allied Combined Bomber Offensive, the Fw 190 would meet increased competition in the skies. The USAAF B-17 and B-24 bombers were large aircraft that could absorb a lot of fire, and flying in formation they could defend themselves with their large array of guns, as the German Fw 190s needed to pass dangerously close multiple times in attempts to shoot them down. Fw 190 pilots learnt to attack the bombers 'head on' where armament was weakest. The Fw 190 was developed further with increased firepower, when the Fw 190A-8, nicknamed '*Sturmbock*' ('Battering Ram'), was modified to use two larger cannons in the outer wing position. But the cannon required the pilot to close to within 600 ft of the bomber, which meant extra armour for the Fw 190 was needed. Although there was some initial success, once the Allies had long-range escort fighters like the Mustang, it soon proved to be too vulnerable to the newer Allied fighters.

By 1944, the Germans were becoming desperate with both the Western Allies and Soviets forcing the borders of the Reich slowly back to Germany. Hitler conceived a plan to fight back in the west. A surprise attack in December 1944 in the Ardennes Forest led to the Battle of the Bulge and in the air with Operation Bodenplatte, where the Luftwaffe attempted to destroy Allied air forces on the ground in France and the Low Countries, with the Fw 190 taking a leading part in the operation. Although the plan was initially successful, losses to the German Luftwaffe were less easily replaced, and especially with the loss of experienced Fw 190 pilots. From the end of 1944, the effectiveness of the Luftwaffe as a fighting force continued to dwindle in the face of overwhelming Allied air power. Even with the improved Fw 190-D, with its fast top speed at high altitude, it couldn't be deployed in significant enough numbers to stem the increasing Allied tide, ultimately leading to the defeat of Nazi Germany in May 1945.

With the end of the war in Europe, many Fw 190s were destroyed or abandoned. But this remarkable aircraft, whilst ending the war in defeat, resulted in the 'Butcher Bird' being one of the finest piston aircraft to fly in World War II.

Northeast of Brussels in Belgium, a German Focke-Wulf Fw 190A-8 fighter lies abandoned on an airfield liberated by British troops.

GERMANY

The German Focke-Wulf Condor. Originally designed as a long-range commercial airliner, it was adapted to a maritime reconnaissance and anti-shipping aircraft against Atlantic convoys for the Luftwaffe.

#42

Focke-Wulf Fw 200 Condor

The Focke-Wulf Fw 200 Condor was a German four-engine all-metal-skin monoplane that was originally designed as a long-distance airliner for transatlantic flights.

It was adapted for wartime service as a maritime patrol aircraft that engaged in anti-shipping bombing, as well as in transport roles for the Luftwaffe. Although it was disruptive to Allied shipping, sinking many ships and coined the 'Scourge of the Atlantic', increased air protection for the Allies and their Atlantic convoys, and the limited handling characteristics of the Condor, would lead to it being sidelined to a transport role later in the war.

Origins and Operations

The Condor first flew in July 1937. It was designed for long-range Atlantic crossings at a time when aircraft on long sea routes were usually seaplanes. The design was an aerodynamic fuselage with four Pratt & Whitney Hornet engines, which were built under licence as BMW 132 engines, and a large wing, to allow it to cruise at just under 10,000 ft over long distance with an unpressurised cabin. Although it proved its capability by flying to New York in 1938 in just over 24 hours, there was little initial interest from airlines, with the German state airliner, Lufthansa, having no need for its range on shorter routes around Europe.

However, with war on the horizon and German planners looking at how to disrupt Allied shipping routes, the Condor was selected as a possible maritime patrol candidate. Focke-Wulf had been working on a modified Condor for the Imperial Japanese Navy, which carried 60 per cent more fuel and over 4,000 lb of bombs and defensive machine guns. The Model Fw 200-B was converted to an Fw 200C-0, and work began on producing further aircraft as war broke out with the Fw 200C-1.

The Condor, named after the bird due to its long wing, operated in support of Germany's invasion of Norway in 1940. But with the capture of Atlantic coastline, following the German defeat of France, it moved to an airfield at Bordeaux, on the edge of the Bay of Biscay. The force of Condors available to the Luftwaffe was never large, often just having a dozen available to fly. However, it was initially very successful in sinking Allied ships, with most convoys lacking air cover, even though it had limited manouverability at low altitudes when required to attack. As the Allies began to use long-range or convoy escort aircraft such as Hurricanes that were catapulted from merchant ships, by mid-1941 losses were mounting and the Condor was switched to a patrol role helping to guide U-boats to attack Allied convoys instead.

The Condor would also serve as a transport aircraft, with one adapted for Hitler's personal use, but it struggled in combat against more agile aircraft. After initial success in the Battle of the Atlantic, the Condor would end the war largely forgotten, with just 276 being built.

A pair of Focke-Wulf Fw 200C Condors. The 'Atlantic Scourge' was eventually countered by air cover provided by Allied escort carriers.

#43
Heinkel He 111

The Heinkel He 111 was a twin-engine German bomber.

It formed the backbone of the Luftwaffe bomber force in the early war years, before Allied air superiority from 1943 saw it moved to a transport role. It would serve in all major German areas of war, famously used extensively during the Blitz on Britain in 1940–1. Its fully glazed nose and elliptical wing made it one of the most recognisable German bombers of World War II.

Heinkel He 111 bombers in formation.

Origins and Operations

GERMANY

The He 111 was originally designed as a fast civilian mail plane, but in part it was always destined to be a bomber, as restrictions placed on the Germans meant it could not openly be displayed as a bomber by the new, secretly formed pre-war Luftwaffe.

It first flew in 1935 and was powered by two BMW VI engines. Although ten were built, it was not deemed powerful enough as a bomber and an updated version began with a Daimler-Benz DB 600CG engine. Defensively, it had three machine guns, in the front and on top and underneath the fuselage, and could carry around 3,300 lb of bombs. The bombs had to drop through the wing-supporting structure, which limited the size of bombs used; later, as war erupted, larger bombs had to be carried under the wings.

Against limited fighter opposition, the He 111 was operationally successful for the Condor Legion during the Spanish Civil War. This led to further development of the 'P' variant, which had a fully glazed stepless cockpit and nose, which housed the pilot and bombardier, and gave it a unique and identifiable design. The bomber also featured self-sealing fuel tanks. The fuel tanks were wrapped in three layers, first leather and then two layers of rubber; if a bullet or metal pierced the tanks, the fuel reacted with the outer rubber, which would swell and form a seal to stop the fuel leaking. This helped in the lightly armed bomber in the early German operations of the war as the He 111 came up against few fighters, but did not help so much when the He 111 finally encountered the Spitfire and Hurricane.

The invasions of Poland and Norway saw the He 111 successfully support German forces with bombing missions. But during the Battle for France, and especially during the Battle of Britain, the losses of He 111s when facing modern fighters were stark, leading to it being changed to night-bombing missions during the German Blitz on Britain. The lack of further bomber development by the Luftwaffe meant the He 111 would serve throughout the war from the Soviet Union to the Mediterranean, carrying a variety of weapons including torpedoes and even an air launched V-1 Flying Bomb. Ultimately, with the advent of Allied air superiority, the He 111 became obsolete, but was forced to continue as dwindling German production and aircraft losses saw it pressed into ever-more desperate service.

A Heinkel He 111 bomber flying over the East End of London at the start of the Luftwaffe's evening raids on 7 September 1940, the first day of the Blitz.

The Junkers Ju 88A-1, the original bomber version of the highly adaptable Junkers 88 aircraft.

#44

Junkers Ju 88

The Junkers Ju 88 was a German twin-engine medium bomber, operated in a variety of roles throughout the conflict.

It could be termed 'multi-role', helping to form the backbone of the Luftwaffe during the war. It was initially built slowly but eventually over 14,000 were produced, making it one of the most manufactured German bombers of the war.

A Junkers Ju 88A-5 in RAF markings in flight over the English countryside.

Origins and Operations

GERMANY

The Junkers Ju 88 was designed in 1935 and first flew in December 1936 as a fast medium bomber, aiming to be so fast that it could evade fighters.

It had room for four crew in the cockpit. It had a glazed nose section and could carry around 1,100 lb of bombs in a bay and a further 6,600 lb of bombs under its wings, with defensive armament of five machine guns. In 1937, partly due to the success of the Ju 87 Stuka, the Ju 88 was developed without the glazed nose to provide dive-bombing capability. As the conflict began, operational needs saw further variants developed, including an attack bomber using heavy-calibre autocannon to attack Russian tanks, a night fighter with on-board radar, a reconnaissance version and one that could conduct a maritime anti-ship role.

At the start of the war the Ju 88 saw limited numbers participate in the invasion of Poland, before taking part in the Battle of France. Here it was used in a dive-bombing role, often targeting the French rail network to hinder the French army's organisation. The Ju 88 was used extensively in the Battle of Britain but at great cost. After suffering high losses, whilst bombing targets by day along the south of England, Ju 88 units were switched to night bombing during the Blitz. The Ju 88 A-1 was proving a difficult aircraft to fly, but this was improved with a longer wingspan that appeared in the A-4 type. The Ju 88 was principally used in the German invasion of the Balkans and Soviet Union in 1941, where Ju 88s inflicted great damage on the first day of the invasion by attacking the Soviet Air Forces on the ground.

The Ju 88 continued to evolve throughout the war. It was particularly successful against Allied convoys delivering aid to the Soviet Union through the Arctic Ocean, where limited fighter cover was available to the Allied ships. It would serve the Luftwaffe with distinction, but with the defeat of Germany it now remains a largely forgotten aircraft.

The wreckage of a Ju 88 in Normandy. The Ju 88 bomber failed to inflict any damage to the Allied invasion fleet on D-Day.

#45
Junkers Ju 87 Stuka

The Junkers Ju 87 Stuka was a German monoplane dive bomber and one of the key aircraft used in the German blitzkrieg that was so successful for German forces in the early years of the war in Europe.

A *Sturzkampfflugzeug* (dive bomber) aircraft, this was abbreviated to 'Stuka' and the name became synonymous with the Ju 87. Although the Stuka served throughout the war, its initial success would soon diminish when it came up against modern Allied fighters, where its limited defensive armament meant it could not easily survive without German air superiority or fighter cover. However, as a ground attack weapon the aircraft would become one of the most terrifying and identifiable aircraft of World War II.

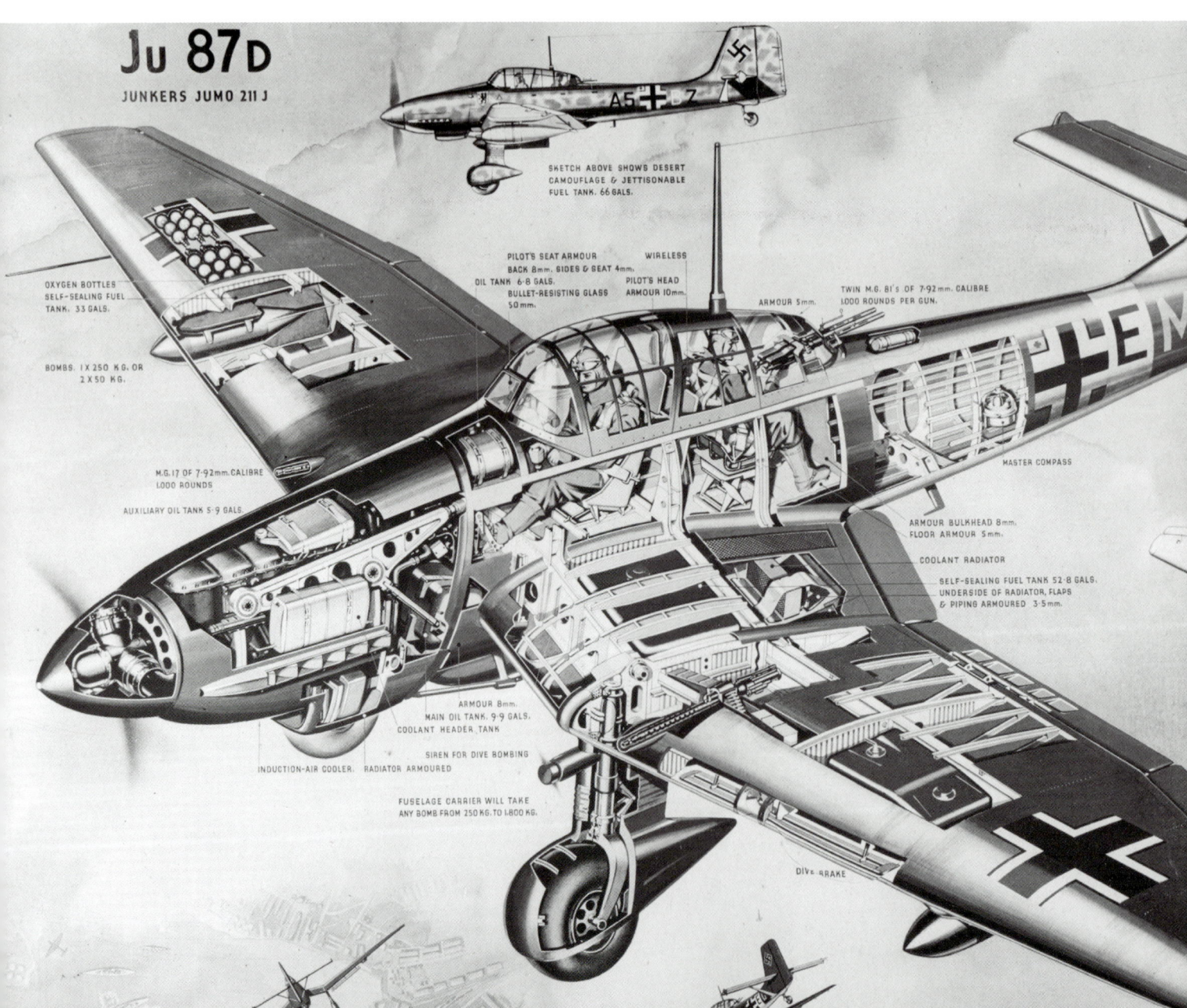

Origins

The Ju 87 was built to support Nazi Germany's doctrine of a fast and mobile 'lightning war', blitzkrieg, using a dive bomber as a form of 'flying artillery'.

It was designed at Junkers by Hermann Pohlmann and a prototype first flew in 1935. The basic design was a single-engine all-metal-skin monoplane with a fixed undercarriage, powered by a Jumo 210A 'inline' engine. The fixed wheels initially had large 'trousers', which were modified through later versions, and a 'gull wing' shape to ensure strength when diving. The Ju 87 would approach a target at a medium height of around 15,000 ft and then dive onto the target using air brakes to dive at a 90-degree angle. As the Ju 87 dived at upwards of 370 mph and 6 G-force, an altimeter in the cockpit would indicate when it was at the correct height and the pilot would release the bomb, which was swung from a cradle to clear the propeller dropping on to the target. Then an automatic pull out process was initiated, which closed the dive brakes and allowed the pilot to pull up before hitting the ground.

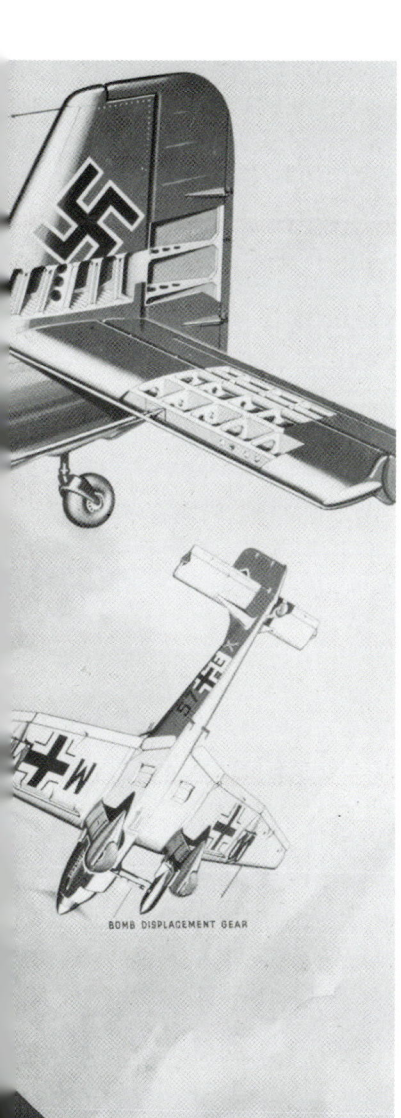

The Ju 87A entered service in 1937 and though lightly armed defensively, with just three machine guns, it could carry up to nearly 4,000 lb of bombs. This was dependent on whether there was one pilot or an additional crew member who sat in the rear, worked the radio and operated a machine gun. The first mass-produced version of the Stuka was the Ju 87B series, which started in 1937. It had a more powerful engine and saw sirens fitted for the first time. These were called 'Trumpets of Jericho', so-named after a legend about the capture of Jericho in Palestine in 13 BCE by the Hebrews, when the sound of the trumpets saw the walls collapse. They were small wind-driven propellers at the top of the fixed wheel legs that produced a 'wailing' sound as the Stuka dived. The sirens reduced the speed of the aircraft by 10–15 mph, but apart from providing an audible reference of the diving speed of the Stuka for the pilot, it would have significant psychological impact during the blitzkrieg for those on the ground. Especially for those soldiers or civilians that had survived an earlier attack, it would terrifyingly signify what was to come.

Although the Stuka's shortfalls were exposed during the Battle of Britain, the lack of a successor dive bomber forced the Luftwaffe to develop the next main variant: the Ju 87D, which entered service by late 1941. The design was altered to reduce drag and it went on to serve in North Africa and on the Eastern Front with the German invasion of the Soviet Union. As 'flying artillery' the Stuka had its greatest successes on the Eastern Front, especially in the first two years when the German army pushed the Soviets back and faced few modern fighters. One of the greatest Stuka aces was Hans-Ulrich Rude. He became one of the key proponents of the Stuka, served on the Eastern Front and contributed to the development of the next major version: the Ju 87G.

As the Soviets introduced more modern fighters, including those by Lend-Lease, the Stuka once again became vulnerable and the 'G' version was developed as an anti-tank weapon to stem the tide of massed Soviet armour that was reversing the earlier German gains in the Soviet Union. This updated version had an upgraded engine and two 37-mm cannon. Small numbers were introduced around the Battle of Kursk in 1943, but could not alter a decisive German defeat. As the war declined further for Nazi Germany, and its homeland was threatened by growing Allied bombing, production of the Stuka was to end in December 1944, as the Focke-Wulf Fw 190 had demonstrated its ability as a fighter bomber. The Ju 87 Stuka would continue to serve in a reduced role in the ever-diminishing Luftwaffe until the end of the war in 1945.

OPPOSITE: A cutaway illustration of a Junkers Ju 87D. It highlights the 'gull-wing' design, with its fixed wheels, and the small propeller above the wheel, the wind-driven siren named 'Trumpet of Jericho'.

Operations

As the Ju 87A entered service, it was sent to the Condor Legion to fly operational missions in the Spanish Civil War for General Franco between 1938 and 1939.

It excelled as a tactical bomber against limited fighter opposition, and allowed crews to perfect their use of the Stuka and hone tactics. The ability and success of the Stuka in the Spanish Civil War convinced the Luftwaffe that dive bombing would become integral to the coming Continental war, so much so that new aircraft being developed were required to have the ability to dive bomb. However, this developing doctrine of a dive bomber supporting ground forces stymied the development of large high-altitude bombers for the Germans that were being developed by Britain and the United States in this pre-war period. This would later hinder German attempts to hit back at the Allies when their own Bomber Offensive began.

The Stuka flew the first aircraft missions of World War II when three Stukas attacked near a bridge over the Vistula River on 1 September 1939, some ten minutes before Germany had officially declared war on Poland. For the invasion, the Germans now had nine *Gruppen* (groups) of Stukas; these had a devastating effect on the Poles, who were suffering from a lack of anti-aircraft artillery, and saw the rapid defeat of Poland.

The Ju 87 also supported the Nazi seizure of Norway in April 1940, with significant success against British ships with an expeditionary force that landed in northern Norway. Meanwhile, the psychological effects of the Stuka with its sirens is recorded in contemporary newsreels that captured the attacks of the Stuka during the German invasion of France and the Low Countries in May 1940, especially on civilians fleeing along roads. The Stuka flew missions against French artillery as the German panzers attempted to break out from the Ardennes Forest in Belgium, flying numerous missions above the key battle at Sedan, which saw the Germans break out and unleash blitzkrieg. As the Allies crumbled, the Stuka faced little concentrated fighter opposition, but the first hint of its vulnerabilities became apparent when encountering Allied fighters.

The Battle of Britain from July 1940 was to highlight the Stuka's limitations thoroughly. Tasked with knocking out the British radar defences, code-named 'Chain Home', losses when facing the RAF's Spitfire and Hurricane were catastrophic. In a ten-day period alone, 66 Stukas were shot down, even when accompanied by the Bf 109 fighters. Speed was principally its 'Achilles heel'; with a top speed of 196 mph it had little chance against a 336 mph travelling Hurricane.

Despite losses in the Battle of Britain, where it was withdrawn early from the battle, the Stuka had considerable success in the Mediterranean and North African desert. This included the German airborne invasion of the island of Crete in 1941, acting as 'flying artillery' in support of lightly armed German paratroopers. Some Stukas were flown by the Italian Air Force against British convoys at Malta, but its main success was during the invasion of the Soviet Union in 1941, when it was able to operate 'freely' against limited opposition, flying as 'artillery support' with three vast German armies that reached to within just 25 miles of Moscow.

As Allied and Soviet air power increased, and the Luftwaffe prioritised fighter production to defend the German Reich, the Stuka became increasingly obsolete, but it was still being used until the end of the war. As a potent symbol of the blitzkrieg and a terrifying weapon of war, the Ju 87 Stuka remains one of the most recognisable aircraft of World War II.

Bombs falling away from a Ju 87 Stuka dive bomber. The Ju 87 was the leading aircraft supporting the German army in the early battles in Poland, Norway, France and the Soviet Union, used as 'flying artillery' during the blitzkrieg.

Junkers Ju 87 dive bombers on the way to attack British tanks in the Western Desert, North Africa. The Ju 87 performed well in the Mediterranean and North Africa with both the Italians and Germans before the Allies gained air supremacy.

A Bf 109V3 (w. NR 760) third prototype in flight over Augsburg, Germany in 1936.

#46

Messerschmitt Bf 109

The Messerschmitt Bf 109 was a German single-seat fighter and one of the most-produced fighters in aviation history, with around 34,000 built.

It served throughout the war with the Luftwaffe and with other Axis-aligned air forces. It went through a series of adaptions, producing many variants as the war progressed, capable of roles such as interceptor, bomber escort, fighter bomber, night fighter and in reconnaissance. As the mainstay of the Luftwaffe fighter force, it saw action in all areas of German operations, becoming the defining 'classic' single-seat fighter of the war for the Germans.

View of a Bf 109E-1. The Bf 109 performed well during the Spanish Civil War, leading to further development.

Origins

The Messerschmitt Bf 109 was developed in the mid-1930s concurrently with the formation of the new German Air Force, the Luftwaffe, in response to a requirement to provide the Germans with a modern fighter aircraft.

In 1933, the German Air Ministry issued research projects for key aircraft that the future Luftwaffe would need, and a single-seat monoplane fighter was one such necessary requirement. German aircraft designer Wilhelm Emil 'Willy' Messerschmitt designed the Bf 109 alongside Walter Rethel. It was based on an earlier low-wing monoplane, the Bf 108, to be a powerful yet lightweight monoplane fighter interceptor. It was designated 'Bf' to show it was built by Bayerische Flugzeugwerke (Bayern Aircraft Works). It first flew in May 1935, with the first prototype (V1) powered by Rolls-Royce Kestrel engines as German engines were not ready, before the next prototype used the Junkers Jumo 201A engine.

The Bf 109 was trialled against other German prototype aircraft, including the Arado AR 80 and Focke-Wulf Fw 159. It successfully won the competition and an initial batch was put into production. Although a rival aircraft had also been selected by the Reich Aviation Ministry for further development, the He 112, it was the Bf 109 that eventually won the race to be manufactured. With a lighter airframe than its rival, it was slightly faster and had superior climbing and diving performance, which led to the original production aircraft the Bf 109A being ordered for the Luftwaffe.

The first production aircraft were sent in 1937 for evaluation as part of the German Condor Legion that fought in the Spanish Civil War, before an updated version with a Daimler-Benz DB 600 engine was built in 1938. The design used Willy Messerschmitt's principles of 'lightweight construction', which aimed to reduce the number of separate parts that could be found in the aircraft, with an uncomplicated structure. As the war progressed and more powerful engines were added or adaptions made due to combat, the lightweight airframe would suffer from reduced manoeuvrability as the weight of the aircraft increased.

The success of the Bf 109 in the early part of the war was down to its fast engine, lightweight airframe and the addition of cannon armament alongside wing-mounted machine guns, which had been added in response to the British Hurricane receiving eight machine guns in its own pre-war development. This gave the Messerschmitt Bf 109 a firepower advantage over the early versions of RAF fighters of the Spitfire and Hurricane. The Bf 109 was superior to anything except the Spitfire in the early war years, and although it was superseded by the Fw 190 in Western Europe from 1943 onwards in battles against British and American aircraft, it still served as the principal fighter on the Eastern Front against Soviet forces, until the eventual defeat of Germany in 1945.

Variants

Pre-war variants saw changes to engines, designated B–D in the series, but the first main production version was the Bf 109E, or 'Emil'.

This had structural changes to accommodate a more powerful Daimler Benz DB 601 engine, before being delivered in large quantities to the Luftwaffe. Over 3,000 were delivered by the end of 1941, making the 'Emil' the key fighter version during the German blitzkrieg campaigns from 1939. Painted with a distinctive yellow nose section to help with aircraft recognition, it had four machine guns and a cannon firing through the propeller hub, before the cannon was moved to the wings as the central nose cannon caused some engine problems.

The 'Emil' was the main version that fought the Battle of Britain for the Luftwaffe, where it would come up against its main RAF adversary, the Spitfire. There is much debate to this day as to which was the better aircraft, but at the time of the Battle of Britain, the Spitfire was slightly faster with a greater turning arc and rate of climb. However, the 'Emil' Bf 109 could dive faster due to its fuel-injected engine and had heavier armament with the use of cannon versus the Spitfire's eight machine guns. The 'Emil' was also fitted in some variants with a fuel drop tank to increase its range for fighter bombing and reconnaissance missions.

The next major variant of the Bf 109 was the 'F' series, or 'Friedrich', which was developed in 1939–40 and began to be delivered to German front-line units from May 1941. This design had new wings, engine cover and a larger propeller hub to make the most of the more powerful DB 201 N/E engines, and was aerodynamically the most streamlined Bf 109 to feature in the war. However, despite its fluid looks and fantastic handling for pilots, some preferred the 'Emil' as the 'Friedrich' had just one cannon and two machine guns along the nose, fewer than the earlier 'Emil'. As a result, some crews modified it by situating two cannons under the wings to increase its firepower.

The next variant was the 'G' series, or 'Gustav'. This version combined the 'Friedrich' airframe with another more powerful engine, the DB 605, which made the 'Gustav' the most successful version of the Bf 109. It was produced in large numbers from 1942 until 1945, with over 23,000 being built. 'G' versions featured a pressurised cockpit, which would become crucial as the Luftwaffe engaged the Allies in defence of the Reich. Later 'Gustav' versions also featured an MW-50 water-injection boost (a 50/50 mix of water and methanol injected into the engine to produce better power performance) and superchargers, just about keeping the Bf 109 able to compete with new Allied aircraft. The last version was the 'K', or 'Kurfürst', with further improvement on the 'G' series seeing it fitted with a more powerful DB 605D engine, keeping the Messerschmitt Bf 109 operational right up to the end of the war.

British soldiers pose with a Messerschmitt Bf 109E-4 which crash-landed in Kent, 24 August 1940. The pilot was captured unhurt. The aircraft's cannon can be seen to the right, in the wing.

GERMANY

Pilots of the Luftwaffe JG 53 'Pik As' fighter wing with their mascot dogs in front of one of their Messerschmitt Bf 109 planes, 1940.

Operations

At the start of the war, the Bf 109, as with the German army, swept away all before it.

Alongside the Stuka dive bomber it became a potent symbol of German blitzkrieg, using tactics that had been developed when the Bf 109 had fought during the Spanish Civil War. The Battle of Britain would see the Bf 109 matched by the Spitfire, but it was superior to the Hurricane. The Luftwaffe's defeat over the skies of Britain in 1940 can be attributed to the tactics of both sides, rather than the inferior performance of the Bf 109.

The Bf 109 played a crucial role in the Nazi invasion of the Soviet Union in 1941, where it shot down large numbers of Soviet aircraft in the first phase of the invasion, and in the Mediterranean and North Africa, where the Bf 109F supported the German Afrika Korps. The Focke-Wulf Fw 190 began to take over later in the war over Western Europe, but the Bf 109 carried on as production became gradually hindered by Allied air raids on the Bf 109 factories, and the increase in Allied air power brought eventual air supremacy for the victorious Allies.

Yet the Bf 109, for its pilots, was a reliable aircraft and it would be attributed with more aerial victories than any other aircraft in the war. As Luftwaffe pilot Günther Rall recalled: 'I was very familiar with that plane and looking at the 109 today I never could figure out how I could survive or fly that for five and a half years because it was a very narrow cockpit, very tiny and the view to the back was very limited … But if you get used to it you know, we flew it in Russia, out of snow and mud and everything and I felt familiar.' The record of the Bf 109 would also become familiar to generations following the war and secure its place in World War II aviation history.

A Messerschmitt Bf 109G-6/U2, one of two aircraft that landed in error at Manston in Kent on 21 July 1944. Both fighters were on a night '*Wilde Sau*' ('Wild Boar') operation against RAF bombers. This was a Luftwaffe tactic to engage RAF night bombers attacking Germany, using day fighters like the Bf 109, with the help of ground-based searchlights, to shoot down the British bombers. Although there was initial success, the loss of valuable Luftwaffe fighters saw the tactic discontinued by spring 1944.

GERMANY

#47
Messerschmitt Bf 110

The Messerschmitt Bf 110 was a large twin-engine German fast and heavily armed fighter with a crew of three.

It was designed to be a long-range *Zerstörer* (destroyer), clearing the skies of enemy fighters by sweeping in front of Luftwaffe bombers. However, after initial success in the early months of the war, when it finally came up against more manoeuvrable single-seat Allied fighters, it suffered heavy losses. This resulted in the aircraft's role being adapted to that of a night fighter against Allied bombers, equipped with new on-board radar. Although just over 6,000 were produced before the end of the war, it did prove to be an adaptable aircraft when used in the right circumstances, but could not deliver any significant victories to prevent the defeat of Germany in 1945.

Origins and Operations

GERMANY

The Bf 110 was designed in response to a 1934 requirement by the Reich Aviation Ministry for a heavy fighter capable of sweeping away all enemy fighters before it to pave the way for its bombers.

The Bf 110 first flew in May 1936. It was initially faster than its contemporary, the Bf 109 single-seat fighter, but testing and development meant it did not see action in the Spanish Civil War like so many other Luftwaffe aircraft. The Bf 110 was heavily armed, with four machine guns found in the nose section and two wing cannon. When the improved Daimler Benz 601A-1 engine was added to the 'C' version, it could reach a top speed of 348 mph.

When the Bf 110 flew in the skies over Poland in 1939, it swept all before it, escorting the He 111 bombers and avoiding dogfights with more agile Polish fighter aircraft. It was also successful against early RAF daylight bombing raids, with Bf 110s shooting down 11 out of 22 Wellington bombers over Wilhelmshaven in December 1939, in part prompting the RAF to switch to night bombing raids. But during the Battle of Britain, it performed badly. Initially it could out-climb the Spitfire and avoid the Hurricane with its speed, sweeping forward of the bombers at 22,000 ft. But as the Luftwaffe lost more bombers it was forced to fly in support of them at the slower bomber's speed, which made it vulnerable to RAF fighters. In August 1940, 120 Bf 110s were lost in the battle and a further 83 in September. Despite the losses the Luftwaffe was forced to continue to use them as escorts, regardless of their obvious shortcomings in that role. At some stages of the battle, single-seat Bf 109 fighters had to escort the Bf 110 fighters.

The Bf 110 had more success in a fighter bomber role. It was moved to the Mediterranean, North Africa and the Soviet Union before it was withdrawn from the Eastern Front and fitted with radar, which gave it a new lease of life as a night fighter in its 'G' model variant. It proved to be a constant problem for RAF Bomber Command, but it did not live up to its promised *Zerstörer* role.

A Messerschmitt Bf 110C showing its armament in the nose.

A Messerschmitt Bf 110C of III/NJG 3 with shark's-mouth markings.

A Messerschmitt Me 163B Komet. The Komet was a short-range rocket interceptor introduced in late 1944, which had a phenomenal rate of climb and speed but only a few minutes' flight duration at full power. Its explosive fuel mixture and skid landing gear meant accidents were common.

#48
Messerschmitt Me 163 Komet

The Messerschmitt Me 163 Komet was an interceptor aircraft designed to intercept Allied bombers flying at high altitudes and was the only rocket-powered aircraft to see action during the war.

Using volatile rocket-engine fuel, this rocket-powered aircraft was less successful than the jet-powered Me 262.

It took great bravery to fly, as the fuel would lead to many crashes on take-off and landing, due to the lack of a wheeled undercarriage and reliance on a skid sledge landing gear on top of the volatile fuel, which became a dangerous mix. Despite its technological advances and supreme speed, the impact of the Komet on the Allied bombing campaign was virtually non-existent.

Origins and Operations

GERMANY

The development of the Komet began in 1937, when aeronautical engineer Dr Alexander Lippisch began work on a new delta-wing glider aircraft design that was fitted with a rocket engine, the Walter I-203 rocket motor, at the Deutsche Forschungsanstalt für Segelflug (German Institute for Glider Research).

In early 1939, Dr Lippisch and his team were transferred by the Reich Aviation Ministry to Messerschmitt to further develop his design into a rocket-powered fighter as part of Project X. In August 1940 Lippisch's design, the DFS 194, flew for the first time, equipped with the HWK R-1-203 rocket motor and reaching a top speed of 340 mph. Although the engine required further development, early trials showed the aircraft demonstrated good handling and glide characteristics. Further trials saw the prototype reach 497 mph, with subsequent launches reaching 621 mph and nearing the barrier of sound.

Development work continued and in September 1941 the prototype Me 163A aircraft took to the skies for the first time. In December that year work began on the Me 163B, designed to be easy to mass produce, and equipped with the HWK 109-509 bipropellant rocket engine. The HWK 109-509 was powered by two fuels: 'T-Stoff' (hydrogen peroxide and water) and 'C-Stoff' (hydrazine hydrate and methanol). Both fuels were highly toxic and corrosive, with ground crew required to wear special protective clothing, and water being flushed through the fuel tanks after each flight. The explosive combination pushed the Komet to speeds in advance of anything else flying in the war, but it could only sustain powered flight for seven or eight minutes. Despite this limitation the Me 163 entered service with the Luftwaffe in May 1944.

Now equipped with two 30-mm cannons in each wing, the Me 163 could blast to 39,000 ft in just over three minutes at 550 mph, dive to attack bomber formations with its cannon and glide back to base with its engine fuel spent. In action it was disappointing, not least as the ability to hit a target in just a few seconds when speeding past bombers had been underestimated. The first engagement against Allied bombers took place in August 1944. Despite hitting a bomber it ended with one Me 163 being shot down by a B-17 tail gunner and another lost to a P-51 Mustang. The flawed idea of a jet-powered interceptor became clear. Despite 364 Komets being built, only 16 Allied bombers were shot down before the end of the war for the loss of 13 Komets, with a further 200 lost in accidents during take-off and landing. A technological marvel that broke the mould, the dawn of jet-powered aircraft would eclipse the brief impact of this rocket-powered aircraft experiment.

Aircraft apprentices training at RAF Halton in Buckinghamshire rebuild a Messerschmitt Me 163B Komet rocket-powered aircraft. This aircraft is now on display at the Science Museum in London..

#49
Messerschmitt Me 262

The Messerschmitt Me 262 was a technological first, taking its place in aviation history as the first operational jet fighter aircraft and the first to see combat during the war.

It would rival anything the Allies could put in the sky, but it entered service late. Production delays with both the technology and a lack of materials, coupled with shortages of fuel, meant it was unable to change the course of history in the air war.

A Messerschmitt Me 262 A-1a *Schwalbe* ('Swallow'). The ultimate Luftwaffe fighter, the Me 262 jet was also employed as a fast bomber, a role for which it was not as well suited. As a fighter it had no equal, but despite being produced in large numbers in the last year of the war, only a few hundred ever became operational.

Origins and Operations

The Me 262 can trace its development back to 1938 when Messerschmitt was asked to produce an aircraft design to make use of new turbojet engines that were being developed. The subsequent design would use two BMW jet engines, as contemporary thinking in Germany, as in Britain, was that any design would require two jet engines as one would not be sufficiently powerful. However, despite the airframe being ready, the BMW 003 turbojet engine took longer to refine and did not enter production until 1944. During the development stage a small number of Me 262 development aircraft were fitted with the BMW 003 engine, but these proved to be unreliable and prone to failure.

The development of the Me 262 continued in 1942, with the BMW engines replaced by two Junkers Jumo 004B turbojet engines, but progress was inevitably slow. Delays in production, combined with interference from Adolf Hitler who favoured the Me 262 being developed as a bomber rather than a defensive fighter, resulted in the Me 262 not entering service with the Luftwaffe until the summer of 1944. Following Hitler's preference for a bomber variant, and subsequent attempts to delay production of the Me 262 as a fighter, two variants were produced: the Me 262 A '*Schwalbe*' ('Swallow') fighter and Me 262 B '*Sturmvogel*' ('Storm Bird') fighter bomber. Around 1,400 Me 262 aircraft were built, but only around 300 of these entered service with the Luftwaffe, partly as the jet engines were still unreliable and susceptible to combat fatigue.

In April 1944, the first Me 262 aircraft were delivered to the Luftwaffe. The aircraft's first air-to-air combat took place in July 1944, when Leutnant Alfred Schreiber damaged a Mosquito photo reconnaissance aircraft of No.540 Squadron RAF. On 8 August 1944 Leutnant Joachim Weber claimed to have shot down another Mosquito of No.540 Squadron, with the loss of the pilot and navigator. This incident is considered to be the first successful downing of an enemy aircraft by an Me 262. It was not until March 1945 that sufficient numbers of the Me 262 were operational to enable the Luftwaffe to mount a large-scale attack on Allied bomber formations. Tactically, Me 262 pilots targeted the Allied bomber streams by approaching rapidly from the rear above the bombers, diving to a level with them that enabled the Me 262 to slow sufficiently enough to fire at the Allied bombers with their four 30-mm cannons in the nose, before diving again and escaping at speed from accompanying Allied fighters.

A Messerschmitt Me 262 V3 (third prototype) taking off, 1943.

Later Me 262s were equipped with additional unguided rockets with devastating effect on bomber streams. Capable of easily outrunning Allied piston aircraft, although not as manoeuvrable or able to turn as well, the Me 262 was most vulnerable when at low speed, particularly when taking off and landing. Consequently, heavy flak guns and Fw 190 fighters guarded Me 262 bases as lurking Allied fighters such as the Hawker Tempest hunted them, often successfully.

Overall, the Me 262 was a groundbreaking innovation in terms of the development of jet-powered aircraft and as a result is of considerable historic significance. Although the Me 262 did not change the course of the war, examples captured at the end of the war and evaluated by the Allies were to play a crucial role in the development of jet aircraft in the post-war decades.

#50
Mitsubishi A6M Zero

The Mitsubishi A6M Zero was a Japanese long-range carrier-based fighter aircraft that served with the Imperial Japanese Navy from 1940 to 1945 and is often regarded as one of the most effective aircraft of World War II.

The aircraft's flying range and manoeuvrability enabled it to easily surpass contemporary Allied fighters, making the Zero a decisive factor in the early Japanese victories in the Pacific.

As the war progressed, however, and the need grew for more powerful engines to combat the rapid improvement of Allied aircraft, the Zero's capabilities in the skies diminished. The air of 'invincibility' reputation that it had gained at the start of the war was challenged, with the Zero pressed into desperate kamikaze suicide attacks. The supreme dogfighting aerial prowess of the Zero was no longer sufficient to maintain Japanese superiority in the skies.

The Japanese Mitsubishi A6M Zero fighter was a formidable opponent for Allied forces during World War II because of its excellent manoeuvrability and exceptional range.

JAPAN

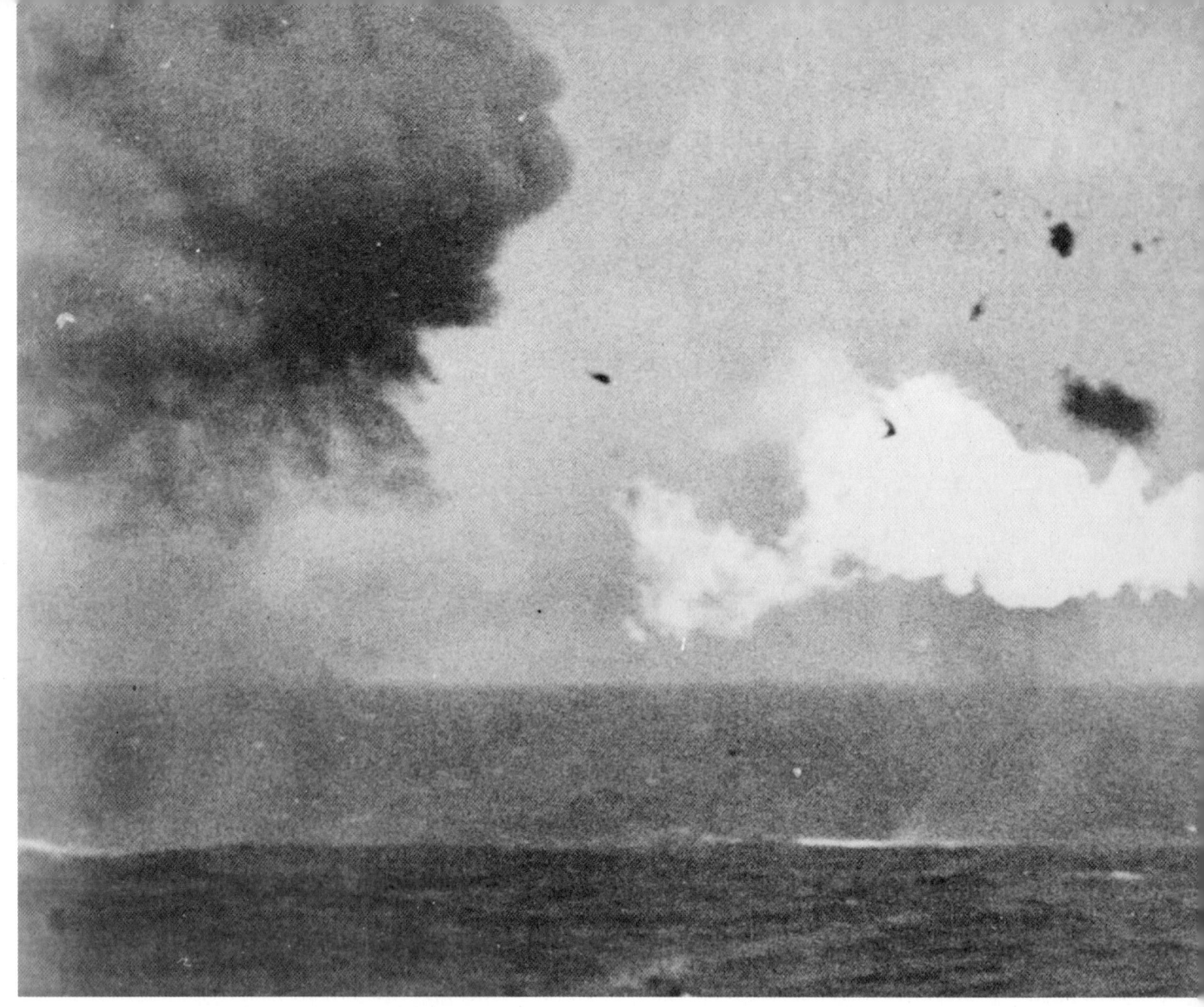

Origins and Variants

The Mitsubishi A6M Zero was designed by Jiro Horikoshi, chief engineer at Mitsubishi Aircraft Company, in the late 1930s.

This was in response to an Imperial Japanese Navy 1937 requirement for a replacement to the A5M 'Claude' aircraft that had only entered service in 1937 and itself was already a vast improvement on earlier Japanese biplanes. However, the Imperial Japanese Navy determined that any future conflict would require a fighter that could fly far and operate over the vast distances of the Pacific Ocean, requirements that the A5M could not meet. Horikoshi's new design was designated the A6M ('A' for aircraft carrier, '6' for the sixth aircraft produced, and 'M' for the manufacturer Mitsubishi). As it was to enter service in the 2,600th Japanese imperial year (1940) it was known as the '0' Navy Type Carrier Fighter or 'Rei-sen' (Zero), representing the last digit of the imperial year. It was also named 'Zeke' by the Allies, as well as being known as 'Zero'.

The design was very lightweight to allow it to operate at long distances due to primarily being constructed using extra super duralumin (ESD). This new aluminium alloy was lighter and stronger than other alloys developed by Sumitomo Metal Industries in 1936. The lightweight design also sacrificed armour plating to protect the pilot and self-sealing fuel tanks, which were becoming more common on other contemporary aircraft. This fed into the Japanese military machismo psychology of fast,

JAPAN

A Japanese A6M Zero explodes over water after being hit by anti-aircraft fire. The lack of armour and self-sealing fuel tanks meant the Zero was likely to explode if hit by Allied gunfire.

manoeuvrable and fearless warfare, for how could an Imperial Japanese pilot ever be shot down? This lack of aircraft protection would lead to high losses later in the war as the Zero was challenged in the skies by Allied aircraft with far better pilot protection.

The success of the A6M-1 prototypes led to the full production of the A6M-2 Zero Model 21 in 1940, which included folding wing tips to help with storing them on aircraft carriers. The A6M-2 Zero would gain almost mythical status in the first months of the war following the Japanese attack on Pearl Harbor in Hawaii, as its long range, powerful armament and great manoeuvrability ensured the aircraft's success in the Pacific theatre. Despite later variants being equipped with a larger, more powerful engine, the A6M-2 variant remained in service until the end of the war.

As the Zero's success against Allied aircraft began to decline, new variants were introduced to counter the growing Allied success in the skies. The A6M-5 removed the folding wing tips and became the most-produced version of the Zero, entering service in October 1943. The Imperial Japanese Navy had few aircraft carriers remaining following its losses during the Battle of Midway (before sub-versions of the A6M-5 belatedly included armour protection for pilots and their fuel tanks) and the extra weight of the A6M-5 meant it would soon become out-classed by Allied fighters.

Operations

When it entered service the Zero soon became the dominant aircraft in the Pacific.

It flew in support of the Japanese bombers in the surprise attack on the American forces at Pearl Harbor and in the South West Pacific as the Japanese pushed through island chains, including New Guinea. Although the Spitfire was faster than the Zero it could not out-turn it, and other American aircraft, such as the Brewster Buffalo and P-40, were no match for the Zero.

Despite the Allies' shock at the long-range performance and acrobatic prowess of the Zero, their pilots soon developed tactics to counter this initial shortfall in performance. Engaging a Zero in a dogfight was fruitless, so Allied pilots learnt to 'boom and zoom' down on the Zero (dive from height and shoot a burst of fire), which with its light airframe would be enough to down the Zero. Another tactic was the 'Thach Weave', devised by US pilot 'Jimmy' Thach, which saw two Allied aircraft, such as the F4F Wildcat, fly side by side about 200 ft apart. When a Zero attacked one of the aircraft, the two Wildcats would turn towards each other, allowing the accompanying aircraft to fire on the Zero and shoot it down.

As the war of attrition continued in the Pacific, improved Allied aircraft, tactics, and trained pilots, began to gain superiority over the Zero, which led to it being adapted to be used on kamikaze suicide missions against Allied ships. The arrival of the powerfully armed P-38 Lightning, F6F Hellcat and F4U Corsair meant the Zero was becoming obsolete. A lack of a replacement for the Zero would see it pressed into increasingly desperate service by the Imperial Japanese Navy as the war ended with Japanese surrender in 1945.

With over 10,000 Zeros being built, it was the superior long-range fighter aircraft at the start of the Pacific war. But the sacrifice of defensive features for lightweight long-range gain would lead ultimately to the loss of many Japanese pilots.

A Japanese Mitsubishi Zero fighter plane attempting a kamikaze crash into the deck of the American battleship USS *Missouri* off Okinawa in April 1945. The pilot was unsuccessful, hitting only the battleship's hull.

Index

Page numbers in **bold** refer to image captions.

A

A.V. Roe & Co. Ltd 17, **18**
'A' wing 189
Aarhus Raid 87, **87**
Abbeville airfield 131
aces 111, 131, 134, **172**, 173, **190**
Admiralty 106
Africa 62, 71
   see also North Africa
Air Fighting Development Unit (AFDU) 161, 162
Air Ministry 14, 61, 83, 84, 114, 186, 197
   Specifications 32, 103, 124, 128–9, 142, 175, 179, 183, 196
Air Transport Command 38
air-cooled engines 217
Alaska 38, 41
Allard, Sergeant G. 'Sammy' **130**
Allied Combined Bomber Offensive 47, 50, 53, 164, 220, 230
Allied Expeditionary Force **116**
   First Allied Airborne Army **97**
Allied Supreme Headquarters directive 25
Allies 212, 216, 219–20, 222–5, 227–30, 234, 236, 238–44, 246–7, 249
   air superiority 25, 47, 50, 53, 72, 126, 164, 194, 216, 224, **231**, 236
   aircraft 9–208
   see also Britain; Soviet Union; United States
Allison engines 37–8, 79, **79**, 150, 161, 170–1
Alps **173**
American Volunteer Group ('Flying Tigers') 80
Anglo-French Purchasing Board 71
anti-aircraft rockets **127**
Arado AR 80 233
Arctic Ocean **104**, 227
Ardennes Forest 220, 230
Argentan-Falaise gap **145**
Ark Royal (aircraft carrier) 106
Armstrong Whitworth 16
Arnhem 88, 97, 127, 140
Arnsberg **26**
astrodomes 94
Atlantic, battle of the 19, 69, 71, 77, 106–8, 135, 179–81, 199, 223
Atlantic Ocean 71, 77, 87, **104**, 105, 146, 212, 222–3

'Atlantic Wall' 126
atomic weapons 10, 54, **54**, 58, **58**, 77, 165
   'Little Boy' 58
Augsburg **232**
Austin Motors 140
Australia 72, 80, 147, 154, 194
Avro Anson 147
Avro Lancaster 10, 12–32, **17**, 174, 175–6, 198
   and the Avro Manchester 34, **34**
   B Mk 1 **3**, **19**
   B Mk I **22**, **26**
   B Mk I (Special) **31**
   B Mk III **14**
   bomb bay 18, 26
   bomb load 16
   BT308 prototype 17
   crews 28–31, **28–9**
   and the 'Dambusters' 21, **21**
   development and manufacturing 16–18
   and the Halifax 123–4, **124**, 126–7
   Mk I **7**, 14, 16
   Mk III 26, 29
   Mk III, EE173, 'K for King' 29, 31
   operations 19–25
   origins 14
   rear fuselage **18**
   specialist bombs 26–8
Avro Manchester 14, 32–4, 124
   Mk I 32, 34, **34**
   Mk IA 34, **34**
   Mk III (renamed 'Lancaster') 14, 34
Axis powers 60
   aircraft 211–49

B

Bader, Sqn Ldr Douglas 134, **134**
Balkans 227
ball turrets **41**, 42, 52
   'Sperry' **41**, 42
   'ventral' 70
Bamberger, Cyril 189
Bangkok 57
Banham, John 188
Battler (escort carrier) **108**
Bay of Biscay 62, 71
Bayerische Flugzeugwerke 233
Bazenville **96**
Beaverbrook, Lord 16, 84, 130
Belgium 25, **88**, 108, 110, 115, **115**, 158, **220**, 230
Bell Aircraft Corporation 55
Bell P-39 Airacobra 36–8, **37–8**
   Mk I **36**

Bell P-63 Kingcobra 10, 38, **38**
   P-63A 38
Bendix Corporation 42
Benghazi 72
Berlin 21–2, 29, 34, 38, 151, 160, 164, 167, **176**, 198
   battle for 22
Berlin airlift crisis 94
Bermuda Triangle 123
'Big Week' 48–50, **50**
'big wing' formation 134, **134**, 165
Bismarck (battleship) 77, 107
Bismarck Sea, battle of 51, 62, 151
'Black Week' 48
Blenheim Type 142/142M 65
'blister' windows **44**, 75–6, **76**
Blitz 62, 65, 135, 168, **214**, 224–5, **225**, 227
'blitzkrieg' (lightning war) 65, 131, 212, 228–30, **230**, 234, 236
'Blockbuster' bomb 198
BMW engines 217, 223, 225, 243
Boeing B-17 Flying Fortress 10, 13, 40–53, **40**, **47–8**, **50**, **53**, 55, 69, 71–2, 164, 172, 220, 241
   B-17A 41
   B-17E **41**, 42, **42**
   B-17F 42
   B-17G 42, **51**
   and 'Big Week' 48–50, **50**
   bomb bay **45**, 70
   cockpit view **43**
   costs 44
   crew 52–3
   Model 299 B-17 (prototype) 41
   Norden Bombsight 44–5, **45**
   operations 47–8, 51
   origins 41
   radio operator's position **43**
   steering column **43**
   tail gun **42**
   variants and developments 42–4
   waist gun positions **44**
   YB-17 41
   YB-17A 41
   YB-40 42
Boeing B-29 Superfortress 10, 18, 51, 54–8, **54**, **57**, 72, **166**, 167, 212
   and atomic warfare 58
   B-29A-BN 55
   B-29B-BA 55
   Bock's Car 58, **58**
   bomb bay 55
   Enola Gay 58, **58**
   operations 57–8
   origins 55
   tail gunners **56**

technology 55, **56**
The Big Stink **58**
XB-29 prototype 55
YB-29 55
Boeing Model 247 41
'Bomber Mafia' 40, 45
Bonin Islands 122–3
'boom and zoom' tactic 249
Bordeaux 223
Boscombe Down 34, **114**
Bougainville Island 151
'bouncing bomb' (code-named 'Upkeep') 21, 26, **27**, 196
Bremen **197**
Brest 77
Brewster Buffalo 116, 249
Bristol Aeroplane Company 61, 64
Bristol Beaufighter 60–2, 86
   Mk IC 62
   Mk VIF **60**, **62**
   Mk XIC 62
   TF Mk X (the '*Torbeau*') **60**, 62, **63**
Bristol Blenheim 64–6, 92
   Mk I 65, **65**
   Mk I F 65
   Mk IV **64**, 65, **66**
   Mk IV (the Bolingbroke) 66
Bristol Centaurus 139–40
Bristol Hercules 62, 125–6, 175, 197
Bristol Pegasus 105, 179–80, 197
Britain 10, 48
   aircraft 12–37, 60–6, 82–8, 102–15, 124–45, 174–99
   and the Douglas Dakota 94
   and the PBY Catalina 75, 77
   planned German invasion of 10, 192
   shipping convoys 71
Britain, battle of 62, 65, 113, 128, 130, **130**, 132, **133**, 134–5, 175, 186, 188–9, 192, **193**, 194, 198, 214–15, 225, 227, 229, 230, 234, 236, 239
British Army
   1st Airborne Division 87
   Eighth Army 62
   Royal Dragoon Armoured Division 31
British Direct Purchase Commission 37
British Empire 80, 175
British Expeditionary Force (BEF) 131, 192
British Purchasing Commission (BPC) 92, 147, 161, 163
British Technical and Scientific Mission (Tizard Mission) 169
Brittany 220
Brooklands 197

Brown, Sergeant Navigator Ken 28–31
Browning machine guns 36–7, **37**, 42, 130, **130**, 171, 184, 189
Broxton, Cecil **163**
Brunswick 29
'bubble' canopies 139, **139**, 143, **162**, 163, 167, 171, 173
Bulge, battle of the 169, 220
Burma (Myanmar) 62, 71, 80–1, 96, 158, 165, 173
Bush, George H. W. 122–3

C

'C' wing 189, **190**
C-Stoff 241
'cab rank' system 145
Calshot **183**
Camm, Sir Sydney 128–9, 139, 142–3, **143**
Canada **25**, 38, 71, 130
Canadian Car and Foundry Co. 130
Cape Matapan, battle of 107
carbon monoxide 143
Casablanca Allied conference 47
Castle Bromwich Aircraft Factory 186, **186**
Catapult Armed Merchant (CAM) ships 135, **135**
Chadwick, Roy 14, 16
Chamberlain, Neville 147
Chance Vaught 202, **202**, **205**
  see also Vought F4U Corsair
'Channel Dash' 1942 107–8, **107**, 220
Chichijima 122–3
'chin' gun turrets 42
China 57, 71, 75, 80–1, 96, 110, 158
Christensen, Capt Frederick J. **172**
Churchill, Winston 16, 25, 72, 132, 135, 181, **186**, 192, 194
'clipped' wing 189, **190**
Cold War 94
Coles Crane **129**
Cologne 19, 65, **176**, 199
Colombelles steelworks **159**
Condor Legion 215, 225, 230, 233
Consolidated Aircraft Company 75
Consolidated B-24 Liberator 10, 51, 68–72, **68**, **70**, **73**, 172, 220
  'assembly ships' 72, **73**
  B-24D 70
  B-24H 70
  B-24J 70
  bomb bay 70
  design 70
  operations 71–2
  origins 69
  Very Long Range (VLR) 71
  XB-24 prototype 69
Consolidated Model 31 69
Consolidated Model 32 69

Consolidated PBY Catalina 74–7, **76**
  Mk I **75**, **77**
  PBY-4 75
  PBY-5A 75
  XP3Y-1 prototype 75
'cookie' bombs 83, 86, **197**, 198
Coral Sea, battle of the 99, 117
Crete 230
Cricklewood factory **125**
Cruickshank, Flying Officer John 77
Curtiss 171, 173
Curtiss P-36 Hawk 79
Curtiss P-40 Warhawk 10, 78–81, 79, 150, 161, 249
  'Kittyhawk' Mk III **78**, **80**
Curtiss Wright Corporation 79
Curtiss XP-40 79

D

D-Day 25, 50, 87, 96, **96**, 119, **120**, 140, 145, 151, 155, 158, 165, 169, 173, 174, **227**
  see also Normandy landings
Daily Mail (newspaper) 65
Daimler Benz engines 225, 233, 234, 239
'Dambusters Raid' 21, **21**, 26, **26–7**, 88
Davis, David R. 69
'Davis Wing' 69, 70
daylight air raids 19, 47, 50, **50**, 69, 74, 70, **93**, 126, **126**, 160–1, 170, **214**, 220
de Havilland, Geoffrey 83, **83**
de Havilland DH91 Albatross 83
de Havilland Mosquito 10, 62, 82–8, **83**, 152, 168, 243
  bomb bay 83
  DH98 Mosquito (prototype) 83, 84
  FB 87
  FB Mk VI **85**, 87, **87**
  FB Mk XVIII ('Tsetse') 87, **89**
  II **85**
  IIF **82**
  Mk IV **83**
  Mosquito Mk VI **86**
  NF 86
  NF Mk XIII **84**
  operations 85–8
  origins 83–4
  PR Mk 34 87
  PR Mk I 87
  PR Mk XVI **88**
depth charges 181
Derwent engines 114
Desert Air Force 80, 135
Deutsche Forschungsanstalt für Segelflug 241
DFS 194 241
Dieppe 164
dive bombers 98–9, 212, 228, 230
Doolittle, Major General James 'Jimmy' 49, 158, **158**, 164
'Doolittle Raid' 57, 158

'dope' 111, 129, 184
Dornier Do 17 214–15, **214–15**
  Do 17Z 215
  Do 17Z-10 2 **214**
Douglas A-20 Havoc (Boston) 90–2, **92–3**, 158
  DB-7 92
  Mk I 91
  Model 7B prototype 92
Douglas Aircraft Company 41, 44, 99
Douglas C-47 Skytrain 10, 94–7, **95**, **97**
  Douglas Dakota 94
  Douglas Dakota Mk III **96**
  'Mary Co-Ed II' **97**
Douglas DC-2 94
Douglas DC-3 94
Douglas SBD Dauntless 98–9, **99–100**
  SBD-2 99
  SBD-3 **98**, 99
  SBD-4 99
  SBD-5 99
  XBT-1 prototype 99
  XSBD-1 99
Douglas TBD Devastator 99, 120
Dowding, Air Chief Marshal Sir Hugh 192
'Dowding System' 132, **133**, 134, 192
drag 37, 55, 69, 70, 99, 161, 229
Dresden 25, 53
drop tanks 172
Dunkirk 65, 131, 147, **147**, 192
duralumin 197, 208, 246

E

Eaker, Brigadier General Ira 48, 49
'earthquake' bombs 28
East Anglia 48, 53
East End, London **225**
East Langdon **193**
Eastern Front 25, 36–8, **38**, 81, 92, 135, 194, 207–8, 220, 229, 233
Eder dam 21
Edward VIII 129
Egypt 65, **111**, **146**
Eindhoven 97
Eisenhower, Dwight D. 145
electromagnetic rings 199, **199**
English Channel 107, 140, 172, 219–20
English Electric 125
Enterprise (aircraft carrier) **98**, 99
Esmonde, LCDR 107–8
extra super duralumin (ESD) 246

F

Fairey Albacore 104
Fairey Aviation 125
Fairey Firefly 102–3, **102–3**
  Mk I **102**
Fairey Fulmar 103, 205

Fairey Swordfish 10, 104–8, **104**, **107–8**
  Mk I **104**, 105
  Mk II **107**, 108
  Mk III **106**, 108
  TSR I prototype 105
  TSR II prototype 105
Falaise 145, **145**
Fallingbostel 31
Farnborough 115
Fieseler Fi 103 140
Finback (submarine) 123
firebombing 58
firestorms 21, 25
flak (anti-aircraft fire) 52, **52**, 72, 181
Flensburg airfield **218**
flying boats see Consolidated PBY Catalina; Short Sunderland
Focke-Wulf Fw 159 233
Focke-Wulf Fw 190 85, 143–4, 150, 165, 189, **190**, 191, 207, 212, 216–20, **218**, 229, 236
  Fw 190A 165, 190, 219
  Fw 190A-0 218
  Fw 190A-3 **217**, 220
  Fw 190A-4 144
  Fw 190A-8 220, **220**
  Fw 190D 220
  Fw 190F 189
  '*Langnasen-Dora*' ('Long-nosed Dora') 219
  operations 220
  origins 217–19
  'Ta' designation 219
Focke-Wulf Fw 200 Condor 222–3, **222**
  Model Fw 200B 223
  Model Fw 200C **223**
  Model Fw 200C-0 223
  Model Fw 200C-1 223
Ford factory, Willow Run 69, **70**
former Yugoslavia 155
Formidable (aircraft carrier) **117**
Forward Aircraft Controllers (FACs) 145
France 79, 158, 176, 192, 215, 220, 230, **230**
  aid raids 25, 47
  Allied invasion 87
  and the 'blitzkrieg' 131
  and the D-Day landings 25, 87
  fall of 71, 79, 92, 106, 116–17, 192, 223
  and the Havoc 91–2, **93**
  and the Hudson 146–7
  and the Hurricane 131, 135
  'Rhubarb' raids 163
  troop evacuations from 131, 132
France, battle for 131, 225, 227
Franco, Francisco 214, 230
Free French Air Force 155
Freeman, ACM Wilfrid 84
French Army 227
French Navy 106, 116–17
'friedly invasion' 48
'friendly-fire' 31
Frise, Leslie 61

G

General Motors 120
geodetic airframes 197–8, **197**
German Army 173, 229, **230**
    Afrika Korps 236
German High Command 21
German Navy 198, 220
German Prisoners of War 22, 25, 31
Germany 16, 19, 21–2, 28, 38, 42, 57, 81, 107, 115, 126, 147, 158, 164, **166**, 173, 198, 212
    air defences 22
    air superiority 228
    aircraft 212–43
    and the Balkans 227
    and 'blitzkrieg' 65, 131
    defeat 233
    invasion of France 71, 79, 223
    invasion of Norway 223, 225, 230, **230**
    invasion of Poland 10, 32, 212, 214–15, 225, 227, 230, **230**, 239
    and the Netherlands 25, 50
    and the Normandy landings 25
    planned invasion of Britain 10, 192
    Soviet invasion 10, 227, **230**, 236, 239
    and the Spitfire 191
    and the V-1 Flying Bomb 140
    see also Nazi Germany
Gestapo 87, **87**
Gibson, Wg Cdr Guy 21, **26–7**, 88
glider tugs 127, **176**, 215
gliders 127, 241
Gloster Aircraft Company 110, 113, 140
Gloster Gauntlet 111, 177
Gloster Gladiator 10, 64, 110–11, **111**
    Gloster Sea Gladiator 110, **110**
Gloster Meteor 10, 112–15, **113**
    F.1 114
    F.3 114, **115**
    F Mk I **114**
    Gloster E28/39 'W4041' prototype 114
Gneisenau (battleship) 107
Goldenberg power station **66**
Great Marianas Turkey Shoot 119
Greece **65**
Grumman Aircraft Engineering Corporation 119
Grumman F4F Wildcat 10, 116–17, **116–17**, 119, 205, 249
Grumman F6F Hellcat 118–20, **118–19**, 201, 205, 249
    XF6F-3 prototype 119
Grumman TBF Avenger 120–3, **120, 122–3**
    TBM Avenger 120
Guadalcanal 72, 96, 205
Guadalcanal, battle of 117, 122
Guam 57
'gull wing' 201–2, 229, **229**

H

Habbaniyah, Iraq **111**
Hamburg 21, **22**, 25, 31
Hamilcar (glider) 127
Hamilton Standard 202
Handley Page factory **125**
Handley Page Halifax 32, 124–7, **125–6**, 174–6
    B Mk II **127**
    H.P.57 'Halifax' prototype 124
    Mk I L7245 (second prototype) 124
    Mk II 127, **127**
    Mk III 125, 126
    Mk VI 127
    Mk VII 127
    Special Operations 127
Hanson, Lt Bob 205
Harris, ACM Sir Arthur 19, 21, **27**
Hawaii 41, 51, 81, 123, 212, 247
    see also Pearl Harbor
Hawker Aircraft Limited 128, **141, 143**
Hawker Fury 128
Hawker Hurricane 10, 14, 80, 110–11, 128–35, **130, 133–4**, 173, 184, 188, 192, 215, 217, 223, 225, 230, 233, 236, 239
    and the Battle of Britain 132
    and the 'big wing' formation 134, **134**
    design and production 129–30
    Hawker Sea Hurricane **128**, 135, **135**
    K5083 prototype 129
    Mk I **130**
    Mk IIB **129**
    Mk IIC **137**
    Mk IID **136**
    operations 131
    origins 128–9
Hawker Tempest (originally Hawker Typhoon II) 138–41, 165, 243
    Mk I 139
    Mk II 139, 140, **141**
    Mk III 139
    Mk IV 139
    Mk V 114, **138–9**, 139, **141**, 191
Hawker Typhoon 31, 138–9, 142–5, **143**, 173
    Mk IB **142, 144**, 145
HE (high explosive) bombs **199**
Heinkel 184
Heinkel He 111 **130**, 214, 224–5, **224–5**, 239
    'P' variant 225
Heinkel He 112 233
Heligoland Bight 198
helmets, flying **193**
M3 52, **52**
Henshaw, Alex 186
Heydekrug 31
Hibbard, Hal 150
Himalayas 57, 96
Hiroshima 54, 58, 165
Hispano cannons **60**, 114, 139, 189

Hitler, Adolf 21–2, 53, 147, 198, 220, 223, 243
Holland, Henry Philip 110
homing pigeons 25
Horikoshi, Jiro 246
Hornet (aircraft carrier) 99, 122, 158, **158**
humanitarian missions 25, 50
HWK rocket motors 241

I

Ijmuiden 155
Illustrious (aircraft carrier) 106, **107**
Imperial Japanese Navy 99, 106, 123, 151, 158, 223, 244, 246–7, 249
Imperial War Museum Duxford 18, 53, **113**, 134, 188, 192
    American Air Museum **43, 44**
Imphal 158
incendiary ammunition **60, 163**
incendiary bombs 25, 57, 106
Indefatigable (battlecruiser) 103, **103**
India 57, 62, 65, 71, 96, 199
Indianapolis (heavy cruiser) 77
Iraq 65, **111**
Irish Sea **75**
Italian Air Force (Regia Aeronautica) 110, 194, 230
Italian Navy (*Regia Marina*) 106, 180
Italy 50, 62, 72, **93**, 106, 107, 111, 155, 158, **173, 184**, 190, 194
Iwo Jima 165

J

Jagdbombers (Jabos) 145
Japan 25, 51, 55, 57–8, **57**, 66, 77–8, 98–9, 122–3, 135, 147, 154, 169, 173, 212
    and the A6M Zero 116–19, 151, 194, 205, 212, 244–9
    atomic warfare against 54, 58, **58**, 165
    and Australia 80
    and the B-25 Mitchell 158, **158**
    and the Battle of Bismarck Sea 62
    and the Battle of Midway 122
    and China 75, 80–1, 96, 158
    and the end of the war 25
    and the F4U Corsair 201, **201**, 205
    oil supplies 103, **103**
    and the P-38 Lightning 149, **149**, 151
    and the P-51 Mustang 165–7, **166**
    and Pearl Harbor 72, 99, 106, 149, **149**, 151, 154, 158, 212, 247, 249
    unconditional surrender **58**
Japanese Army 158
Japanese Supreme War Council **58**

Java 147
jet aircraft 113–15, 240–1, 242–3
Jet Power Limited 113
Johnson, Clarence 'Kelly' 150
Johnson, Gerald 173
Johnson, Wg Cdr J. E. **190**
Joyce, William ('Lord Haw-Haw') 31
Junkers Ju 87 Stuka 212, 227–30, **230–1**
    Ju 87A 229, 230
    Ju 87B 229
    Ju 87D 229, **229**
    Ju 87G 229
Junkers Ju 88 117, 226–7, **227**
    Ju 88 A-1 **133, 226**, 227
    Ju 88 A-4 227
    Ju 88 A-5 **226**
Junkers Jumo engines 219, 229, 233, 243
Jutland 147

K

kamikaze pilots 212, 244, **249**
Kartveli, Alexander 170–1
Kawasaki Ki 56 147
Kindelberger, James Howard 161
Klimov engines 208
Korea 58, 103, 207
Korean War 163, 165, 205, **205**
Krumme, Lake 31
Kursk, battle of 229

L

laminar flow 38, 69, 70, 139, 161
Lane, Sqn Ldr Brian 'Sandy' **192**
Lawson, Flt Lt Walter 'Farmer' **193**
'Leigh Lights' 71, 199
Leipzig 29
LeMay, General Curtis 57
Lend-Lease initiative 38, 81, **118**, 135, 147, 158, 162–3, 194, 229
Life magazine 151
Lille-Seclin **130**
Lippisch, Alexander 241
Lockheed 44
Lockheed Hudson 10, 146–7, **147**
    Mk VI **146**, 147
Lockheed Model 14 Super Electra 147
Lockheed P-38 Lightning 10, 149–51, **150–1**, 249
    P-38E **149**
    XP-38 prototype 150
Lofoten Islands 77
London 134, 140, 147, 168, 192, **192, 214, 225**
Low Countries 131, 220, 230
Lufthansa 215, 223
Luftwaffe 10, 40, 47–50, **50**, 62, 134, 215
    and the B-26 Marauder 155
    and the Bf 109 233–4, **235–6**, 236
    and the Bf 110 238–9
    and the Blenheim 65
    and the Blitz 168

factory targets 17
and the Fw 190 216–17, 219–20
and the Fw 200 Condor 222–3, **222**
and the Halifax 126
and the He 111 224, **225**
and the Hurricane 128, 131
Jagdwaffe (fighter force) 220, **235**
and the Ju 87 Stuka 229, 230
and the Ju 88 226, 227
and the Me 163 Komet 241
and the Me 262 **242**, 243
and the Mosquito 86, **86**
Nachtjäger III/NJG 3 **239**
and the P-38 Lightning 151
and the P-40 Warhawk 78, 80
and the P-51 Mustang 163–5
and Poland 212
and the Spitfire 186, 189–90, 192, 194
and the Stirling 175–6
and the Swordfish 107
and the Thunderbolt 171–3, **173**
and the Typhoon 144
and the Wellington 198
'Wilde Sau' operation **236**
and the Yak-9 207–8
Luqa, Malta 62

M
M4 cannon 156
MacGill, Elizabeth 'Elsie' 130
Magruder, Peyton M. 152
Malaya 103, 147
Malta **62**, **85**, 135, 194, 230
siege of 111
MAN factory, Augsburg 19
'Manhattan Project' 58
Manston **236**
Marauder B-26 156
Marianas Islands 57, **57**, 58
Martin B-26 Marauder 152–5, **153–5**
B-26B 152
B-26C (Marauder II) 155
B-26F 152
Martin Company 41, 55, 152
mascots 53, **235**
Matford Automotive **93**
Mediterranean 62, 65, **77**, 104, 106–7, 110–11, 146, 149, 151, 155, 180, 191, 194, 199, 225, 230, 236, 239
'Meredith effect' 161
Mers-el-Kébir 106
Messerschmitt, Wilhelm Emil 'Willy' 233
Messerschmitt Bf 108 233
Messerschmitt Bf 109 107, 128, 131–2, 140, 150, 165, 186, 189, 207, 212, 217, **217**, 219, 230, 232–6, **235**, 239
Bf 109A 233
Bf 109E ('Emil') 234
Bf 109E-1 **233**
Bf 109E-4 **193**, **234**

Bf 109F ('Friedrich') 234, 236
Bf 109G ('Gustav') 234
Bf 109G-6/U2 **236**
Bf 109K ('Kurfürst') 234
Bf 109V3 prototype **232**
operations 236
origins 233
variants 234
Messerschmitt Bf 110 199, 238–9
Bf 110C **239**
Messerschmitt Me 163 Komet 240–1
Me 163A 241
Me 163B **240–1**, 241
Messerschmitt Me 262 25, 113, 114, 140, 165, 212, 240, 242–3
Me 262 A '*Schwalbe*' ('Swallow') **242**, 243
Me 262 B '*Sturmvogel*' ('Storm Bird') 243
Me 262 V3 **243**
MG 17 machine guns 218
Mid Atlantic Gap 71
Midway, battle of 77, 99, **100**, 117, 122, 154, 158, 247
Midway Island 72, 77
MiG aircraft 58
Mildenhall, Suffolk **199**
mines 127
magnetic 199, **199**
Ministry of Aircraft Production 16, 130
Ministry of Defence 31
Ministry of Information 198
Missouri (battleship) **249**
Mitchell, Gen William 'Billy' 156
Mitchell, Reginald Joseph 183–4, **183**, 186, **186**, 188, 194
Mitsubishi A5M 'Claude' 246
Mitsubishi A6M Zero 10, 81, 116–19, 151, 194, 205, 212, 244–9, **244**, **247**, **249**
A6M-1 247
A6M-2 Zero Model 21 247
A6M-5 247
operations 249
origins 246–7
variants 246–7
Mitsubishi Aircraft Company 246
Mitsubishi G4M 'Betty' 151
Möhne dam 21, **27**
Molins anti-tank cannon 87, **89**
Monnington, Walter Thomas **141**
Montabaur, Germany **154**
Monte San Elmo **93**
Montgomery, Gen Bernard 96
Morris Motors 186
Mortain 145
Motor Torpedo Boats (MTBs) 220
Multi-Role Combat Aircraft (MRCA) 82
see also de Havilland Mosquito
Munich Crisis 1938 61, 130
Munster 48
Musashi ('super' battleship) 122

N
Nagasaki 54, 58, **58**, 165

Naito, Takeshi 106
Napier Sabre engines 139, 143
Nash & Thompson turrets 198
Naval Construction Battalion ('Seebees') 57
Nazi Germany 10, 53, 161, 196, 207, 216, 229
and the Allied Combined Bomber Offensive 47
defeat 13, 28, 31, 220, 229
defiance against 13
oil supplies 72, 126, **126**
and the RAF bomber threat 21
rearmament 14
shrinking borders of 25
and the sinking of the *Bismarck* 77
Nazis 10, 22, 192, 230, 236
Netherlands 25, 50, 96, **97**, 155
New Britain 154, 158, 205
New Guinea 99, 151, 154, 205, 249
Newchurch, Kent **141**
Nicolson, Flt Lt James 132
night fighter/intruder missions 65, **86**, 91–2, 168–9, 183, **214**, 238–9
night raids 19, 21–2, 25, 29, 47–8, 50, 55, 58, 62, 198, 239
Nijmegen 97
Norden, Carl 44
Norden Bombsight 44–5
Normandy 26, **159**, 190
Normandy landings 25, 50, 96, **96**, **108**, **116**, 119, **144**, 145, 160, 173, 191, **227**
see also D-Day
North Africa 57, 62, 72, 78–80, 92, **92**, 110, 117, 135, 149, 151, 155, 158, 189, 194, 229–30, **231**, 236, 239
North American Aviation 156
North American B-25 Mitchell 10, 154, 156–8, **173**
B-25A 156
B-25B 156
B-25C 156, **157**
B-25G 156, 158
B-25J 156
NA-62 prototype 156
North American P-51 Mustang 10, 38, 72, 78, 139, 156, 160–7, **160**, **162–7**, 216, 220, 241
and the B-17 40, **40**, 42, **48**, 49, **50**, 53
engines 162–3
Mustang Mk I 161
NA-73X prototype 161
operations 163–7
origins 161
and the P-38 Lightning 150–1
P-51 A 162
P-51 B 162, 163
P-51 B/C (Mustang III) 162–3
P-51 K 163
P-51C 162, 165–7

P-51D (Mustang IV) 162–4, **162**, **164**, 167
variants 162–3
X prototype 162
XP-51B prototype 162
North Coates 62
North Sea 87, 108
Northrop 99
Northrop A-17 99
Northrop P-61 Black Widow 62, 168–9, **169**
Norway 62, 77, **85**, 103, 105, 123, 147, 180, 223, 225, 230, **230**
'nuisance' raids 86, 163, 190
Nuremberg 22

O
Oban Bay **178**
Okinawa 165, **249**
Operation Airthief 220
Operation Argument 50
Operation Bodenplatte 220
Operation Chastise ('Dambusters Raid') 21, **21**, 26, **26–7**, 88
Operation Dynamo 131
Operation Exodus 25, 31
Operation Gomorrah 21
Operation Manna 25, 50
Operation Market Garden 96, 127
Operation Overlord **51**, 145
see also D-Day
Operation Starvation 58
Operation Tidal Wave 72
oxygen masks 52, 143, **193**

P
Pacific arena 25, 51, 54–5, 59, 62, 65–6, 71–2, 77, 81, 96, 98, 103, 106, 116–20, 122–3, 149, **149**, 151–2, 154–6, 158, 165, **166**, 169, 173, 194, 201, **201**, 205, 212, 244, 246–7, 249
central 99, **201**
South West 71–2, 78, 80, 151, 154, 249
Pacific Ocean 74–5, 119, 246
Packard 162
Packard-Merlin engines 79, 191
Pangkalan Brandan **103**
Papau New Guinea 80, 158
parachute drops 94, 96, **96**, **97**, 230
partisans 155
Pattle, Sqn Ldr Marmaduke Thomas St John 'Pat' 111, **111**
Pearl Harbor 51, 55, 72, 81, 99, 106, 122, 149, **149**, 151, 154, 158, 212, 247, 249
Peirson, Rex 196
Philippine Sea, battle of the 119
Philippines 51, 72, 92
'Phoney War' 131
photo reconnaissance 87–8, **88**
Pinckney, Captain Phillip 220
Ploesti, Romania **70**, 151
Pohlmann, Hermann 229
Pola (cruiser) 107

253

Poland 10, 32, 212, 214–15, 225, 227, 230, **230**, 239
'porpoising' 188
Port Moresby 80, 99
Potsdam Declaration 1945 **58**
Pratt & Whitney engines 41, 55, 70, 76, 117, 119, 147, 152, 169, 170–1, 181, 201–2, 223
precision bombing 26, 40, 44–5, **45**, **50**
Pretoria Castle (liner) **102**
Project X 241
Pulman, Sgt Arthur 31

Q

'Queen Mary' trailer **129**
Quill, Jeffrey 186, 220

R

Rabaul, New Britain 154, 205
radar 50, 55, 62, 99, 238, 239
    Air to Surface Vessel (ASV) 62, 71, 105, 147, 180–1
    Airborne Interceptor (AI) 65, 82, **84**, 86, 92, 168–9, **169**
    'Chain Home' 230
    and the 'Dowding' home defence system 132
    'stealth' radar invisibility 85
    'Window' 176
    and wooden aircraft 85
radiators 161
radome 62
RAF Cranwell 114
RAF Culmhead 115
RAF Duxford **36**, **113**, 134, 144, 188
RAF Halton **241**
RAF Kenley **192**, 215
RAF Pembrey 220
RAF Waddington **7**
railways 25, 126, 227
Rall, Günther 236
Regensburg 48, 164
Reich 21, 165, 212, 220, 230, 234
Reich Aviation Ministry (*Reichsluftfahrtministerium*) 215, 217, 233, 239, 241
Reiner Aerodrome 31
Republic Aviation Corporation 170
Republic P-43 Lancer 170
Republic P-47 Thunderbolt 10, 78, 114, 119, 144, 170–3, **171–3**, 201
    AP-4 prototype 170
    AP-10 prototype 170
    P-47B 171
    P-47C 171
    P-47D (Mk I and II) 171
    P-47M 171
    XP-47B prototype 171
resistance groups 87, 127
Rethel, Walter 233
Rhine 96, 97, 127
'Rhubarb' raids 163
Richards, Vernon R. **160**
rocket projectiles (RPs) 87

Rockets Assisted Take Off (RATO) 105, 135, **135**
Rolls-Royce 114
Rolls-Royce Goshawk engines 183
Rolls-Royce Griffon engines 103, 139, 191
Rolls-Royce Kestrel engines 233
Rolls-Royce Merlin engines 14, 16, 49, 83, 84, 124, 126, 130–1, **162**, **162**, 164, 171, 182, **184**, 188–91, 194, 197
Rolls-Royce V-12 engine (later the 'Merlin' engine) 184
Rolls-Royce Vulture engines 14, 16, 32, 143
Rolls-Royce/Packard Merlin engines 165
Romanian oil fields **70**, 72, 151
Rommel, General Erwin 80
Rose, Flight Sergeant Morris **141**
Rothermere, Lord 65
Royal Air Force (RAF) 10, 19, 22, 212
    aircraft
        A-20 Havoc (Boston) 91, 92
        B-24 Liberator 70, 71
        B-25 Mitchell 158, **159**
        B-26 Marauder 152, 155
        Beaufighter 61–2
        Blenheim 64, 66
        Boeing B-17s 47
        Gladiator 110, **110**
        Halifax 126
        Hawker Tempest 138, 140
        Hurricane 128–31, **130**
        Lockheed Hudson 146–7
        Meteor **113**, 114–15
        P-39 Airacobra **36**, 37
        P-40 Warhawk 'Tomahawk/Kittyhawk' Mk III 78, **78**, 80, **80**
        P-47 Thunderbolt 171–3
        P-51 Mustang 161, 162–4
        PBY Catalina 77, **77**
        Spitfire 182, 188–9, 191–2, **192**
        Stirling 175–6
        Sunderland 181
        Typhoon 143–5, **145**
        Wellington 196–8
    'area bombing' strategy 22–5
    Army Cooperation Command 161
    Banff Strike Wing **85**
    and the Bf 109 233, 234, **236**
    and the Bf 110 239
    Commands
        RAF Bomber Command 16, 19, 21, 22–5, **22**, 28–9, 34, 86, 124, 126, 174–6, 197, 199, 239
        RAF Coastal Command 62, 71, 77, 87, 127, 147, 199
        RAF Fighter Command 128, **130**, 131, 132, **133**, 135, 198

        RAF Southeast Asia Command 173
    and the Do 17 214–15, **215**
    and the Fw 190 220
    and night raids 48, 50
    Operational Training Unit (OTU) 28
    Pathfinder Force 19, 126, **127**, **176**
        Light Night Striking Force 86
    Photo Reconnaissance Unit (PRU) 85, 194
    Royal Observer Corps 132, **133**
    Second Tactical Air Force (TAF) 87, 144, 145
    Squadrons
        No.3 Sqn 140
        No.17 Sqn **133**
        No.19 Sqn 188, **192**
        No.50 Sqn 13
        No.56 Sqn 144
        No.64 Sqn **192**
        No.71 'Eagle' Sqn **133**
        No.98 Sqn **159**
        No.119 Sqn **106**
        No.140 Sqn **88**
        No.181 Sqn **145**
        No.207 Sqn 29, 32, **32**
        No.272 Sqn **62**
        No.303 Sqn (Polish) 132
        No.310 Sqn (Czech) 220
        No.540 Sqn 243
        No.601 Sqn **36**
        No.610 Sqn 164
        No.616 Sqn 115, **115**
        No.617 Squadron 21, 26
    Tactical Flight (T-Flight) 115
    see also RAF bases
Royal Aircraft Establishment 38, 131
Royal Australian Air Force (RAAF) 61–2, 80, 158, 181, 194
    No.467 Squadron **25**
Royal Canadian Air Force (RCAF) 66, 80, 158, **194**
Royal Navy 77, 104, 107, 110, 118
    and the 'Channel Dash' 220
    and the F4F Wildcat 'Martlet' 116, 117
    Fleet Air Arm 102, 105, 110, **118**, 123, **123**, **128**, **202**, 205, **205**
    Naval Air Squadron 103
    Pacific Fleet 103, 205
    and the Sea Hurricane **128**, 135, **135**
    and the Seafire 191, **191**
    and the TBF Avenger 'Tarpon' 123, **123**
Royal Netherlands Air Force 158
Royal Netherlands Navy 103
Royal New Zealand Air Force, No.486 Sqn 140
Rude, Hans-Ulrich 229
Ruhr 21, **126**

S

Saipan 57
Sandefjord **85**
Sangatte beach 192
Saxilby 34
Scapa Flow 117
Scharnhorst (battleship) 107, 126
Schmued, Edgar 161, 162
Schneider Trophy 183, **183**
Schreiber, Leutnant Alfred 243
Schweinfurt 48, 164
Scotland **60**, 71, **135**, 178
'search and rescue' missions 77
Sedan, battle of 230
semi-elliptical wing 184, **185**, 186, 189
Seversky P-35 170
'shadow factories' 175, 186
Shenstone, Beverley 184
Shilling, Beatrice 131
'Shilling' restrictor valve **130**, 131
shipping convoys 71, **104**, 135, 179, 199, 222–3, 227
    Atlantic **104**, 222–3
Shokaku (light aircraft carrier) 99
Short Brothers 175
Short Empire 179
    S23 C Class Empire **180**
Short Stirling 174–6, **174**
    B Mark III **176**
    Mk I **175–6**
    Mk III 176
    Mk IV 176
    S.29 prototype 175
Short Sunderland 10, 175, 178–81
    Mk I **178**, 179, 180, **181**
    Mk II 180
    Mk III 180, **180**
    Mk V 181
Siberia 38
Sicily 62, 96, 155, 158, 194
'Silverplate' fleet 58
Sinclair, Gordon 188
Singapore 65, 135, 179
Sittang 173
'Skunk Works' 150
Smiter (aircraft carrier) **191**
Smith, Joseph 186, 188, 194
Smolensk, battle of 208
Solomon Islands 122, 158, 205
Sorpe dam 21
South African Air Force (SAAF) 80, 110, 152, 155
    No.24 Squadron **92**, **93**
Southeast Asia 96, 106, 135, 146–7, 165, 173, 194, 205
Soviet Air Forces 36, 37, 38, **38**, 92, 227
Soviet armies 25, 31
Soviet Union 10, 38, 81, 135, 194, 212, 220, 225, 230
    air superiority 207
    German invasion 10, 227, 229, **230**, 236, 239
    and the Yak-9 207–8, **207**, **209**
Spaatz, General Carl 48
Spanish Civil War 212, 214, 225, 230, 233, **233**, 236, 239
Special Operations Executive (SOE) 127, 176

Spilsby, Lincolnshire 29
Stalag 357 31
Stalag Luft VI 31
Stalingrad, battle of 208
stepless cockpit 65, **65**
Sto-Wing 117, **117**, 120
Suez Canal 80
Sumatra 103, **103**, 147
Sumitomo Metal Industries 246
Supermarine Aviation Works 183
Supermarine S.4 184
Supermarine S.5 seaplane **183**
Supermarine SB.6 seaplane 183
Supermarine Spitfire 10, 13–14, 47, 84, 110, 114, 161, 165, 171, 182–94, **184**, **186**, **189**, 215, 216
   and the A6M Zero 249
   and the Bf 109 233, 234, 236
   and the Bf 110 239
   in Burma 173
   and the Fw 190 220
   and the He 111 225
   and the Hurricane 128–31, 132
   and the Ju 87 Stuka 230
   K5054 prototype 186, **186**, 188
   Mk I 184, 186, 188–9, **189**, 192
   Mk II 188, 189
   Mk III 189
   Mk IX 162, 190, **190**, 220
   Mk V 171, 188, 189, 190, **190**, 194, **194**, 220
   Mk VB **182**, **185**, 191
   Mk VC **190**
   Mk VIII 194
   Mk XII **190**, 191
   Mk XIV 191
   Mk XVI 191
   Mk 24 186, 188
   operations 192–4
   origins 183–4
   production 186
   'Seafire' (naval version) 182, 186, 191, **191**
   Type 300 prototype 183–4, 186
   types/variants 188–91
Supermarine Type 224 183

T
T-Stoff 241
'Tallboy' (bomb) 26
'Tallboy Large' bomb ('Grand Slam') **26**, 28
Tank, Kurt Waldemar 217–18, 219
Taranto 106, **107**, 180
Tarawa Atoll **201**
Teltow 31
terror bombing 25
'terrorflieger' (terror fliers) 22
Thach, Jimmy 249
'Thach Weave' tactic 117, 249
Thailand 57
Tibbets, Colonel Paul **58**
Tilson, John 164
Tinian 57, 58, 77
'Tip and Run' raids 144

Tirpitz (battleship) 26, **27**, 103, 205
Tito 155
Titre, Mike 171
TNT 181
Tokyo 49, 57, 58, 158, **158**
Torpex 181
trawlers **63**
Trumpeter (aircraft carrier) **123**
'Trumpets of Jericho' 229, **229**
Tunisia 136, **194**
turbojets 113–15

U
U-boats 19, 71, 77, 87, 105, 108, 123, 147, 179–80, 180–1, **180**, 223
   U-625 **180**
United Aircraft 202
   see also Vought F4U Corsair
United States 21
   aircraft 10, 38–58, 68–81, 90–101, 116–23, 146–73, 200–5
   atomic weapons 58
   enter the war, 1941 47
   and Pearl Harbor 249
United States Army
   82nd Airborne Division 97
   101st Airborne Division 97
United States Army Air Corps 37–8, 41, 45, 55, 69, 79, 92, 150, 156, 168–70
   Circular Proposal 39-340 152
United States Army Air Forces (USAAF) 38, 115, 220
   7th Photographic Reconnaissance Group **157**
   425th Night Fighter Sqn **169**
   and the A-20 Havoc (Boston) **91**, 92
   and the B-24 Liberator **68**, 69, 70, **70**, 71
   and the B-25 Mitchell 156, 158, **158**
   and the B-26 Marauder 152
   and the Beaufighter 61–2
   and the Boeing B-17 40, 42, 44, 47–50, **47–8**, **50–2**, 53
   and the Boeing B-29 54, **54**, 55, **56**, 57, 58
   Bombardment Groups 44
     22nd BG 154
     91st BG **40**, **47**
     93rd BG **68**, **73**
     96th BG 53
     100th BG 48, 50, **51**
     303rd BG **41**
     306th BG 52
     320th BG **155**
     322nd BG **154**, 155
     381st BG **48**, **53**
     497th BG **57**
   Bombardment Wings
     58th BW 57, 59
     73rd BW 57
   costs **54**
   Fighter Groups
     20th FTR GP **151**

     55th FTR GP **167**
     56th FTR GP 172, **172**, 173
     339th FTR GP **165**
     355th FTR GP **48**
     361st FTR GP **160**, **164**
     405th FTR GP 171
   Forces
     5th Air Force 62, 154
     8th Air Force 44, 47, 48–50, **50**, **52**, 53, 151, 164, 172
     9th Air Force 155
     12th Air Force **173**
     15th Air Force 50, 70
     20th Air Force **54**, **56**
     Far East Air Force 51
     and the P-47 Thunderbolt 170–1
     and the P-51 Mustang 160–7
   Troop Carrier Groups, 434th **97**
United States Marine Corps 99, 158, 201, **201**, 205
United States Navy 45, 75, 99, 116, 118–20, 147, **201**, 202, 205, 217
   Bureau of Aeronautics 202

V
V-1 Flying Bombs 87, 115, 126, 140, **141**, 164–5, 171, 191, 194, 199, 225
V-2 rockets 26, 88
Valletta **62**
Vengeance (aircraft carrier) **205**
Vickers Wellington 196–9, **197**, 239
   DWI variant 199, **199**
   III **199**
   Mk I 197, **198**
   Mk IV **197**
   Type 271 prototype 197
Vickers-Armstrong 16, 183, 186, **197**
Victoria Cross 77, 107–8, 132, 199
Victorious (aircraft carrier) 106–7
von Ohain, Hans 113
Vought F4U Corsair 118–19, 200–5, **201–2**, 249
   F4U-5 **205**
   XF4U-1 (V-166B) prototype 202

W
Waddington **28**, 32
Wake Island 72, **98**
Wallis, Barnes 26, **27**, 28, 196
Walter I-203 rocket motor 241
Wanne-Eickel, Ruhr **126**
Ward, James 199
Weber, Leutnant Joachim 243
West Africa **147**
Western Desert 62, **64**, **129**, **231**
Western Front 25, 239
Whittle, Air Cdre Sir Frank 113, **113**

Wilhelmshaven 65, 239
'Window' 176
women in war 38, **186**
wooden aircraft 83–5, 88, 111
Wright cyclone engines 42, 55, 99, 120
Wroath, Sammy 129

Y
Yakovlev, Alexander Sergeyevich 208
Yakovlev Yak-1 207, 208
Yakovlev Yak-7 208
Yakovlev Yak-9 10, 207–8, **207**
   Yak-9D **209**
   Yak-9U 208
Yamamoto, Admiral 149, **149**, 151
Yamato ('super' battleship) 122
Yeadon factory 16–17
Yorktown (aircraft carrier) 99

Z
Zemke, Major Hubert 163
'Zemke Wolf Pack' **172**
Zerstörer concept 238–9

Acknowledgements

My thanks go to all my colleagues at Imperial War Museums who helped with this book, including Madeleine James, Lara Bateman, and Rebecca Harding. Thanks also to all the team at HarperCollins, especially Gerry Breslin and Craig Balfour for bringing the book to life. As ever, thanks to my wife for all her love and support. Finally, I would like to dedicate this book to the memory of RAF Sergeant Navigator Ken Brown, and all those crew members who served in the Aircraft of World War Two.

Image Credits

t (top), m (middle), b (bottom), l (left), r (right)

Imperial War Museums

P11 CH8785; **P12** TR1156; **P15** CH21121; **P17** TR1386; **P18** TR1384; **P19** TR198; **P20** TR1128; **P22** HU63075; **P23** CH8792; **P24** TR1795; **P25** TR193; **P26**(t) CH15375; (m) TR1127; **P27**(tl) HU92132; (tr) C4873; (ml) IWM_FLM2340; (mr) CH9687; (br) CH9683; **P28** TR186; **P29** CH15362; **P30** MH30791; **P33** COL205; **P34** CH3890; **P35** CH3880; **P36** CH3723; **P37**(tr) CH3729; (br) CH3720; **P39** FRE10381; **P40** FRE5652; **P41** FRE1109; **P42** CH7817; **P43**(t) 010297; (bl) DUX10298; (br) DUX10300; **P44** DUX10301; **P45** DUX10299; **P46** FRE7604; **P47** FRE5669; **P49** FRE6247; **P50** HU4052; **P51** EA31796; **P52** FRE9885; **P53** FRE6251; **P54** FRE11984; **P56** FRE11989; **P57** FRE11987; **P58** HU44878; **P59** MH2629; **P60** CH17873; **P61** CE22; **P62** TR1061; **P62**(t) CH9755; (b) C4639; **P64**(t) CM3108; **P65** CM292; **P66** C2020; **P67** CH364; **P68** FRE11426; **P70** FRE9245; **P71** FRE8757; **P73** FRE780; **P74** CH2455; **P76** CH5559; **P77** CM6524; **P78** TR978; **P79** TR824; **P80** TR975; **P82**(t) TR1090; (b) RAEO876; **P83**(tr) TR930; (mr) TR1426; (br) CH12621; **P84** CH16606; **P85**(t) TR1076; (b) HU93037; **P86** HU107770; **P87** C4762; **P88** C4995; **P89** CH14114; **P90** COL371; **P92** TR856; **P93**(t) C2282; (b) CNA900; **P95** FRE7025; **P96** CL3885; **P97**(t) K7570; (b) FRE7452; **P99** MH5088; **P102**(t) EMOS1367; (b) A26502; **P103** A27167; **P104** A3536; **P105**(t) A19308; (b) A22058; **P106** CL2277; **P107**(t) A12870; (b) TR1138; **P108** A24983; **P109** A16649; **P110** MH5091; **P111**(t) ME_RAF1260; (b) CM774_B; **P112** MH28313; **P113** TR3737; **P114** ATP15023_B; **P115**(bl) CL2936; (br) C5658; **P116** A24529; **P117** TR285; **P118** A24533; **P119** A30070; **P121** A24944; **P122** A26077; **P123** A24282; **P124** HU107792; **P125**(t) D7123; (b) D7080; **P126** (t) C4713; **P127**(t) CH17867; (b) COL185; **P128**(t) A9534; **P129**(b) CM2240; **P130**(t) TR1273; (b) HU106301; **P131**(t) CI178; (b) C1512; **P132**(t) HU73745; (b) C1288; **P133**(t) CH2401; (b) TR1443; **P134** CH1406; **P135** A9423; **P136**(t) TR869; (b) TR1012; **P137** COL186; **P138** HU2173; **P139** CH14095; **P140**(t) CH14091; (b) CH13428; **P141**(t) IWM_ART_LD_4588_A; (b) COL44; **P142** CH11583; **P143**(t) HU90326; (b) CH11573_1; **P144** CL3839; **P145**(bl) C4571; (br) CL570; **P146** TR1; **P147**(t) TR902; (b) C1722; **P148** OEM5182; **P150** FRE13873; **P151** FRE5441; **P153** FRE14185; **P154** FRE13727; **P155** FRE14187; **P157** FRE5372; **P158** NY7343_B; **P159**(t) CH13734; (b) CL217; **P160** FRE6210; **P161** FRE11499; **P162** FRE7584; **P163** FRE10310; **P164** FRE6428; **P165**(t) FRE5998; (b) FRE7016; **P166** FRE6075; **P167** FRE12836; **P168** FRE10389; **P169** FRE7461; **P170** TR1411; **P172**(t) FRE5564; (b) FRE2552; **P173** FRE9674; **P174** TR35; **P175** CH17086; **P176**(t) TR36; (b) CH11641; **P177** TR37; **P178** CH839; **P180**(t) ATP8906_B; (m) CH21577; (b) C4287; **P181** CH807; **P182** COL188; **P183** H_AM323; **P184** TR1537; **P185** CH2929; **P187**(t) MH5214; (b) H14259; **P188** HU104755; **P189** CH1458; **P190**(tl) CH12753; (bl) CNA2102; (br) CL604; **P191** A27603; **P192**(t) HU54420; (b) CH1366; **P193**(t) CH1361; (b) HU73433; **P194** TR845; **P195** COL190; **P196** TR11; **P197**(t) CH5974; (b) CH7350; **P198** CH17; **P199**(t) TR106; (b) CM5312; **P200** NYF_041740; **P203** A_021398; **P204**(b) A_028909; **P214**(t) HU108214; (b) C5423; **P215** PL8096; **P216** MH4190; **P218** CL3307; **P221** CL1104; **P222** HU39426; **P223** CH16122; **P224** MH6547; **P225** C5422; **P226**(t) MH6115; (b) HU93021; **P227** TR2107; **P228** CH9829; **P230** GER18; **P231** MH5591; **P232** HU67699; **P233** HU67693; **P235**(t) HU76052; (b) HU67704; **P237** CH15662; **P238** HU108211; **P239** HU108215; **P240** CH15664; **P241** RAF_T2663; **P242** CH15714; **P243** MH24073; **P246** FRE15209; **P248** NYF70679

Alamy

P3 Avpics / Alamy Stock Photo; **P4** Shawshots / Alamy Stock Photo; **P6** PA Images / Alamy Stock Photo; **P98** Shawshots / Alamy Stock Photo; **P100** public domain sourced / access rights from D and S Photography Archives / Alamy Stock Photo; **P210** Sueddeutsche Zeitung Photo / Alamy Stock Photo; **P213** Shawshots / Alamy Stock Photo

Getty Images

P204(t) Scott Germain/Stocktrek Images/Getty; **P206** Sovfoto/Getty; **P208** Sovfoto/Getty; **P245** Museum of Flight Foundation/Getty

Shutterstock

End papers Everett Collection/Shutterstock; **P8** Granger/Shutterstock

Cover images

Front: Avpics / Alamy Stock Photo; Sergei A. Tkachenko/Shutterstock
Back: CH3880/Imperial War Museums; H14259/Imperial War Museums; A22058/Imperial War Museums